Macroeconomics

Helmut Merklein

University of Dallas
Irving, Texas

Wadsworth Publishing Company, Inc.   Belmont, California

Designer: Russ Leong

Editor: Kevin Gleason

Technical Illustrator: Mark Schroeder

ISBN–0–534–00175–0

L. C. Cat. Card No. 72–80403

Printed in the United States of America

1 2 3 4 5 6 7 8 9 10–76 75 74 73 72

Preface

The very complexity of our national economy requires an advanced degree of abstraction to make its workings comprehensible. To really understand current macroeconomic theory requires training in all aspects of economics. This book, however, is intended to be more than an intermediate treatise on economic theory. Its main objective is to provide an education in macroeconomics sufficient for the reader to understand most of the current issues facing our economy. It is, if you wish, a nonmathematical aggregate supply-and-demand model with heavy emphasis on stabilization policies.

However, as impressive as is modern macroeconomic thinking, beginning students too often get lost in its detailed mathematics. I believe that there is a way of presenting present-day macroeconomic theory in nonmathematized terms, and that this theory is important enough to justify a broader and more easily accessible approach.

Relevance to the real world was the guiding principle in the writing of this book. As a result, many widely debated and subtle issues of a strictly theoretical import have been omitted. The liquidity trap is one example of such an omission. Similarly, negative rates of interest are not discussed in the text. Negative rates of interest are a phenomenon of greatly troubled times, when lives are in jeopardy, property rights unenforceable, and the national entity of a people in question. In those times, our neat macroeconomic models — let's face it — are worthless.

The sequence in this book is somewhat unorthodox. The usual approach is as follows: GNP, the mechanics of money, the model, applications. But two things have always bothered me about this sequence.

First, after the GNP, when the model should logically follow, there is an interruption on the order of three to four weeks to discuss money. Thereafter, when the model does follow, what has been said about the GNP is somewhat remote and the connection between the GNP and the model is less easily discerned.

Second, that part of the course that students like most, monetary and fiscal policy discussions, tends to get short shrift. It is usually offered at the end of the course, as a sort of filler for remaining class time. There is often little time to extend policy discussions to the real world.

This book has the following sequence: Part One deals with the GNP; Part Two develops the model; policy applications are the core of Part Three; finally, the mechanics of money are relegated to Part Four. Discussion of policy applications is made possible simply by selling on faith the idea that the money supply can be increased or reduced, and leaving the discussion of how this is done to the end of the book. This strategy, I believe, yields a rapidly moving and cohesive succession of concepts from the GNP to the model to the workings of the model.

While Part Four is taught in the last four or so weeks of a course, there is time to discuss Parts One through Three in the light of current economic developments. In fact, our students at the University of Dallas are required to read pertinent articles from the *Wall Street Journal* and to be prepared to discuss them in class in terms of the model as soon as Parts One through Three have been covered. This, perhaps more than anything else, makes the student aware of the fact that what he has learned is relevant.

The book is aimed at two distinct fields: undergraduate economics programs and graduate business administration programs. In fact, the expanded chapter on money is addressed to the needs of business schools. In undergraduate economics programs, the money section is ordinarily handled separately in a special course in economics programs, but not in graduate business schools, where typically only two economics courses are offered: micro and macro. Because the money section is in Part Four, i.e., toward the end of the book, the instructor teaching economics majors may simply omit it without loss in continuity.

No textbook in economics has ever been written in a vacuum, and the present book is no exception. To name all the people, living or dead, who have influenced my writing would be an impossible task. However, the initiated will have no trouble in detecting one predominating influence, namely that of Thomas Saving at Texas A&M University.

I would like to take this opportunity to express my gratitude to the many people who have read and commented on parts or all of the manuscript, in particular Professor Paul E. Junk, of the University of Missouri, and Professor Philip W. Cartwright, of the University of Washington. If errors remain, they are entirely mine.

Contents

Part One   National Wealth

1   Introduction   1

2   Wealth   4
    The Price Index   9
    The GNP-Deflator   14
    National Income Defined   17
    Problems   23
    Suggested Readings   24

3   The U.S. National Income Accounts   26
    Measurement Problems   31
    Income Distribution   34
    Problems   36
    Suggested Readings   38

4   The U.S. Economic Track Record   39
    Problems   52
    Suggested Readings   53

Part Two   The Model

5   Introducing the Model   54
    Problems   59
    Suggested Readings   59

6   The Aggregate Supply Curve   60
     The Labor Market   65
     Aggregate Supply   67
     Problems   75
     Suggested Readings   76

7   Components of Aggregate Demand   77
     The Commodity Market   79
     Consumption Spending   79
     Investment Spending   86
     Government Spending   90
     Equilibrium in the Commodity Market   91
     Problems   97
     Suggested Readings   98

8   Money, Credit, Aggregate Demand   100
     The Money Market   101
     Demand for Money   103
     Supply of Money and the LM-Curve   107
     The Aggregate Demand Curve   112
     The Credit Market   113
     Problems   118
     Suggested Readings   119

Part Three   Income Stabilization Policies

9   The Depressed Economy   120
     Problems   131
     Suggested Readings   131

10   Fiscal Policies   132
     A. Increase in Government Spending
        Financed by Taxation   134
     B. Increase in Government Spending
        Financed by Borrowing   137
     C. Stimulation of Private Spending by
        Cuts in Corporate or Income Taxes   139
     A Final Note on Fiscal Policies   141
     Problems   143
     Suggested Readings   145

11   Monetary Policies   146
     A. Stimulating a Depressed Economy   147
     B. Anti-Inflationary Monetary Policy Actions   149
     A Practical Note on Monetary and Fiscal Policies   150
     Lags   150
     Quantification of Policies   153
     Problems   154
     Suggested Readings   155

12	*Current Macroeconomic Issues*	*157*
	Demand-Pull, Cost-Push Inflation	*157*
	The Wage-Price Spiral	*163*
	Empirical Evidence on Cost-Push Inflation	*164*
	Wage and Price Controls	*168*
	Our National Debt	*172*
	Problems	*175*
	Suggested Readings	*176*
13	*Important Macroeconomic Concepts*	*177*
	The Keynesian Multiplier	*178*
	The Accelerator	*180*
	Automatic Stabilizers	*181*
	1. Unemployment Compensation	*181*
	2. Induced Deficit Spending	*181*
	3. Dissaving	*182*
	The Phillips Curve	*182*
	Keynesian versus Non-Keynesian—Post-, Pre-, Anti-, Pro-, Neo-Keynesian?	*185*
	Problems	*187*
	Suggested Readings	*188*

Part Four   Money and Credit

14	*Money*	*190*
	The Mechanics of Money	*192*
	The Federal Reserve System	*197*
	The Structure of the Fed	*198*
	Federal Reserve Policies	*202*
	Open Market Operations	*202*
	The Discount Window	*205*
	Changes in Reserve Requirements	*206*
	Independent Factors Changing Bank Reserves	*209*
	1. Changes in Currency Holdings	*209*
	2. Changes in Treasury Deposits	*210*
	3. Foreign and Other Deposits	*211*
	4. Changes in Gold Holdings	*211*
	5. Federal Reserve Bank Float	*213*
	A Final Note on the Federal Reserve System	*213*
	The American Banking System	*214*
	Problems	*217*
	Suggested Readings	*217*
15	*Credit*	*219*
	Financial Intermediaries	*222*
	Instruments of the Credit Market	*223*
	Different Rates of Interest	*225*
	Types of Credit Instruments	*231*
	Problems	*232*
	Suggested Readings	*233*

16   *Long-Term Macroeconomic Problems*   *234*

Appendices

A   *Present Value Tables*   *239*

B   *Partial Differentials*   *248*

C   *Financial Intermediaries*   *250*

D   *Short-Term Credit Instruments*   *258*

E   *Sample Articles from the Wall Street Journal*   *263*

Index   *276*

Part One
National Wealth

1 Introduction

The size and complexity of a modern-day economy are staggering. In the United States, there live at present over two hundred million people. Of these, eighty-six million belong to the labor force. Each year they produce goods and services worth one trillion dollars, and their output is rising.

The term one trillion dollars is easily pronounced. Yet it practically defies comprehension. If you were asked to count out one trillion dollars in Federal Reserve Notes of one million dollar denomination made especially for this experiment, and if you could count these notes at the rate of one per second, eight hours per day, five days per week, it would take you approximately seven weeks to finish your task (not counting coffee breaks and other social, natural, or institutional interruptions).

The composition of this nation's output is even more perplexing. It has been estimated that 200,000 different goods are currently being produced, ranging from penny candies to multi-million-dollar airplanes. The average U.S. supermarket carries several thousand different items on its shelves. To produce this tremendous variety of goods, different skills and machines are needed. Thus, the complexity of output demanded in the market requires an equally complex assortment of inputs.

In this country, the great majority of goods and services are produced in relatively free markets. Somehow, without guidance or central planning, these goods and services appear when needed, remain as long as they are demanded, and fade away when obsolescence or shifting tastes make them no longer wanted. In the face of this ever-changing flow of goods and services, one would think it impossible to make any generalizations and thus to capture and, perhaps, theoretically describe this complicated animal called the U.S. economy. Conversely, any comprehensible description of this economy appears doomed to such a level of abstraction or theoretical simplification that it will no longer relate to the real world it attempts to describe. So why not leave the economy alone? The answer is, of course, that your well-being and mine, plus that of another 199,999,998 people hang in the balance. In 1943, a frightening total of 1.6 million people died of starvation in Bengal. Why? In post-World-War-I Germany, there were times when a dollar earned one day was not worth a dime the next day. Why? During the peak of the Great Depression, 25% of the U.S. labor force was out of work and reduced to poverty. Why?

If we can understand why people starve, why they see their savings and pensions reduced to nothing, why they must beg for jobs when they are able-bodied; if we can understand the reasons for these anomalies, then there is hope that we can prevent them. There is *hope* — no more. Whether we can wipe out human suffering we don't know. But we do know that we cannot unless we are prepared to grapple with the problem.

This is not a book on economic development. The American people are not faced by immediate threats of wholesale starvation and, thanks to not-too-far-removed breakthroughs in economic theory, the Great Depression may not repeat itself. Still, the U.S. economy is not as healthy as we would like it to be. In spite of the many cures that have been suggested and attempted, and in spite of the many doctors who have suggested them, The Great Medicine has not yet been found, and very likely never will be. At the time of this writing, unemployment is running at the alarming rate of 5.9%. Incredibly, prices are rising simultaneously, and they are rising faster than at any time in the past two decades. Recession and inflation used to be mutually exclusive events, but now no longer. The recession-inflation, or reflation, is born. It has hurt enough people so that neither the public nor the economic profession can or do ignore it any longer.

The well-being or welfare of the people is at the bottom of economic theory — *all* economic theory. Unfortunately, the bewildering number of economics courses and special disciplines we have managed to create tend to obscure this fact. There exist the two broad fields of microeconomic theory and macroeconomic theory; there are the fields of international trade, regional economics, spatial economics (having to do with terrestrial space, not galaxies), and, of course, a specialty of its own called welfare economics. All of these disciplines make valid contributions, but the pursuit of any one of them is worthwhile only to the extent that it benefits mankind.

If the welfare of the people is our concern, how then do we measure it? What makes people well off? How can they be made better off? What is this stuff called welfare that people have to varying degrees? If the truth must be known, we economists have no answer to these questions. We don't even have good approximations. Certain material aspects of welfare are dealt with by a rather elaborate theory. What we have to say in this book rests in part on that theory. But material goods and services are not the only items in an individual's welfare portfolio, which includes such intangibles as religious freedom and personal bliss or misery derived from noneconomic and nonmaterial goods that are patently nonquantifiable. In fact, welfare itself cannot be quantified, has no dimensions, and thus escapes statistical evaluation.

Economists know all this. As human beings they will tell you that you are asking too much, that the exact quantification of well-being requires nothing less than to fathom the human soul. This is a task better left to philosophers and religious leaders. However poor, there is a substitute for measuring how well off a people is. From necessity rather than from virtue the following measuring device is used by economists: the living standard of a people, their ability to consume, their real income, their wealth, call it what you like. Admittedly, this measuring rod does not do justice to the intricate and highly subjective scale of human well-being, but it is better than nothing, and it is the best we have.

The wealth of a people or their ability to consume real goods and services, then, will be our measuring device of well-being through much of this book. This point deserves emphasis, because it tends to escape the student. There will be pages and whole chapters devoted to total output, employment, price levels, and other important phenomena. These matter only insofar as real wealth, and more precisely per capita real wealth, is concerned. And real wealth matters because through it, however deficiently, we measure human well-being.

Though on theoretical grounds per capita real wealth is a poor measure of well-being, on pragmatic grounds it does have redeeming features. From 1965 to 1970, per capita real wealth in the United States rose by about 10%. On the other hand, during the Great Depression per capita real wealth declined by approximately 40% in the short span of four years.[1] Few will deny that on the whole the American people went through a period of increasing well-being in the first instance and a period of diminishing well-being, to put it mildly, in the second instance.

This book is concerned with more than the definition and measurement of a nation's aggregate well-being. We are not simply passive participants in the big game of economics. To a degree, we can govern economic developments, we can take evasive action when on a collision course with calamity. The recognition of impending trouble and the implementation of preventive policies are the main topic of this book.

There are many pros and cons for using per capita real wealth as a measure of well-being. Some of these we will touch upon later, but first let us take a closer look at wealth, how it is defined, and how it is measured. After we have done this, we will be in a position to take up some of the issues surrounding this concept.

---

[1] Based on a decline in real per capita national income from $720.9 in 1929 to $426.7 in 1933, expressed in constant 1929 dollars. The preceding figures were calculated from national income and population data listed in the *Historical Statistics of the United States, Colonial Times to 1957*, U.S. Department of Commerce. More will be said in Chapter 2 on the use of national income as a measure of wealth and, ultimately, of well-being.

2 Wealth

If the wealth of a people, as we have said, to a large extent determines their well-being, we must first define the term wealth and devise a means of measuring it. To implement policies aimed at controlling the wealth of the people, we must have an objective and statistically reliable method of measuring it. We must know at all times what the people's wealth is and what it can reasonably be expected to be in the near future.

Wealth can be expressed either as a stock variable or as a flow variable with time dimensions attached.[1] There is nothing mysterious about these terms, as will become clear from the following example. Suppose you receive a letter from your lawyer advising you that in appreciation of your outstanding performance in the study of economics, some kind benefactor who shall remain unnamed has set up a trust fund in your name. This fund is in the amount of $100,000, and you may either cash it in today or leave it at the bank, where it is guaranteed to yield 6% interest in perpetuity.

Obviously, whichever option you exercise, you are wealthier as a result of this donation than you were before. Suppose you decide to cash in your trust fund. You then hold a stock of monetary wealth worth $100,000. This is the stock equivalent of your new wealth. This wealth is not likely to remain in

---

[1]Needless to say, our concept of wealth as a proxy for well-being differs from the wealth concept used, for example, by the Department of Commerce, which is, by definition, a stock variable consisting of land; residential, business, and public structures; and durable goods and inventories. In regard to the equivalence of income and wealth, see the books by B. P. Pesek and T. R. Saving, M. J. Bailey, and D. Patinkin, cited at the end of this chapter.

the form of money. After all, you must have had a reason to want all the money now. Chances are, you wanted to spend it. Suppose you spend every penny of it. You buy a home and a new car and a 20-foot runabout. You are still wealthier than you were before you received your donation. The economist would say that your stock of *real* wealth, as opposed to *monetary* wealth, has increased by the equivalent of $100,000.

Suppose, however, that you decide instead to leave the principal intact. In that case, at an interest rate of 6%, the $100,000 trust fund will yield an annual income of $6000. This is the flow equivalent of your new wealth. It has a time dimension attached to it. If you express your new wealth in dollars, i.e., $6000 per year, you are referring to your monetary income, which buys so many goods and services in the market. Therefore, if you prefer to express your new wealth in terms of real income, you will make reference to the actual goods and services that your new monetary income will buy.

It really makes no difference whether you express your new monetary wealth as a stock variable ($100,000) or as a flow variable ($6000 per year). Both terms describe exactly the same concept. Therefore, if you were asked to declare your wealth, you would probably use the variable that is more easily quantifiable. And that is precisely what the U.S. Department of Commerce does in measuring the wealth of this nation. For statistical simplicity, they use the flow variable called National Income—usually expressed in billions of dollars per year.

Admittedly, wealth is popularly defined as a stock variable: We speak of millionaires, not of $100,000-after-tax income recipients. In fact, most people probably do not know of the equivalence of flow and stock variables in expressing wealth. Why, then, does the U.S. Department of Commerce use national income as a measure of aggregate wealth?[2] The answer is that the aggregate stock of wealth is not statistically quantifiable, while aggregate income is.

Broadly speaking, income can be derived from two sources: human labor and nonhuman productive equipment. Few difficulties exist in expressing as a stock variable the wealth represented by a given machine: It is simply the value of the machine. In fact, the machine derives its value from the income stream it generates. Thus, it makes no difference whether we say that a given machine is worth $100,000 or that it produces a net income of $13,600 per year over the next ten years.[3] The only major problem is shifts in demand: Suppose, for example, that contrary to projections our machine generates an annual income of $13,600 for only five years and that this income stream is subsequently

---

[2] Actually, while the U.S. Department of Commerce does measure national income, it does not necessarily agree that this variable is a measure of aggregate well-being. Theirs is an accounting approach, ours is conceptual.

[3] This assumes an interest rate of 6% and zero scrap value of the machine after 10 years. Under these conditions, if the machine generates a net income of $13,600 per year for a period of 10 years, the present value of this income stream, and thus the value of the machine, is $100,000. See present value tables in Appendix A, in particular Table 3.

diminished to $5000 a year for the remaining five years, due to an unantici-
pated decline in demand for its product. This reduces the present value of the
machine to $73,000.[4] However, since the machine was purchased for $100,000,
a capital loss is incurred in the amount of $27,000. Alternatively, an increase
in the value of our machine after it has been purchased would be in the nature
of a capital gain.

In the case of productive equipment, then, reporting wealth as income
rather than as stock eliminates the need to make adjustments for capital
gains or losses. These adjustments would be required retroactively if the initially calculated present value of the machine were used as an indicator of the
stock of wealth represented by the equipment. Such adjustments would be
cumbersome but not impossible.

For the nation as a whole, its wealth as represented by the value of its
productive equipment would be subject to correction for as long as that equipment lasts. Suppose we agree that the relevant time span is ten years. Then a
nation's stock of wealth as represented by its productive equipment could only
be established unambiguously with a ten-year lag. In the interim, preliminary
wealth estimates would have to be subject to constant adjustments in an upward or downward direction.

What about the second source of income? The present value of human
labor cannot possibly be calculated with any degree of reliability. Mathematically speaking, the present value of my labor services is equal to the discounted value of my future incomes, and therein lies the problem:[5] A man's
future income stream cannot possibly be estimated with any accuracy. Death,
incapacitation, unemployment, job changes, and similar events cannot be
predicted. As a result, human wealth cannot be expressed as a stock variable.
However, it can easily be expressed as a flow variable, i.e., in current income.
In the aggregate, the incomes of all people in an economy can be calculated
with relative ease.

A nation's wealth consists of its human and nonhuman wealth. Human
wealth, as we have seen, cannot be expressed as a stock variable; nonhuman
wealth can be so expressed, but with reservations. Both kinds of wealth can
easily be determined if the relevant flow variables are used. This is the reason
why the U.S. Department of Commerce uses the flow variable called national
income to calculate this nation's wealth.

The student might object that there is more to wealth than the income

---

[4] Again, this figure can be found with the present value tables in Appendix A. Thus, the
present value of a five-year annuity in the amount of $13,600 is equal to 4.21 × 13,600 or $57,250,
using an interest rate of 6%. Similarly, the present value of a five-year annuity, in the amount of
$5000, starting in the sixth year and ending in the tenth year, is equal to (7.36 − 4.21) × 5000 or
$15,750. The student should check these calculations to make sure he understands them.

[5] Note carefully that we are talking about the present value of income streams derived from
human labor, not the value of human life. For example, at an interest rate of 6%, if a 45-year old
employee expects to earn $10,000 per year for another twenty years, and nothing thereafter, the
present value of his future income is 11.4 × 10,000 or $114,000. This does not mean that this
man's life is presently worth $114,000. The value of a human life is not an economic issue, since it
cannot be determined objectively.

stream derived from human and nonhuman resources. After all, such a definition of wealth is oriented toward the present and future and neglects wealth accumulated in the past. This objection is valid, and an adjustment is required to allow for accumulated wealth. Let us first discuss this idea in terms of a stock variable.

The present stock of wealth, then, consists of two items: (a) assets accumulated and currently owned by the people and (b) the present value of the future income derived from human and nonhuman factors of production. For an individual, this can be expressed mathematically as follows:

$$W_s = A_s + \sum_{t=1}^{1} \frac{1}{(1+r)^t} \cdot (I_{t,h} + I_{t,p}), \qquad \text{2-1}$$

where W_s = an individual's stock of wealth,

A_s = his accumulated assets,

$I_{t,h}$ = his future income from human labor in year t,

$I_{t,p}$ = his future income from productive equipment in his possession, year t,

r = interest rate,

t = time, years,

1 = our individual's remaining lifetime.

The problem now is what to include in our individual's assets. We have already decided that it is more convenient to treat as a flow variable that part of his wealth which will be derived from his labor or from his possession of productive equipment. If we were to also count the value of his machines into his asset holdings A_s, we would be guilty of double-counting. Using the example of our $100,000 trust fund, such an accounting would be equivalent to the assertion that the recipient of the fund has increased his wealth by asset holdings worth $100,000 plus an increase in income in the amount of $6000 per year. Obviously, this kind of reasoning would overstate the newly acquired wealth.

Since the income stream from human and nonhuman productive resources, i.e., from all productive resources, is already contained in the terms $I_{t,h}$ and $I_{t,p}$ in equation 2-1, productive resources can no longer be counted into the asset holdings A_s. Thus, A_s stands for nonproductive assets that have been accumulated in the past. As we will soon see, in national income accounts this means durable consumer goods, and not even all of those. Houses, cars, refrigerators, lawn mowers, furniture—in short, all consumer goods ordinarily lasting longer than one year—are examples of durable consumer goods.

Equation 2-1 expresses the wealth of one individual; the wealth of all people, the nation's wealth if you wish, is the sum of the wealth held by all individuals in that nation. Conceptually, this presents no problem. If, however, we wished to express an individual's wealth entirely as a flow variable, we would have to convert equation 2-1 into its flow equivalent, expressed in dollars per year, for example. Since the terms $I_{t,h}$ and $I_{t,p}$ are already expressed as flow variables, the only problem remaining is to convert the stock variable A_s (nonproductive assets) into its flow equivalent. In equation form, an individual's wealth may thus be expressed as a flow variable as follows:

$$W_f = A_f + (I_h + I_p),\qquad\qquad 2\text{-}2$$

where W_f = an individual's wealth as a flow variable,

A_f = the flow equivalent of our individual's nonproductive assets.

The question now arises how, in practice, the stock variable A_s in equation 2–1 is converted into its flow equivalent A_f in equation 2–2. An example may serve to illustrate how. Let there be an individual whose only nonproductive asset is his home, which he owns outright. The basic question is, what income does he derive from his own home? The imputed income flowing from his home is equal to the rental payments he would have to make, if he did not own the place. That is, our man is assumed to rent the house from himself, and the imaginary rental payments are included in the national income accounts. In fact, in these accounts the payments are specifically listed under the heading "rental income of persons." As a matter of interest, this item is surprisingly large. In 1969, for example, the rental income of persons exceeded military wages and salaries by approximately $3 billion annually and it lagged behind corporate dividends by less than that.

Let us pause for a moment to consider what we have accomplished so far. We have reluctantly agreed that wealth is an important determinant of the well-being of people. We have found that wealth can be measured as a stock or a flow variable and that in fact it is measured as a flow variable by the U.S. government. Most of our discussion has been in monetary terms—that is, we thought of income as so many dollars per year. The trouble is, we really could not care less, individually and as a nation, how many dollars a year we make. What we do care about is the goods and services that our income will command in the market. In other words, it is the real income that matters.

Suppose a man makes $1000 per month. In that case, ignoring taxes, social security, and other mandatory deductions, his monthly paycheck shows the figure $1000, and that amount allows our man a very definite living standard. Now suppose that the dollar is outlawed, and the cent remains as the only legal denomination. Our man's paycheck would now be in the amount of 100,-000 cents. Except for the disappearance of a decimal point on the paycheck, nothing has happened; the 100,000 cents command the same amount of goods and services in the market as the $1000 used to. Thus, in real terms, our man is as well off now as he was before the dollar was outlawed.

The relevance of a man's real income can be brought into sharp focus by another example. Suppose the man from our previous example wakes up one morning and finds out that the price level has doubled overnight. His next paycheck will be in the amount of $1000 as usual. That is, his monetary income has not changed, but since the purchasing power of money has been cut in half, his paycheck will buy only half the goods and services it used to buy. In real terms, then, our man's income has been cut in half, and he is likely to take notice, since his real wealth has been reduced as a result.

Since we are basically interested in the real, not the monetary, income we receive, why do we measure the people's well-being in terms of monetary income? We do this as a matter of convenience. The alternative to using money income would be to express real income as the goods and services that the money income will buy in the market. Thus, our $1000-a-month paycheck from the preceding example may be said to represent a real monthly income of 5 lbs. of steak, 10 lbs. of hamburger meat, 20 lbs. of potatoes, 10 gallons of milk, 3 fifths of bourbon, 700 car-miles, the use of 1500 square feet of housing, etc., etc. Obviously, this is a totally impractical approach, much too cumbersome to use in practice. So, for simplicity we measure income in money. Money, however, is a rubbery yardstick. During inflationary periods, that is, in times of rising price levels, it overestimates the real value of monetary income; in times of falling price levels, it underestimates it. Needed, then, is a method of compensating monetary income for price-level changes. This is accomplished through the so-called price index.

The Price Index

There are several methods of measuring changes in price levels. The most important one of these, and the only one we will consider in detail in this text, is the so-called consumer price index, henceforth referred to simply as the price index. This index is calculated and published monthly by the U.S. Department of Labor. Almost without exception, references to rising price levels or inflationary trends, as made in the press and in government releases, are based on this consumer price index.

Basically, the price index measures the cost of a given combination of goods and services in one year as compared to some earlier, "base" year. This combination of goods and services is called a "market basket" and reflects average U.S. consumption patterns. The relevant question in connection with the price index is: How much do I have to pay this year for a given market basket that cost $100 last year or some other preceding base year? A sample calculation, shown in Table 2–1, will do much to clarify the procedure used in calculating the price index.

The market basket, column 1 in Table 2–1, contains bread, butter, and milk. Column 2 shows the average quantities of these goods consumed yearly by an average American family. Given the prices of the goods in the base year and in the year in question, the consumption expenditures can be calculated for both years. It should be noted that the quantities consumed remain constant. Furthermore, the Department of Labor goes to great trouble to make sure that the quality of the consumer items also remains the same. With quan-

Table 2–1
The Consumer Price Index

Market Basket		Base Year		Next Year	
Good	Quantity	Price, $	Expenditures, $	Price, $	Expenditures, $
(1)	(2)	(3)	(4)	(5)	(6)
Bread	200 lbs.	.20	40.00	.25	50.00
Butter	50 lbs.	1.00	50.00	.90	45.00
Milk	100 Gals.	1.10	110.00	1.20	120.00
			Total 200.00		Total 215.00

tities and qualities the same, any changes in consumption expenditures are a reflection of the cumulative effect of price changes.

In Table 2–1 the new market basket costs $215, while the base year's had cost $200. This can be expressed in two ways: The cost of living has risen, or the purchasing power of the dollar has been diluted. The price index measures the increase in the cost of living, expressed as an index figure. In the case at hand, the price index is equal to $(215/200) \times 100 = 107.5$. Thus, according to Table 2–1, the price index has risen by 7.5%.[6] (Note that the price index has risen even though the price of butter has declined, because the price increases of bread and milk more than offset this decline.)

In real life, the Department of Labor market basket includes approximately

---

[6] Mathematically, the price index may be expressed as follows:

$$P.I. = \frac{\sum\limits_{i=1}^{n} p'_i \cdot x^0_i}{\sum\limits_{i=1}^{n} p^0_i \cdot x^0_i} \times 100,$$

where $P.I. =$ price index,

$\sum\limits_{i=1}^{n} p^0_i \cdot x^0_i =$ cost of the market basket in the base year,

$\sum\limits_{i=1}^{n} p'_i \cdot x^0_i =$ cost of the market basket in the year under investigation,

$x =$ goods and services,
$p =$ prices,
subscript $i =$ identifies goods and services over which the summation is made,
superscript $^0 =$ relative to base year,
superscript $' =$ relative to year in question.
The student will notice that Table 2–1 is nothing but an application of the above formula.

400 different goods and services, and is revised periodically to bring it up to date; since 1935, for example, four such revisions have been made, most recently in 1964. Sales taxes, when applicable, are reflected in the price index.

Figure 2–1 shows the rise of the consumer price index over the last thirty years. Also shown are price increases of several major subgroups that are part of the market basket. Actually, the Department of Labor uses a base *period* rather than a point in time for a price-level reference; the average price of a market basket over a given period, rather than at a given date, determines the price base. In Figure 2–1, the price index of all items and of the various subgroups uses the base period 1957–1959. This is why the various price indexes are approximately equal to 100 in 1958.

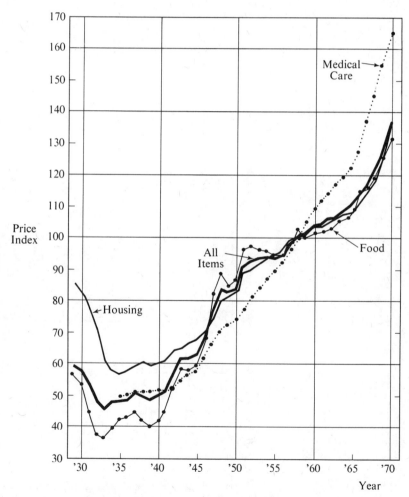

Figure 2–1   *The Consumer Price Index*
(1957–59 = 100)

Source: *Handbook of Labor Statistics 1970*, U.S. Department of Labor.

Table 2-2
Consumer Price Index, All Items and Major
Groups, U.S. City Average, 1935–69
[1957–59 = 100]

Period	All Items	Food	Housing	Apparel and Upkeep	Transpor-tation	Medical Care	Personal Care	Reading and Recreation	Other Goods and Services
1935	47.8	42.1	56.3	46.5	49.4	49.4	42.6	50.2	52.7
1936	48.3	42.5	57.1	46.9	49.8	49.6	43.2	51.0	52.6
1937	50.0	44.2	59.1	49.3	50.6	50.0	45.7	52.5	54.0
1938	49.1	41.0	60.1	49.0	51.0	50.2	46.7	54.3	54.5
1939	48.4	39.9	59.7	48.3	49.8	50.2	46.5	54.4	55.4
1940	48.8	40.5	59.9	48.8	49.5	50.3	46.4	55.4	57.1
1941	51.3	44.2	61.4	51.1	51.2	50.6	47.6	57.3	58.2
1942	56.8	51.9	64.2	59.6	55.7	52.0	52.2	60.0	59.9
1943	60.3	57.9	64.9	62.2	55.5	54.5	57.6	65.0	63.0
1944	61.3	57.1	66.4	66.7	55.5	56.2	61.7	72.0	64.7
1945	62.7	58.4	67.5	70.1	55.4	57.5	63.6	75.0	67.3
1946	68.0	66.9	69.3	76.9	58.3	60.7	68.2	77.5	69.5
1947	77.8	81.3	74.5	89.2	64.3	65.7	76.2	82.5	75.4
1948	83.8	88.2	79.8	95.0	71.6	69.8	79.1	86.7	78.9
1949	83.0	84.7	81.0	91.3	77.0	72.0	78.9	89.9	81.2

Year									
1950	83.8	85.8	83.2	90.1	79.0	73.4	78.9	89.3	82.6
1951	90.5	95.4	88.2	98.2	84.0	76.9	86.3	92.0	86.1
1952	92.5	97.1	89.9	97.2	89.6	81.1	87.3	92.4	90.6
1953	93.2	95.6	92.3	96.5	92.1	83.9	88.1	93.3	92.8
1954	93.6	95.4	93.4	96.3	90.8	86.6	88.5	92.4	94.3
1955	93.3	94.0	94.1	95.9	89.7	88.6	90.0	92.1	94.3
1956	94.7	94.7	95.5	97.8	91.3	91.8	93.7	93.4	95.8
1957	98.0	97.8	98.5	99.5	96.5	95.5	97.1	96.9	98.5
1958	100.7	101.9	100.2	99.8	99.7	100.1	100.4	100.8	99.8
1959	101.5	100.3	101.3	100.6	103.8	104.4	102.4	102.4	101.8
1960	103.1	101.4	103.1	102.2	103.8	108.1	104.1	104.9	103.8
1961	104.2	102.6	103.9	103.0	105.0	111.3	104.6	107.2	104.6
1962	105.4	103.6	104.8	103.6	107.2	114.2	106.5	109.6	105.3
1963	106.7	105.1	106.0	104.8	107.8	117.0	107.9	111.5	107.1
1964	108.1	106.4	107.2	105.7	109.3	119.4	109.2	114.1	108.8
1965	109.9	108.8	108.5	106.8	111.1	122.3	109.9	115.2	111.4
1966	113.1	114.2	111.1	109.6	112.7	127.7	112.2	117.1	114.9
1967	116.3	115.2	114.3	114.0	115.9	136.7	115.5	120.1	118.2
1968	121.2	119.3	119.1	120.1	119.6	145.0	120.3	125.7	123.6
1969	127.7	125.5	126.7	127.1	124.2	155.0	126.2	130.5	129.0

Source: *Handbook of Labor Statistics 1970*, U.S. Department of Labor.

That the price indexes are approximately, not exactly, equal to 100 is better seen in Table 2–2, a reproduction of the consumer price index in the *Handbook of Labor Statistics 1970,* published by the U.S. Department of Labor. Outstanding in Figure 2–1 and Table 2–2 is the accelerated price increase of medical care.

The GNP-Deflator

In early 1971, our nation's gross national product, or GNP,[7] surpassed the one-trillion-dollar mark. This event was duly heralded in the press. For the first time in the history of this nation, we were told, the total U.S. output of goods and services had reached such proportions that it would take a trillion dollars to buy it in the market. In a narrow sense, this is the truth—but it is not the whole truth, since a great deal of this apparent increase in GNP reflects rising price levels.

The index used to adjust the GNP for price-level changes is the so-called GNP-deflator. As we will see in Chapter 3, some 60% of our nation's GNP consists of consumer goods and services. As a result, we would expect increasing consumer prices to coincide with an increase in the GNP-deflator. And this is generally the case. While they are not usually numerically the same, the consumer price index and the GNP-deflator move together.

The United States has been experiencing a practically continuous price-level rise since the Great Depression, or more precisely since 1933, the year in which the Great Depression reached bottom. Thus, if we were to compare an after-1933 GNP, expressed in current or nominal dollars, with the GNP of 1933, the more recent GNP would be overstated.

The fictitiously large increase in the nominal GNP due to rising price levels is dramatically brought into focus by Table 2–3. Column 2 shows the nominal GNP for certain years of the 1933 to 1970 period. The apparent increase in GNP, relative to the 1933 GNP, is shown in current dollars (column 3) and as a percentage figure (column 4). Using the GNP-deflator in column 5, the real GNP, expressed in 1958 dollars, is listed in column 6. From this column the increase in real GNP was calculated (columns 7 and 8).

As can be seen in Table 2–3, the nominal GNP in 1933 was $55.6 billion; by 1940 it had risen to $99.7 billion. Thus, in the period 1933–1940, the GNP had apparently risen by $44.1 billion or 79%. In the same period, however, the price level had risen, causing the GNP-deflator to increase by over 11%, from 39.3 to 43.9. This made the 1940 nominal GNP fictitiously large, relative to 1933. In constant 1958 dollars, the real 1933 GNP was $141.5 billion, com-

---

[7]The GNP is often used to measure the performance of an economy. An exact definition of this and other national income accounting terms will be given shortly.

Table 2-3
Our Inflated GNP
(Billions of Dollars)

Year	Nominal GNP	Apparent Increase in GNP, Relative to 1933		GNP-Deflator 1958 Base Year	GNP expressed in 1958-dollars (Real GNP)	Deflated or Real Increase in GNP, Relative to 1933	
		$	%			$	%
(1)	(2)	(3)	(4)	(5)	(6)	(7)	(8)
1933	55.6	–	–	39.3	141.5	–	–
1940	99.7	44.1	79	43.9	227.2	85.7	61
1945	211.9	156.3	281	59.7	355.2	213.7	151
1950	284.8	229.2	412	80.2	355.3	213.8	151
1955	398.0	342.4	616	90.9	438.0	296.5	210
1958	447.3	391.7	704	100.0	447.3	305.8	216
1960	503.7	448.1	805	103.3	487.7	346.2	245
1965	684.9	629.3	1132	110.9	617.8	476.3	337
1970	974.1	918.5	1652	135.3	720.0	578.5	409

Source: Survey of Current Business, U.S. Department of Commerce, July 1971, p. 46, Table A.

pared to $227.2 billion in 1940. Thus, the growth of this nation's real GNP in the period 1933–1940, expressed in constant 1958 dollars, was only $85.7 billion or 61%.

We have seen that more recent nominal GNPs are overstated relative to preceding years in times of rising price levels. Suppose, however, we wish to compare previous GNPs with a more recent GNP, using the latter as a basis of comparison. In this case, if a period of rising price levels is under consideration, the previous GNPs will be understated and have to be corrected upward to compensate for the loss in purchasing power during the period in question. For example, both the nominal and real GNPs amounted to $447.3 billion in the base year of 1958. In 1955, however, the nominal GNP was $398.0 billion. But since the price level had been rising during the relevant three-year period, the purchasing power of the dollar had been reduced, i.e., the 1955-dollar was worth more than the 1958-dollar. In fact, Table 2–3 indicates that 398.0 billion 1955-dollars correspond to 438.0 billion 1958-dollars (columns 2 and 6).

Also worth noting in Table 2–3 is that the discrepancy between nominal and real GNPs increases as the relevant time interval is increased. Thus, the uncorrected GNP almost doubled during the last decade ($503.7 billion to $974.1 billion); after correction for price-level changes, the rate of increase is found to be only about one half the uncorrected rate, a still impressive 48% ($487.7 billion to $720.0 billion). If we go back to 1950, the nominal increase in GNP, as of 1970, is 242%, compared to a real increase of 103%. Finally, the uncorrected 1970 GNP is approximately 16.5 times larger than the corresponding 1933 GNP. In real terms, the growth was limited to a factor of four. These and other figures in Table 2–3 point to the importance of a correct assessment of price-level changes.

Let us recapitulate what we have accomplished so far: The wealth of the people can be measured as a stock or a flow variable, and is in fact measured by the U.S. government as a flow variable called national income. The nominal level of national income, or more precisely of the gross national product, reflects the combined effect of changes in real GNP and in the price level. To isolate the change in real GNP, and through it the change in wealth, an independent method of quantifying price-level changes is needed. This method was developed in our discussion of the price index and the GNP-deflator. Knowing the relevant GNP-deflators, we can adjust any year's nominal GNP in terms of the base year's GNP. This enables us to make a meaningful comparison of the GNP or the national income, and thus of aggregate wealth, at various points in time.

Two important questions still remain unanswered in our discussion. We know that national income can be used to measure aggregate wealth, and that GNP-deflators can be used to facilitate meaningful comparisons of aggregate wealth at different points in time. But we do not yet know how, in practice, the flow variable measuring this aggregate wealth, namely national income, is defined and how it is measured. To answer these questions, let us first turn to the definition of the national income.

National Income Defined

Let us once more take up our example of the trust fund; the recipient of that fund had the option of taking his newly acquired wealth in the form of either a stock variable ($100,000) or a flow variable ($6000 per year). Suppose that he makes arrangements to have his income from the fund increased to $10,000 per year. Does such an arrangement make him wealthier? Of course not. The only difference is that he is using up his principal. What really happens to his principal is illustrated in Table 2–4.

Table 2–4
Consumption of Principal

Year	Beginning Capital Stock, $	Interest, $ ($r = 6\%$)	Income Payments, $	Out of Principal, $	Remaining Capital Stock, $
1	100,000	6,000	10,000	4,000	96,000
2	96,000	5,750	10,000	4,250	91,750
3	91,750	5,500	10,000	4,500	87,250
4	87,250	5,250	10,000	4,750	82,500
5	82,500	4,950	10,000	5,050	77,450
6	77,450	4,650	10,000	5,350	72,100
7	72,100	4,340	10,000	5,660	66,440
8	66,440	3,980	10,000	6,020	60,420
9	60,420	3,630	10,000	6,370	54,050
10	54,050	3,250	10,000	6,750	47,300
11	47,300	2,840	10,000	7,160	40,140
12	40,140	2,410	10,000	7,590	32,550
13	32,550	1,960	10,000	8,040	24,510
14	24,510	1,470	10,000	8,530	15,980
15	15,980	960	10,000	9,040	6,940
16	6,940	420	7,360	6,940	-0-

Table 2–4 shows that if our trust-fund recipient insists on being paid an annual income of $10,000, he will consume his principal in 16 years. The original stipulation of the fund was that the recipient could either cash in the total amount at once, i.e., take his new wealth in the form of a stock variable, or opt for the equivalent flow variable, namely $6000 per year in perpetuity. The key

lies in the term "in perpetuity," since it implies that the trust fund remains intact. If our man withdraws more than $6000 per year from the fund, the fund does not remain intact. As Table 2–4 shows, the yearly income payments of $10,000 are not the equivalent of our recipient's newly acquired wealth.

The perpetuity clause, then, becomes critical in defining our trust-fund recipient's newly acquired wealth as a flow variable. This perpetuity concept could be formally incorporated into a definition of income or national income, but it is not. Rather, the equivalent concept of an unimpaired source of funds is used in this definition. The newly acquired wealth of our trust-fund recipient may then be defined as the maximum stream of income payments that may be derived from the fund while leaving the fund itself intact.

The preceding definition is, in effect, the one used in our national income accounts. Replace the trust fund of our example with the term "capital stock" or "producing capacity," and replace the recipient's income with the term "national income," and the following definition emerges:

Our national income, and therefore our nation's wealth, is the maximum income that can be obtained in a given year while leaving the capital stock (the producing capacity) intact.

Unfortunately, our definition of national income still contains the term "income"; hence, some clarification is required. Let us discuss this concept at first in real terms. Suppose we are dealing with an economy as shown in Table 2–5. That is, our economy, henceforth called Slobovia, has a capital stock of 100 machines and produces 210 market baskets in a given year.

Table 2–5
Slobovia's Economy

Time	Capital Stock	Consumer Goods
Beginning of Year 1	100 machines	210 market baskets
End of Year 1	100 machines	

Clearly, in accordance with our definition, Slobovia's national income is 210 market baskets. At the beginning of year 1, Slobovia had a producing capacity of 100 machines and at the end of the year, the producing capacity has remained intact. Using this producing capacity, Slobovia has produced 210 market baskets to be consumed by the Slobovians (henceforth called Slobs for brevity).

This does not mean, of course, that no machines have been produced in Slobovia. Suppose, for example, that of the 100 initial machines 20 wore out during year 1 and had to be replaced by new machines. This means that total output in Slobovia was 210 market baskets and 20 machines. But since the 20 machines were used to replace worn-out machines, i.e., to keep the producing capacity intact, these machines are not counted into Slobovia's national income. In national income accounting terminology, Slobovia's total output or gross national product is 210 market baskets and 20 machines. Slobovia's national income is 210 market baskets.

The capital stock of a nation does not usually remain the same; it increases in normal times. But since national income is based on the concept of a constant capital stock, any *net* increase in capital stock is added to national income and any *net* decrease in capital stock is deducted from it. In our trust fund example, if the recipient opts to withdraw only $2000 at the end of the first year, does this reduce his newly acquired wealth? That wealth, as we have seen, is $100,000 or $6000 per year; it cannot be affected by the manner in which the new owner disposes of it. If he withdraws only $2000 of the $6000 he has coming, his principal is increased by $4000. His wealth, as defined above in terms of income, now consists of two parts:

1. Withdrawal of $2000, and
2. Net addition to the fund of $4000.

His income, then, is $6000 per year. A real-life economy makes an equivalent adjustment in determining its income. This is illustrated in Table 2–6.

Table 2–6
Slobovia's Growing Economy

Time	Capital Stock	Consumer Goods
Beginning of Year 2	100 machines	210 market baskets
End of Year 2	110 machines	

Slobovia's national income in year 2 is 210 market baskets and 10 machines. That is, the Slobs withdrew from their economy, i.e., consumed, 210 market baskets. In addition, there was a net increase in capital stock in the amount of 10 machines.[8] Suppose we want to know Slobovia's GNP in year 2. Table 2–6 does not show sufficient information from which to calculate Slobovia's GNP. Needed is the number of machines that wore out and were replaced in year 2. Let us again assume that 20 machines are involved. Then the total output or GNP of Slobovia is 210 market baskets and 30 machines.

Machines and market baskets are cool expository devices, but we already know that they won't do in real life. For one thing, they can't be added, a property they share with apples and oranges. For another thing, there are many different kinds of machines, and machines are not the only items that make up a nation's capital stock. In the consumer goods area, market baskets present similar problems. Thus, instead of being expressed in real terms, the GNP and national income are usually shown in monetary terms. Let us illustrate this for Slobovia with the aid of Tables 2–5 and 2–6, assuming a market price of $2 per machine and $1 per market basket.

In year 1 (Table 2–5), Slobovia's national income of 210 market baskets will be shown as $210. The Slobs' GNP, on the other hand, is $250, since their total output also includes 20 machines at $2 a piece. Similarly, in year 2 (Table 2–6), the Slobovian economy experienced a national income of $230 and a GNP of $270.

Actually, the national income and GNP can be determined independently, and their difference can be reconciled by means of a double book entry system. This cannot be shown with our trust fund example, since no real production takes place in it. Anyhow, we have gotten all the mileage out of this example that we could hope for, and we are, therefore, dismissing it for good. But our Slobovian example portrays a producing economy and thus lends itself to a double entry system of national income accounting. Let us relate this system to Table 2–6.

We will recall that 20 machines wore out in Slobovia during year 2. Also, the price of market baskets was assumed to be $1 per unit, compared to a price of $2 per machine. Since the Slobs produced a total output of 210 market baskets and 30 machines, twenty of which went to replace the worn-out ones, Slobovia's GNP was calculated to be $270. This number appears on the right-hand or GNP side of the national income accounts. In fact, this side of the U.S. income accounts shows all finished goods produced in a given year plus

---

[8]This discussion opens up an avenue we will not pursue at this time, namely the concept of economic growth. In our trust fund, the less the recipient withdraws for present consumption, the faster his principal, and thus his future income, will grow. Likewise, the less a national economy withdraws for present consumption, the faster its capital stock, and thus its future wealth, will grow. For example, Japan's phenomenal growth after World War II is attributable to a net investment, i.e., a net addition to its capital stock, of over 20% of its national income. An underdeveloped country, on the other hand, oftentimes cannot achieve sufficient growth because it is compelled to withdraw for consumption most or all of its total output, leaving little or nothing to add to its capital stock. U.S. net investment, by comparison, has been fluctuating between 6% and 10% in the last few years.

gross investment. A detailed description in the following chapter will show a breakdown of these goods as they are listed in the U.S. accounts. For now, it only matters that the dollar value of an economy's total output appears on the right-hand or GNP side of the national income accounts and that this dollar value is labeled gross national product.

An independent determination of national income is based on the fact that the Slobs of our example did not produce their total output for nothing. They had to be paid wages for their labor; their corporations earned profits, part of which were distributed as dividends; interest payments had to be made for the use of borrowed funds; these interest payments, of course, are income to the owners of these funds. In short, the production of total output generated a stream of incomes to the various inhabitants of Slobovia. The aggregate of these incomes is that independent measure of national income. It is listed on the left-hand or national income side of the national income accounts.

If what we have said before is correct, then the national income on the left side and the GNP on the right side of the accounts cannot be equal: Slobovia's national income was $230, its GNP was $270. The reason for this inequality is that the term "national income" is tied to the concept of a constant capital stock or producing capacity. Thus, it ignores the twenty new machines that replaced worn-out machines. If these twenty replacement machines were added to the national income, both sides of our accounts would be equal.

The trouble in real life is how to account for the capital equipment that was produced as replacements. Machines are not simply replaced when they wear out. Newer, bigger, improved machines take their place: The diesel locomotive replaces the steam locomotive; nuclear generators replace conventional electric generating plants. Moreover, new products spring to life that require completely new types of machines and processes. This dilemma is solved in the U.S. income accounting system by the use of an entry labeled capital consumption allowance. Since this item consists almost exclusively (over 90%) of depreciation charges, we will make our discussion easier by using the latter term in lieu of the less familiar term capital consumption allowance.

In the United States, firms are allowed to divert a portion of their revenues into a fund out of which replacement machinery and other capital equipment may be purchased. That is, the firms treat payments into this fund as a cost, called depreciation expenses, even though they retain them.[9] Thus, deprecia-

---

[9] There are several methods of calculating depreciation, but all have one thing in common. Total depreciation charges on a given piece of capital equipment may never exceed the purchase price, net of salvage value, of that equipment. Once the total depreciation charges reach that value, the equipment is said to be "off the books" whether it is still in use or not. The simplest type of depreciation, namely straight-line depreciation, may serve to illustrate the problem. Suppose a machine is purchased for $1000, while the life expectancy of that machine is five years and the salvage value zero. In this case the firm that bought the machine may deduct one-fifth of the purchase price, or $200, each year, so that the funds will be available for a new machine when the existing one wears out. Since most firms use many types of capital equipment, some of which wears out in any given year, what really happens is that each firm pools its current depreciation charges on all capital equipment for the purchase of those machines currently in need of replacement. See any standard accounting text for details.

tion expenses differ from other costs in that they do not constitute an outflow of money. Since depreciation charges are retained by the firms, they are income to no one in the economy. In our national income accounts, therefore, they are not included in the wages, profits, interest payments or other items that make up national income, and that is why national income is less than GNP. If these retained depreciation charges were added to national income, the resulting sum would be theoretically equal to the dollar value of the GNP—theoretically, but not in practice. In practice, minor variations usually do occur due to inaccuracies of measurement. To balance the national income accounts, these variations, normally less than one-half of one percent, are added to the left-hand side of the accounts under the label statistical discrepancy.

Let us review what we have learned so far. The U.S. national income accounts are set up as a double-entry system. On the right-hand or GNP side, the dollar value of the total output is listed and labeled GNP. On the left-hand or national income side, all incomes are listed. Their sum is called national income. Not included in this national income are depreciation charges. These were retained by the firms to replace worn-out capital equipment. When these depreciation charges are added to national income, equality with the GNP results.[10] The national income accounts of our Slobovian economy (Table 2–6) will appear as shown in Table 2–7.

Table 2–7
Slobovia's National Income Accounts

	National Income		Gross National Product	
National Income (Wages, profits, interest, etc., derived from production of 210 market baskets and 10 machines)	$ 230	Consumer Goods (210 market baskets)	$ 210	
Depreciation Allowance (for 20 worn-out machines)	40	Gross Investment (30 machines)	60	
Charges against GNP	270	GNP	270	

This terminates the conceptual part of our discussion of national income and GNP. We are now ready to move on to the empirical part. Chapter 3 deals

---

[10] As we will see in Chapter 3, this is not exactly true. For some unfathomed reason, our national income accountants threw in another term, namely net national product, which separates national income from GNP. At this stage, however, what has been said is good enough. See, for example, T. F. Dernburg and D. M. McDougall, *Macroeconomics*, 3rd edition (New York: McGraw-Hill Book Company, 1968), p. 30.

with the problem of how our national income, and thus our nation's wealth, is measured in practice, and it points up some of the difficulties that are encountered in this area.

Problems

1. There are two equivalent ways of measuring the wealth of an economy. What are they? Which method is normally used? Why is the alternative method not used?

2. As a matter of convenience, most economists use the GNP as a measure of our economy's performance. Conceptually, this is not strictly correct. Why not? What is the difference, definitionally and conceptually, between the GNP and the national income? Why is it permissible to use the GNP instead of the national income?

3. Suppose a hypothetical nation has had the following economic performance:

	Physical Capacity	*Output*
Beginning of Year 1971	70 machines	120 market baskets
End of Year 1971	90 machines	

   What is this nation's real national income? If one machine is valued at $2.00 and one market basket at $1.00, what is the national income in dollars? Suppose the relevant national-income deflator in 1971, relative to the base year of 1960, is 0.90. In 1960-dollars, what is the 1971 national income?

4. Calculate the 1971 price index from the following data:

Goods	*Quantity Consumed*	*Base Year Price, $*	*1971 Price $*
Potatoes	200 Lbs.	0.10	0.10
Steaks	100 Lbs.	0.90	1.10
Milk	100 Gals.	1.00	1.20

5. Suppose you are asked to calculate the GNP-deflator for 1971, using consumer goods, investment goods, government services, and net exports as the major relevant subcategories. Let the percentages of these categories in this nation's GNP, and their corresponding price indices, be as follows:

Subcategory	% of GNP	Price Index
Consumer goods	60	120
Investment goods	18	110
Government services	19	125
Exports	3	115

6. Suppose you are informed by your lawyer that a trust fund has been set up for you out of which you will be paid $10,000 per year for ten years, and nothing thereafter. The first payment is due exactly one year from now. At an interest rate of 8%, how much is this income stream worth today?

7. Monetary units are a less-than-perfect measure of national income. Yes or no? Explain.

8. "By tightening our belts today, we can materially improve our lot in the future." In macroeconomics, what is the meaning of this statement?

9. Suppose you are told of some country having a national income equal to, or almost equal to, its GNP. Do you think this is possible? If so, what does this suggest to you about that country's future?

10. "To measure the people's well-being in so many dollars they receive annually is preposterous. It degrades them to consuming machines and ignores their innate human qualities." Do you agree or not? Justify your position.

11. "Another day, another dollar." As a budding economist you should be able to spot a fundamental weakness in that popular expression. What weakness? To remove the deficiency, how would you rephrase the statement?

12. An increase in the price level redistributes wealth between lenders and borrowers. Who gains, and why?

Suggested Readings

On the equivalence of income and wealth:

B. P. Pesek and T. R. Saving, *The Foundations of Money and Banking* (New York: The Macmillan Company, 1968), Chapter 20.

M. J. Bailey, *National Income and the Price Level: A Study in Macroeconomic Theory,* 2nd ed. (New York; McGraw-Hill Book Company, 1971), Chapter 12.

D. Patinkin, *Money, Interest, and Prices,* 2nd ed. (New York: Harper & Row, Publishers, 1965), Mathematical Appendix 11.

On price-level changes:

H. M. Louison, "Some Problems of Price Indices and the Gains and Losses from Inflation," in W. L. Smith and R. L. Teigen, eds., *Money, National Income, and Stabilization Policy* (Homewood, Ill.: Richard D. Irwin, Inc., 1965).

3 The U.S. National Income Accounts

$\mathcal{N}$ow that we have been introduced to the theory of national income accounting, let us take a look at a real-life account from the year 1969, in Table 3–1. Compare this table with Table 2–7 and note the similarity. Starting with the right-hand or GNP side of the accounts, let us list the individual items and discuss them in the order in which they appear in the table.

Gross national product is the first entry; that is the sum total of the major subcategories shown in bold face print, namely consumption, gross investment, net exports, and government expenditures. This subdivision is of great importance to the model that we will be building in Part 2 and applying in Part 3 of this book. Except for marginal references, we will leave out of our model the international sector, net exports. This leaves the consumption, investment, and government sectors, which will be haunting you through much of this text.

Final purchases are not strictly part of the GNP accounts. They are thrown in for good measure, and there is good reason for our accountants' generosity. The GNP is the total output of an economy in a given year, which is not the same thing as total sales. Lots of things are sold on the first of January — Excedrin headache pills, for example — that were really produced in the preceding year. These pills gave rise to income, not in the new year when they are sold, but in the old year when they were produced. The guy who made the pill certainly did not hang around waiting for his paycheck until the pill got sold. The difference between GNP and final purchases is an indication of changing inventories. In 1969, for example, the GNP was greater than final purchases by $7.4 billion. This indicates a growing inventory stock, which is to be ex-

Table 3-1
The U.S. National Income Accounts (1969)

National Income
(in billions of dollars)

Item	1969
National income	**763.7**
Compensation of employees	**565.5**
Wages and salaries	509.6
Private	405.5
Military	19.0
Government civilian	85.1
Supplements to wages and salaries	56.0
Employer contributions for social insurance	27.8
Other labor income	28.2
Proprietor's income	**67.0**
Business and professional	50.3
Farm	16.8
Rental income of persons	**22.6**
Corporate profits and inventory valuation adjustment	**78.6**
Profits before tax	84.2
Profits tax liability	39.7
Profits after tax	44.5
Dividends	24.4
Undistributed profits	20.0
Inventory valuation adjustment	−5.5
Net interest	**29.9**
National income	**763.7**
Plus: Capital consumption allowances	81.1
Indirect business tax and nontax liability	85.7
Other Items	−1.4
Equals: Gross national product	**929.1**

Gross National Product
(in billions of dollars)

Item	1969
Gross national product	**929.1**
Final purchases	921.7
Personal consumption expenditures	**579.6**
Durable goods	89.9
Nondurable goods	247.6
Services	242.1
Gross private domestic investment	**137.8**
Fixed investment	130.4
Nonresidential	98.6
Structures	34.5
Producers' durable equipment	64.1
Residential structures	31.8
Change in business inventories	7.4
Net exports of goods and services	**2.0**
Exports	55.6
Imports	53.6
Government purchases of goods and services	**209.7**
Federal	99.2
National defense	78.4
Other	20.8
State and local	110.5
Gross national product in constant (1958) dollars	**724.7**
Gross national product	**929.1**

Source: "U.S. National Income and Product Accounts, 1967–1970," *Survey of Current Business;* U.S. Dept. of Commerce; July 1971, pp. 13 and 15.

pected in a growing economy. However, in a deep depression the trend may be reversed. In 1933, for example, when the Great Depression reached its trough, sales of goods and services exceeded production by $1.6 billion.

Personal consumption expenditures make up over 60% of our GNP. They are subdivided into durable goods, nondurable goods, and services. Durable goods are those consumption goods that normally last longer than one year: for example, cars, TV sets, refrigerators, lawn mowers, and furniture. The income derived from the production of these goods is captured in the national income accounts. But what about those durable consumption goods that have been produced and accumulated in the past and are carried over into a new year? They, too, are part of the nation's wealth. The existing stock of these durable goods corresponds to the term A_s of equation 2–1, where it is labeled nonproductive assets.[1] If our national wealth is expressed as income, the stock of accumulated consumer goods or nonproductive assets must be converted into a corresponding flow variable, equation 2–2. In the case of owner-occupied homes, we have seen that this is done on the income side by simply treating the home-owner as though he paid reasonable rent to himself. On the GNP side the imputed rent is included in the value of total consumer goods. The net effect is that the GNP is increased on both sides of the accounts by an identical amount. The trouble is, homes are the only nonproductive assets with which this is done. It is not done on cars, TV sets, or any other durable consumer good. To the extent that this correction is not undertaken, the U.S. national income accounts are understated in an absolute sense. Moreover, since the United States has the greatest accumulation of durable consumer goods—just think of the cars in this country—its GNP or national income is more understated than those of all foreign countries, and the more so the smaller that country's stock of material goods.

Nondurable goods, which last less than one year, such as food and clothing, present no such problem. Of course, some nondurable goods are carried over into a new year, and these goods are, strictly speaking, accumulated wealth. But because there are too many of them and the dollar value involved is relatively small, they are ignored in the U.S. income accounts.

Legal and medical services and car and TV repairs are examples of the last item listed under personal consumption expenditures, services. By definition, services are consumed when produced. (That, by the way, makes repossession extremely difficult.) Since our national income accounts are production accounts rather than sales accounts, and since services cannot be carried over into another year, they do not distort our national income accounts.

Gross private domestic investment, as we have seen, consists of those

---

[1] For the convenience of the reader, equations 2–1 and 2–2 are shown again as follows:

$$W_s = A_s + \sum \frac{1}{(1 + r)^t} \cdot (I_{t,h} + I_{t,p}) \qquad\qquad 2\text{–}1$$

$$W_f = A_f + (I_h + I_p) \qquad\qquad 2\text{–}2$$

capital goods that were used to replace worn-out capital goods, as well as any net additions to capital stock. Overwhelmingly, these goods consist of fixed investment. In this important subcategory, nonresidential or business investment predominates at over 75%. This is something we should remember when we come to Part 2 of this book. Investment, in our model, will be assumed to take place in the business sector. If homes are treated as consumption goods, as they will be in our model, our national income accounts certainly support this assumption.

Nonresidential structures are plants and office buildings; producers' durable equipment is machines, trucks, office equipment, etc. The item labeled change in business inventories has been discussed but not expressly defined. That is the balancing item between the GNP and final purchases. This entry is positive, but need not be; during the Great Depression, for example, it was negative.

Net exports of goods and services, as you might have guessed, are exports minus imports. If we grow a bushel of grain in the United States and export it to France, the grain is a source of income to some American farmer and, therefore, to our economy. Conversely, if I import a bottle of Beaujolais from France, some French winegrower derives an income from my consumption of foreign goods. On balance, if total exports exceed total imports in terms of dollar values, our GNP, and therefore our national income, is increased and vice versa.

Government purchases of goods and services exceed 20% of our GNP. This item, as we will see, can change greatly both in absolute magnitude and in relation to other sectors. Approximately half the government expenditures are incurred by the federal government, which uses almost 80 cents out of every dollar it spends for national defense.[2] The other half of government spending takes place on state and local levels.

The gross national product in constant (1958) dollars is also shown in Table 3–1. As we have seen, such a deflated GNP figure allows a comparison of GNPs at different points in time. For example, the 1968 GNP, expressed in constant (1958) dollars, was $706.6 billion. Thus, the real growth in GNP from 1968 to 1969 has been (724.7 − 706.6)/706.6 or 2.6%.

The left-hand or national income side of the U.S. accounts consists primarily of income streams and capital consumption allowances. Let us discuss the individual entries on the left side of Table 3–1 in the listed sequence.

National income is, of course, the sum of all the income streams that have been generated by the production of net investment and consumer goods (including government goods and net exports); this has been discussed previously and needs no elaboration.

Compensation of employees is by far the most important subcategory of

---

[2]That is on the basis of the U.S. National Income Accounts, as shown in Table 3–1. In terms of the Unified Federal Budget, a little less than 50% of the total federal expenditures went for national defense in 1969. See, for example, *The U.S. Budget in Brief, Fiscal Year 1972*, Executive Office of the President, Office of Management and Budget, p. 61.

national income, of which it makes up approximately 75%. The breakdown into private, military, and government wages is self-explanatory, as is that part of supplements to wages and salaries labeled employer contributions for social insurance. The other half of these supplements, other labor income, is mainly employer contributions to private pension and welfare funds. (Wages and salaries are shown on a gross basis, i.e., inclusive of income taxes, whether these are withheld or not.)

Proprietors' income, the second subcategory of national income, measures the income stream that goes to unincorporated businesses. The first item, business and professional income, is the most important. Business income refers to the small grocery store around the corner and other such proprietorships; professional income is the lawyer's and the doctor's income, among others. This item reflects a peculiarity in the interpretation of U.S. tax laws which in the past would not allow professionals to incorporate their businesses. This situation has been remedied in about 1968, and a part of what used to be professional income is now shown as corporate profits.

Farm income deserves special mention, because it contains an element of imputed income. The greatest part of farm income, of course, is from the sale of farm products. But farmers, more so than any other profession, are largely self-sufficient; they produce a substantial amount of food for their own consumption. In the national income accounts, the value of that food is imputed and counted into the farmers' incomes. That is, the farmers are treated as though they sold all of their products in the market for income and then bought back what they needed for their own consumption. This imputation increases both sides of the U.S. national income accounts by the same amount, the value of farm products consumed by farmers. On the GNP side that value is added into nondurable goods; on the national income side it is added to farm income.

Rental income of persons, discussed previously and needing no elaboration here, is primarily the imputed income derived from owner-occupied homes; also included are rental payments to owners who operate rentals as a sideline. Again, the imputed income from owner-occupied homes is posted on both sides of the national income accounts.

The big, bad corporations receive only about 11% of the U.S. national income — before taxes; after taxes it's only a little more than 6%. Since not all corporate after-tax profits are paid out to the shareholders, two additional items are listed, dividends and undistributed profits. These are self-explanatory.

The item labeled inventory valuation adjustment refers to changes in the value of inventories due to price changes. Suppose a corporation has a constant inventory throughout the year, say 100 units with an initial market price of $1.00 each. If the market price at the end of the year rises to $1.50 a piece, the value of our firm's inventories is increased from $100 to $150, a capital gain of $50. That amount is shown on the corporation's tax statements as a capital gain, but since it has not given rise to a corresponding income in the form of wages, etc., it is deducted from corporate profits in the national income accounts. Alternatively, a loss in inventory valuation is added to corporate profits in the national income accounts.

Interest payments, the last entry under national income, are, like wages, profits, etc., generated by the production of goods and services and constitute income to someone. In the national income accounts they are entered on a net basis as a matter of convenience. Suppose firm A receives total interest payments of $100 for consumer goods sold on credit, and it pays interest of $20 on a bank loan. Its net interest receipts are then $80. The national income accounts show interest payments after netting between all firms and individuals. Interest payments on government debts are not listed in the accounts.

This completes our discussion of national income. A few items listed on the left side of Table 3–1 and not shown as part of national income deserve mention. When we discussed capital consumption allowances earlier, we said that their addition with national income gives GNP. As we see now, this is not exactly right. First, there exists the sizable item called indirect business tax and nontax liabilities. In 1969, a little over one half of these consisted of federal excise taxes and state and local sales taxes, something like 40% was property taxes, the rest was professional and motor vehicle licenses, and the like. The exclusion of this item from national income is somewhat controversial. After all, these taxes have been generated by this nation's total output that generated all other incomes.[3] Moreover, all other taxes are shown as part of the national income, notably personal and corporate income taxes. Thus, if the indirect business tax and nontax liability entry is treated as part of national income, then the assertion that national income plus capital consumption allowance equals GNP is essentially correct.

Essentially, but not exactly. A few minor items remain, including statistical discrepancy, which we have contracted into one entry, but which are not worth getting into. Let us, therefore, turn our attention to some of the problems encountered in the measurement of national income.

Measurement Problems

We have defined national income as the maximum income that can be obtained in a given year while leaving the producing capacity of the economy intact.[4] If we express national income in real goods and services, as ultimately we must, it can be redefined as follows:

---

[3] For still another viewpoint, where *all* taxes paid by enterprises are deducted from national income, see the Kuznets study in the references at the end of this chapter, especially pp. 428–430 and p. 897.

[4] This definition gives analytical content to an otherwise statistical tabulation of data. The definition is by no means universally accepted, nor is it original with this author. B. P. Pesek, T. R. Saving, M. J. Bailey, and D. Patinkin have previously proposed similar ideas. See the references at the end of Chapter 2.

National income is the maximum amount of goods and services that can be produced in a given year while leaving the economy's producing capacity intact.

By goods and services we do not necessarily mean consumer goods and services. We have seen on previous occasions that it does not matter whether an economy chooses to produce consumer goods only, after making provisions for a constant producing capacity, or whether it prefers to forgo some present consumption in favor of future consumption. This, of course, is the meaning of a net increase in capital stock or producing capacity. In the first instance, the total physical output of consumer goods and services constitutes real national income. In the second instance, real national income consists of the above goods and services plus something extra—the net addition to capital stock in lieu of which our economy could have produced, but chose not to produce, consumer goods.

The inclusion of net addition to capital stock does not constitute an element of double counting—at least not if it is the wealth of our nation we wish to measure through our national income accounts. But what about those pieces of capital stock that were built to replace worn-out or obsolete equipment? Let us reemphasize that this part of capital-goods production does not belong in national income, and it is not presently shown as part of it in the U.S. income accounts. The problem is definitional, not conceptual, since wealth is defined on the basis of a constant capital stock, and income is but one way of expressing wealth.

We have previously mentioned in passing that only finished goods are included in both the GNP and national income. Let us elaborate on this point. Most economists use the bread example to explain the reason for this convention, and we bow to custom by accepting this ritual. Suppose the final product, bread, goes through four production stages: The farmer plants and harvests the wheat that he sells to the miller; the miller converts the wheat to flour which he sells to the baker; the baker uses the flour and other ingredients to make the bread which he sells to the retailer who, in turn, sells it to the consumer. Suppose the retailer pays 25¢ for a loaf of bread, and he charges the consumer 33¢ per loaf. Suppose further that the miller charges 15¢ for the flour that goes into one loaf of bread, and he has to pay the farmer 7¢ for the equivalent amount of wheat. The whole chain of transactions results in only one consumption good, namely a loaf of bread worth 33¢. If we were to count all the intermediate goods that went into the bread, we would be guilty of double counting. In money terms, this would amount to saying that national income has been increased by 7 + 15 + 25 + 33¢ or 80¢. In real terms it would mean that this nation's income was increased by so much wheat plus so much flour plus one wholesale bread plus one retail bread. But the people of that nation got to consume only one of these items, namely the retail bread for which they paid 33¢.

If we wish to follow the chain of events through the production cycle, we must make use of the value-added concept. The value added is defined as the increase in price of a given intermediate good for the specific services at each production stage. Suppose, for simplicity, that the farmer starts from scratch, that is, his seed and fertilizer inputs are negligible. Then his value added to one loaf worth of wheat is 7¢. The miller, who charges 15¢ for the equivalent amount of flour, adds 8¢ worth of value to the original wheat for his services. The baker's value added is 10¢ and the retailer's service, which consists of making the bread available to the consumer at a convenient marketplace, results in a value added of 8¢. If the various added values are summed, the final retail price of 33¢ of the bread is obtained. The value added is, in fact, a very important concept in many disciplines of applied economic theory. For example, several European countries levy their taxes on a value-added basis.

Another point that deserves explicit mention is that a sale in the nature of a mere asset transformation does not give rise to income. For example, if you sell me your home, the wealth of the nation is not affected, since the number of homes is the same before and after the transaction. In fact, your wealth and mine are also unchanged. You have simply exchanged 30,000 dollars' worth of home for 30,000 dollars' worth of money, and my asset transformation has been the exact reverse of yours. But note carefully that the sale of bread at the store did give rise to national income since the store performed a productive service in making the sale. Similarly, if a broker is involved in the sale of the house, the national income is increased.

We have already discussed the imputed incomes to home-owners and farmers. For the sake of completeness, let us mention three other economic units that have incomes imputed to them: first, domestic employees and military personnel, both of whom receive income in kind in the form of food and lodging; second, banks, and third, life insurance companies, both of whose income imputations are a bit complicated and will not be pursued here.

We have already mentioned that the U.S. national income is undervalued, since the equivalent income of accumulated durable consumer goods is not captured, except for housing. This makes an international comparison of national incomes, or GNPs for that matter, very difficult. A similar problem presents itself in connection with nonmarket activities. Suppose my wife decides to sew herself a blouse. She gets to wear a new blouse as a result, but the GNP only shows the material and the yarn. Had she bought the blouse, the GNP would have shown a complete blouse. The nation as a whole is wealthier by one blouse, but because she sewed the blouse herself, my wife's value added is not included in the national income accounts. This holds true for house cleaning, dishwashing, etc. If we had a maid, these services would be included in the GNP. But we don't have one and are not very likely ever to have one. Thus, the GNP is undervalued by my wife's and every housewife's services. Thank goodness the women's libs haven't yet caught on to the discriminatory accounting practices of the U.S. Department of Commerce.

On the international level, different societies have more or fewer nonmarket activities as part of their daily routines. Suppose, for example, that housewives bake their own bread in some underdeveloped country. Then this country's GNP is undervalued by the value added of their bread-baking services, relative to the United States, where bread is customarily purchased in stores.

Let us complete this part of Chapter 3 with a word on the use of GNP instead of the more meaningful concept of national income. It is, of course, the national income that we are primarily interested in, since it is the flow equivalent of national wealth. Yet, references in the professional economic and business papers and statements by government officials are mostly to GNP, for two reasons: First, GNP, or the total output of a nation, is more reliably measured; second, we are really mostly concerned with *changes* in wealth, not wealth itself. *Changes* in unemployment, *changes* in price levels, and *changes* in total output are what worry us and what we attempt to control. But the GNP has been running at a fairly constant multiple of national income, 21% to 22% higher than national income in the past decade. Hence, a given percentage increase in national income is reflected by an equivalent percentage increase in GNP. This and the fact that GNP is more easily monitored are the reasons for the preferred use of the GNP.

Income Distribution

The thrust of our argument so far has been that a nation's wealth can be measured by measuring aggregate income. In the aggregate this way of measuring wealth presents no major conceptual problem. What does present a problem is the fact that a nation may be very rich, while the majority of the people in that nation may be poor. The income distribution, in other words, has an important bearing on the well-being of a nation's individuals.

When we speak of a nation's per capita real or money income, we are speaking of an average figure: the aggregate income divided by the number of people who live in that nation. This implies that all people, men, women and children, have the same income throughout the country. Of course, nothing could be further from the truth. Incomes are distributed unequally among the people, more so in some nations than in others. Advanced countries usually show a more equal income distribution than less advanced countries.

One way of graphically demonstrating the inequality of income distribution is by way of the so-called Lorenz chart. This well-known graph is nothing more than a cumulative frequency distribution curve with the cumulative percent of people on the abscissa and the corresponding percent of income on the ordinate. Table 3–2 shows how the national income was distributed among the people in the United States during the year 1967.

Plotting these data onto a Lorenz chart gives the graph shown in Figure 3–1. The dashed diagonal line in this graph represents the Lorenz curve or cumulative frequency distribution that would result if all incomes in the nation

Table 3–2
U.S. Income Distribution 1967

People, %	Cumulative Income, %
0	0
20	5
40	18
60	35
80	59
95	85
100	100

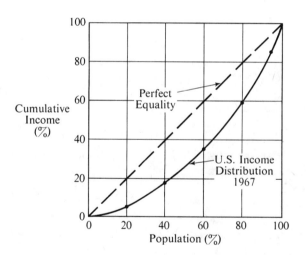

Figure 3–1   The Lorenz Curve
(U.S., 1967)

Source: Current Population Reports, U.S. Department of Commerce, Bureau of the Census.

were equal. The solid line, on the other hand, represents the actual distribution of incomes in the United States in 1967. Clearly, the closer the solid line to the diagonal line, the more equal is the income distribution. A less advanced country typically has a Lorenz curve farther removed from the dashed diagonal line.

Changes in aggregate income are no more equally distributed throughout the nation than is aggregate income itself. Some people are harder hit than others when a nation goes through a depression. In fact, though a few individuals have been known to prosper during the Great Depression, most people suffered from it. If we wanted to capture the distributional effects of aggregate income, we would have to build a model that is capable of allowing for income stratification. Such a model would be unduly complex, and perhaps theoretically untenable. Moreover, empirical data would be very difficult to come by. Our model will not consider income stratification; in fact, we will concentrate our attention on aggregate income. If this aggregate income is reduced — e.g., during periods of recession — we will discuss monetary or fiscal policies that are designed to bring aggregate income back to its pre-recession level. Before we proceed to build our model, however, let us take a look at the economic performance of the United States over the past forty years. This we will do in Chapter 4, which will conclude Part 1.

Problems

1. You are given the following data:

	(Millions of $)
Rental income of persons	2
Gross private domestic investment	9
Net interest	3
Final purchases	78
Capital consumption allowances	5
Government purchases of goods and services	10
Compensation of employees	50
Proprietor's income	8
Net exports of goods and services	1
Indirect business tax and nontax liability	5
Corporate profits and inventory valuation adjustment	7
Personal consumption expenditures	60
Other items	0

a) Set up the left-hand or national income side of our national income accounts. Add up the national income. Without using any of the elements from the GNP side, show how you can calculate the GNP.

b) Set up the right-hand or GNP side of our national income accounts. Calculate the GNP. Without using any of the elements of national income, show how you can calculate the national income from the GNP, by appropriate deductions.

2. The well-known country of Lower Slobovia has just published a list of pertinent national income accounting data. However, they are having trouble setting up the overall accounts. Help them with a double entry system, using the relevant data listed below.

	(Millions $)
Personal consumption expenditures	60
Indirect business tax	7
Proprietors' income	5
Net imports	1
Compensation of employees	55
Corporate profits	8
Government expenditures	21
Rental income of persons	2
Net interest	3
Final purchases	92
Capital consumption allowances	17
Gross investment	18
Other items	1

Be sure your accounts balance. What has been Slobovia's GNP, national income? In looking at your accounts, can you make a statement regarding Slobovia's growth potential, as reflected by last year's performance?

3. In the U.S. national income accounts, there is a term rental income of persons. What is the meaning of this term? Do you think it is really needed in the accounts? Why? Why not?

4. Our GNP is understated in relative and in absolute terms due to certain problems associated with durable consumption goods. Why relative? Why absolute? What adjustments would be required to correct the error?

5. An increase in inventory valuation is shown as a negative figure on our national income accounts. Why?

6. U.S. income accounting fails to measure certain incomes. Generally, which are these? With one exception, these incomes are considered irrelevant. What is the one exception? Why are the other unmeasured incomes thought to be irrelevant?

7. In the U.S. national income accounts, the term inventory valuation adjustment is used. What is the meaning of this term? Actually, when the nation's inventories have been subject to capital gains over the year, the inventory valuation adjustment is shown as a negative entry. That is probably in error, since the firms have received an income, right? Wrong? Explain.

8. Suppose we are experiencing a falling price level over several years. If the real GNP rises over this period, what can you say in regard to the growth rate of the nominal GNP? What can you say if the real GNP declines?

9. The GNP measures goods and services to final purchasers. Why *final* purchasers?

Suggested Readings

The most exhaustive work on national income accounting is:

S. Kuznets, *National Income and Its Composition, 1919–1938* (New York: National Bureau of Economic Research, 1954).

For current information, the following monthly magazine is the *data source:*

Survey of Current Business, issued by the U.S. Department of Commerce; Office of Business Economics.

For excellent secondary treatments, see:

G. Ackley, *Macroeconomic Theory* (New York: The Macmillan Company, 1961), Part I.
T. F. Dernburg and D. M. McDougall, *Macroeconomics,* 3rd ed. (New York: McGraw-Hill Book Company, 1968), Chapters 2, 3, 4.

Two excellent pamphlets on the U.S. budget are:

Economic Analysis of the Budget, issued by the Chamber of Commerce of the United States, Washington, D.C., and *The U.S. Budget in Brief,* issued annually by the Executive Office of the President, Office of Management and Budget.

4 The U.S. Economic Track Record

We mentioned earlier that the GNP is often used instead of the more meaningful national income to monitor the performance of the economy. Suppose we wish to know how our economy has fared in the past. One way to find out would be to compare the year-by-year changes in GNP. Such a comparison is facilitated by plotting the relevant GNPs versus time. This has been done in Figure 4–1, which is based on data published by the U.S. Department of Commerce.

It will be noted that two GNP curves are shown. The solid curve labeled nominal GNP refers to the dollar-GNP as currently measured. The dotted curve labeled real GNP, 1958 prices, shows the GNP after adjustment for price-level changes. Overall, we may state unequivocally that we have been going through a period of sustained economic growth in the period from 1933 to 1970. Of course, since the consumer price index has been rising almost continuously since the Great Depression reached bottom in 1933, the nominal GNP exhibits a faster growth rate than does the real GNP. We have discussed and need not, therefore, elaborate here on the fact that this discrepancy in growth rates is due to the inflation of the more recent nominal GNPs. As a matter of interest it may be pointed out that the annual growth rate of our real GNP in the two decades from 1950 to 1970 has been on the order of 3.6%. Over the same period the annual growth rate of the nominal GNP, by comparison, has been approximately 6.3%.

Two irregularities stand out in Figure 4–1. The first, of course, is the decline in both real and nominal GNPs during the Great Depression, the only period in the twentieth century in which the U.S. economy experienced a

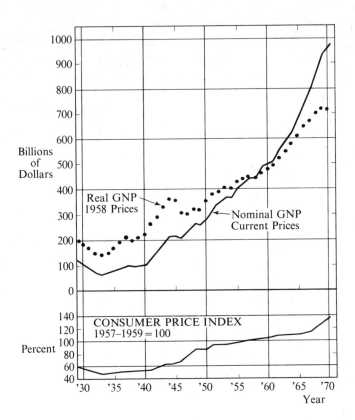

Figure 4–1   *The U.S. Gross National*
Product

Source: U.S. Department of Commerce, Survey of Current Business, July 1971, p. 46.

sustained and substantial fall in the price level. In 1929, the nominal GNP in the United States was $103.1 billion. Four years later, it had fallen to $55.6 billion, a decline of 46%. The percentage decline in real GNP, while substantial, was nevertheless not quite as severe as that in nominal GNP, due to the concurrent price-level fall. Measured in constant 1958 dollars, the real GNP declined by about 30%, from $203.6 billion to $141.5 billion.

The second irregularity in Figure 4–1 is the sudden upswing in real GNP in 1940 and its accelerated growth over a period of four years, during World War II. The increase in real GNP reflects our national war effort. As the bottom curve indicates, the price index remained fairly stable throughout World War II. Unusual situations call for unusual measures; thus, during the war a system of wage and price controls was instituted and maintained. At the end of World War II, these controls were lifted. The result was a rapid subsequent increase in price levels. In spite of the pent-up demand for durable consumer goods, the transition from a war to a peace economy and the release of thousands of men from the armed services brought about a fairly severe recession after World War II. This, in fact, was the first time in recent history that the U.S. went through a period of simultaneous recession and price-level increase. As we can see, the recession-inflation, or reflation, has been around for some time. Yet, when it first raised its ugly head, it passed more or less unnoticed. The discontinuance of price controls and the unleashing of private consumer demands seemed to satisfactorily explain this "one-time" phenomenon.

In 1954 and again in 1958 small-scale recessions occurred. The 1954 recession came in the wake of the Korean War. The 1958 recession, short-lived but severe, had its origin in reduced investment spending and in a highly restrictive credit policy. The 1958 recession was again accompanied by rising consumer prices, but because the inflation rate was visibly reduced in the 1958–1969 period, the apparent paradox of a declining real GNP and a rising price level failed to command the attention it might have deserved.[1]

The sixties were characterized by a period of sustained growth unparalleled in U.S. economic history. In 1968, the price level began to show an alarming rate of increase. By 1970, it reached an annual rate of nearly 6%, while the real GNP declined by $7 billion in six months. This time the economic profession, the public—everyone—took notice. The baby that had been born in 1945 was finally baptized; the reflation was duly registered in the annals of economic history.

The GNP, as we have seen, is very stable in relation to the national income. For that and other reasons discussed earlier the GNP is the most popular measuring device of the performance of our economy. But we are not content with the knowledge that our GNP behaves in certain ways. Descriptive economics is a thing of the past: We need to analyze our economy's behavior. One way to do this is by taking a close look at the various subcategories that make up our GNP: personal consumption expenditures, gross private investment, net exports, and government expenditures. The three larger subcategories are plotted in nominal dollars as a function of time in Figure 4–2. Net exports, which are generally less than 1% of the GNP, would hardly show on the scale used in Figure 4–2. For this reason, their presentation has been deferred to Figure 4–4.

A look at Figure 4–2 tells us that gross private investment took a deep plunge during the Great Depression. In fact, it fell from $16.2 billion in 1929 to $1.4 billion in 1933, a drop of over 90% in the short span of four years. As we will see in a little while, this drastic decline in investment took place in the business sector as well as in the residential housing sector. The fall in consumption expenditures in those four dark years was $31.4 billion or approximately 40%.

Interestingly enough, government expenditures were not greatly affected

---

[1] But it was noticed. See, for example, J. R. Cammarosano in his foreword to M. Friedman's: *A Program for Monetary Stability* (New York: Fordham University Press, 1959).

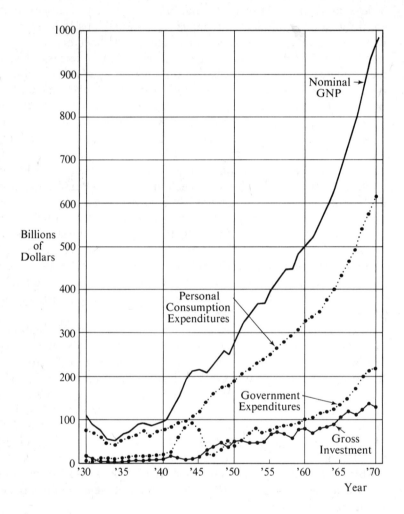

Figure 4-2   The Gross National Product —
Size and Composition (Nominal Dollars)

Source: U.S. Department of Commerce, Survey of Current Business, July 1971, p. 46.

by the Great Depression. To maintain its spending level in the face of declining tax receipts, the government had to borrow funds from the public, a fiscal policy that brings about deficit spending. At that time, deficit spending carried with it the stigma of governmental irresponsibility, even immorality. It was not until 1936, the year in which John Maynard Keynes published his revolutionary book *The General Theory of Employment, Interest, and Money* that deficit spending, under certain conditions, achieved respectability. As we will see in Part 3, in a depressed economy governmental deficit spending may indeed provide a stimulus toward economic recovery.

Not surprisingly, World War II was marked by a substantial increase in government expenditures, reflecting our stepped-up military outlays. Investment spending, which had been rising in the pre-war years, declined rapidly after 1940. Capital investment was limited to industries vital to the defense effort. Since the country was producing at top capacity, the required increase in the production of military hardware necessitated a postponement in the production of nonessential capital goods. For once, the United States had reached the classical position on its production possibility frontier. An increase in the output of guns could be obtained only by a simultaneous reduction in the output of butter. With the very survival of this country at stake, the decision, of course, was made in favor of guns.

The 1954 recession had two primary causes. Termination of the Korean conflict reduced military spending, causing government expenditures to decline. Investment, which had risen vigorously at the beginning of the conflict, had dropped back and remained sluggish for two years or so. This behavior of investment reflects a fall in the purchase of durable goods in 1954, as we will see in Figure 4–3. The U.S. consuming public, fearing that the armed conflict might bring about a shortage of durable consumer goods, had stocked up on them. As a result, the demand for durable goods fell in subsequent years and so did the demand for capital to produce durable goods.

The various subcategories of the GNP in Figure 4–2 display different volatilities. In particular, consumer spending has been rising smoothly and steadily since the Great Depression, while gross investment followed a much more volatile path. Government spending has exhibited a persistent and steady rise, with two notable exceptions of very sharp rise, World War II and the Korean conflict, both periods characterized by unusually heavy military expenditures which raised government spending substantially above its normal level. The fact that consumer spending is the least volatile of the major subcategories in our GNP does not mean that all types of consumer spending exhibit an equally smooth behavior. This is made clear in Figure 4–3, which shows the major subcomponents of consumption spending, namely durable goods, nondurable goods, and services. Services, remember, are consumed when produced; they cannot be placed in inventories, and that makes speculative buying impossible. Services are consumed as steadily as they are needed. As a result, this component of consumption spending exhibits a remarkable stability.

Nondurable goods, by definition, are goods generally lasting less than one year. Their quick turnover in usage and their short life span make speculative buying of these goods difficult. For example, I could purchase at most two months' worth of eggs at a time, given my refrigerator capacity, and then I would be unable to stock up on other food items. That is to say, nondurable

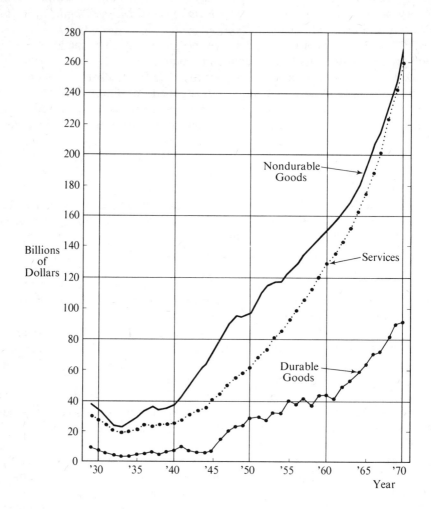

Figure 4–3   Personal Consumption
Expenditures (Nominal Dollars)

Source: U.S. Department of Commerce, Survey of Current Business, July 1971, p. 46.

goods can be inventoried, but only to a limited extent. As a result their volatility hardly exceeds that of services.

Durable goods, on the other hand, can be stored indefinitely and normally last longer than a year; thus, they are subject to speculative buying. An example of such buying has been given in the discussion of the economic repercussions of the Korean conflict. At the outset of this conflict, in early 1950, people rushed to buy up durable goods (see Figure 4–3). For a more distinct illustration of this point, the reader is referred to the Federal Reserve System Historical Chart Book, where purchases are plotted on a monthly basis rather than the crude yearly basis used here.

Just as durable goods can be bought ahead of actual needs, the replacement of such goods can be postponed in times of economic hardship. The Great Depression and the 1958 reflation are clear examples of this, as is the period of World War II, except that the postponement of durable-goods purchases at that time was not imposed by economic hardships. They simply were not produced in the quantities the public wanted, since most of the U.S. productive effort was geared toward military hardware. Whatever the reasons, the fact that durable goods may be purchased earlier or later than needed makes the aggregate consumption of these goods much more volatile than either nondurable goods or services. Moreover, since a great portion of the durable goods are bought on credit, their purchases are influenced to some degree by the cost of credit, i.e., the rate of interest. This is a subject we will take up again when we construct our model.

We have pointed out in our discussion of the national income accounts that homes are not treated as durable consumer goods, as they will be in our model. Rather, the U.S. Department of Commerce treats residential structures as part of gross private investment. Figure 4–4 shows the three major subcategories of gross private investment, business fixed investment, residential structures, and change in business inventories. Typically, business investment and residential structures decline during periods of recession. The years 1933, 1954, and 1958 may again serve as examples. The trough in 1943, of course, is due to the war effort in other areas.

Changes in business inventories play a somewhat ambiguous role in business cycles. Increases in inventories often precede recessions. However, once a recession does occur, business people seem to be intent on reducing inventories. The build-up of inventories may thus be one of the many forces leading to a recession, but they are not necessarily a concomitant of recessions. A look at business inventories in 1933, 1954, and 1958 will support our contention.

There is a very good reason for our concern about inventory changes. As inventories are built up, they give rise to income and employment. Conversely, a reduction in inventories causes income and employment to decline. To see this, let us cite an example and push it to the extreme: Suppose a firm finds itself with a huge stock of inventories that it wishes to unload. One way of doing this is to shut down all manufacturing operations, say for a month, while continuing sales. During that month, then, our firm's employment and income in the manufacturing division is zero. The national income, and the GNP for that matter, is reduced by our firm's reduction of income. What holds true for our firm in the above example holds true for all firms. This is why a reduction in aggregate inventories causes the national income and employment to decline.

Also shown in Figure 4–4 are the net exports of goods and services from the United States. When these are positive, the U.S. balance of trade is posi-

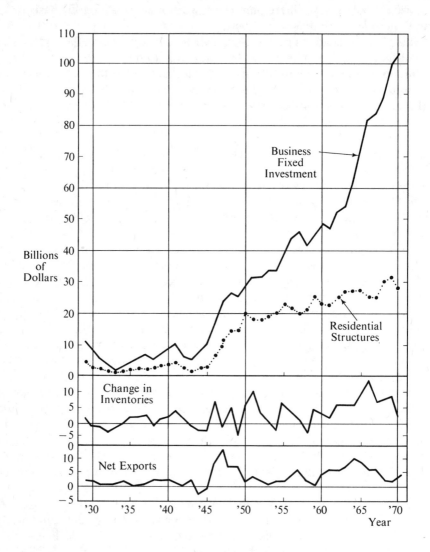

*Figure 4–4   Gross Investment and Net
Exports (Nominal Dollars)*

Source: U.S. Department of Commerce, Survey of Current Business, July 1971, p. 46.

tive. As the figure shows, our balance of trade has been positive in almost every
year since the end of World War II, until the end of 1970. Of course, our balance of payments, which among other things includes capital flows, has been
mostly in the red since 1958.

A comparison of Figures 4–3 and 4–4 reveals that the components of gross private investment are much more volatile than those of personal consumption expenditures. The ability of gross investment to respond quickly and substantially to changing economic conditions makes this category of the GNP a likely candidate for policy measures. The investment tax credit and adjustments in depreciation rates are two examples of such policy measures that are aimed specifically at the business sector via investment spending.

Contrary to the writings of some alarmists, the government is not in the process of taking over the function of private enterprise. In fact, during the period from 1955 to 1970, government expenditures fluctuated at around 20% of the GNP. Moreover, half of all government expenditures are made by local and state authorities. Figure 4–5 clearly shows that federal expenditures have been almost exactly the same as state and local government expenditures during the five-year period from 1964 to 1968. In 1969 and 1970, however, state and local expenditures greatly exceeded federal expenditures, and the gap is widening. This may suggest that state and local government spending is subject to a greater inherent inertia than is federal spending. If this is true, and only time will tell, future efforts to curb government spending may well have to be directed primarily at state and local authorities.

The most striking feature of the federal expenditure curve is, of course, its enormous increase during World War II. In 1944, these expenditures were about 17 times those of 1939. A similar but less ostensive pattern developed during the Korean conflict. This pattern vividly demonstrates the government's ability to increase its expenditures almost at will, and, in fact, a number of macroeconomic policy tools depend on that ability. In our model, this ability will be taken into consideration by treating government spending as an autonomous variable. This will be discussed in detail when we build our model in Part 2.

Before we begin to build our model, let us turn our attention to two more variables that are widely discussed and closely monitored: unemployment and the rate of interest. Unemployment and related data are plotted in Figure 4–6. Over the past forty years, the U.S. labor force has been rising steadily, with the notable exception, again, of World War II, when temporarily it rose much more sharply. This, of course, was because the productive services of many people not ordinarily in the labor force, in particular housewives and retired personnel, were tapped to help in national survival. The solid, labor-force curve in Figure 4–6 includes members of the armed forces, the dotted curve civilians only. This explains the apparent built-in contradiction in Figure 4–6: As the labor force increased during World War II, civilian employment fell, but unemployment fell, too. The reason, of course, is that the ranks of the military increased substantially.

Figure 4–6 clearly shows that, in varying degrees, unemployment has always plagued our nation. This is brought into sharp focus by the two lower panels, where civilian unemployment is plotted both in total volume and as a percent of the labor force. Two characteristics of this latter set of curves deserve mention.

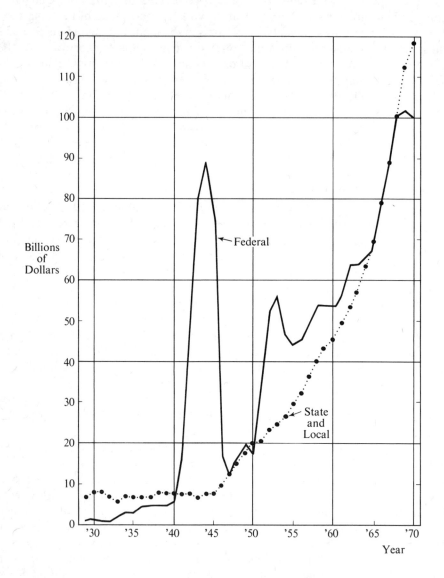

Figure 4–5   Government Expenditures
(Nominal Dollars)

Source: U.S. Department of Commerce, Survey of Current Business, July 1971, p. 46.

First, so far none of the graphs has depicted the severity of the Great Depression as vividly as the unemployment curves. This is in part due to the direct emotional appeal of the unemployment concept. After all, the GNP is a

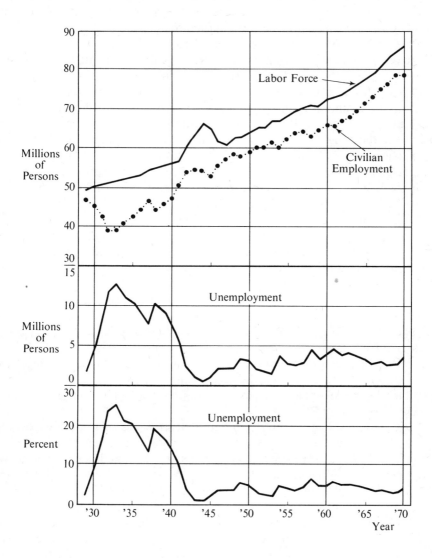

Figure 4–6   Employment

Source: Handbook of Labor Statistics 1970, U.S. Department of Labor.

somewhat abstract and impersonal thing: People do not ordinarily relate it to their personal well-being. Unemployment, on the other hand, is easily understood; on a personal level, it has the unpleasant characteristic of being an all-or-nothing variable: When it strikes in a household, it strikes hard. The Great

Depression and its aftermath were characterized by an unemployment problem unparalleled in modern history. Over a period of seven years, more than ten million laborers, on average, were out of work. The bleakest year of that bleak period showed an unemployment rate of approximately 25%.

The second problem brought out by Figure 4–6 relates to the concept of the maximum acceptable unemployment rate. Not all unemployed people are presently looking for work; some are in transition between jobs, having terminated one job and not yet started at the new job; or a pregnant professional woman must temporarily interrupt her work. Second, there has always been and, I expect, always will be a small element in our population that seems unable to see the enlightenment of work. The problem is to quantify the percentage of our total labor force that can normally be expected to fall into one of these categories. To put the problem into a different concept, at what level of unemployment should our governmental authorities become sufficiently alarmed to deem remedial policy actions necessary? The debate on the maximum acceptable rate of unemployment reveals somewhat that economists do not have all the answers. For example, throughout the 1960s, when economic expansion was the order of the day, most economists agreed that a rate of 4% represents a reasonable unemployment rate. In 1970, when unemployment shot up to almost 6% while the price level continued to rise, strong noises were heard from both the economic profession and governmental quarters that the 4% ceiling may not be so reasonable after all, and the debate goes on. The conventional monetary and fiscal cures that had worked so well for some thirty years could not cope efficiently with this new inflationary recession. Rather than getting at the roots of the problem, a move that was bound to trigger unpleasant political repercussions, the debate followed the path of least resistance by attempting to redefine the term recession. (More will be said on this most interesting subject in Part 3.)

The second macroeconomic variable that deserves separate discussion is the rate of interest. This variable derives its importance from the fact that it is one of the major determinants of investment demand, and investment, as we have seen, is one of the major subcategories of the GNP. Figure 4–7 shows the past performance of two types of short-term interest rates, namely those on prime commercial papers and those on treasury bills. Also shown are the mid-year levels of Federal Reserve discount rates. The precise meaning of these terms has not yet been made clear in this book, but in order to maintain the thrust of our discussion, we will defer a detailed explanation to Part 4. Suffice it to say here that short-term interest rates were chosen as an example because they react more quickly to changing economic conditions than do long-term interest rates. Therefore their behavior more closely parallels the performance of the general economy.

As is clearly illustrated by the recessions of 1954 and 1958, a sluggish economy typically exhibits falling interest rates. The expansionary 1960s generally reflect rising interest rates which apparently peak out in late 1969, when the latest reflation made its appearance. Their close correlation with the

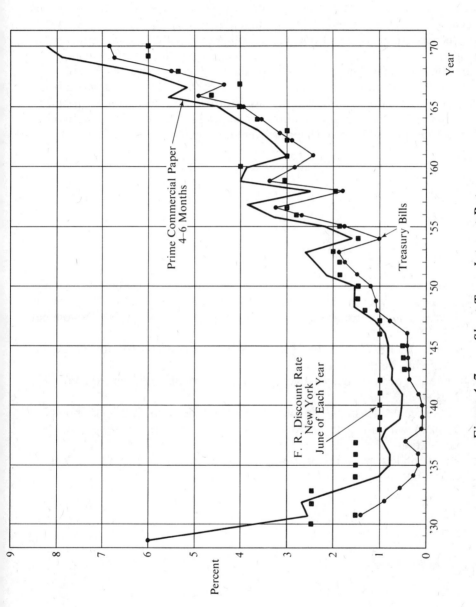

Figure 4–7   Short-Term Interest Rates

Source: Federal Reserve Bulletins, The Federal Reserve System.

performance of the economy makes interest rates a very important monitoring device.

This brings us to the end of Part 1. Lest we forget, what we really care about in macroeconomics is our aggregate well-being, i.e., the real wealth, of the people in our economy. This real wealth we attempt to measure by the simple expedient of measuring and deflating our national income or, more frequently, our GNP. But the GNP is composed of many different types of goods and services, and these are affected by different variables. The discussion of the historical performance of our economy gave us a preliminary glimpse of its complexities. Let us now turn to the task of presenting the interrelations of the primary economic variables in an orderly fashion. In other words, let us proceed to build a macroeconomic model.

Problems

1. Over the last twenty or so years, the nominal GNP in this country has been rising more rapidly than the real GNP. True or false? Why? What has been the approximate annual rate of increase in real GNP, in nominal GNP?
2. During World War II, the U.S. economy was operating on its production possibility boundary. Explain.
3. Durable goods are the least volatile subcategory of consumer expenditures. Yes or no? Explain.
4. Government spending, in our model, will be considered autonomous. Explain why and cite at least one historical instance in support of this contention.
5. Fiscal policy measures are often aimed at investment spending. Yes or no? Why?

Suggested Readings

Important sources or illustrations of historical U.S. economic data are:

Survey of Current Business, U.S. Department of Commerce; Office of Business Economics.

Handbook of Labor Statistics, U.S. Department of Labor, Bureau of Labor Statistics.

Historical Chart Book, Board of Governors of the Federal Reserve System.

For a historical and factual review of many of the concepts that are discussed in Chapter 4, an excellent source is:

T. J. Hailstones, B. L. Martin, and F. V. Mastrianna, *Contemporary Economic Problems and Issues,* 2nd ed. (Cincinnati: South-Western Publishing Co., 1970).

Rather than tackling J. M. Keynes' General Theory *listed in the text, at this stage the student might get more out of:*

A. H. Hansen, *A Guide to Keynes* (New York: McGraw-Hill Book Co., Inc., 1953).

Part Two
The Model

5 Introducing the Model

We have already pointed out, and we will have no trouble whatsoever in convincing the reader, that the U.S. economy is a very complicated system. It can be dealt with at any level of abstraction. The simpler the model, the more easily it is described and understood. But then, a simple model provides less insight into the many interdependencies that we need to capture in order to obtain a workable understanding of our economy. An example may do much to clarify the problem.

Suppose I tell my five-year-old that our car runs because I put gasoline into it and hold the steering wheel. That's his model: gasoline and steering wheel. For my ten-year-old this model won't do. He knows about gasoline and the steering wheel, yes, but he also knows that there are spark plugs, pistons, cylinders, a fuel pump, and various other pieces of equipment. That is, my ten-year-old's model of automotive propulsion is more complicated than his brother's. As for myself, I have a still more complicated model in my mind.

Suppose, now, the car stalls on a family trip. My five-year old, on the basis of his simple model, can trace the trouble to either the steering wheel or the gasoline. The former is still where it always was, ergo it must be the gasoline: We are out of it. A look at the fuel gauge, of course, may tell me that this theory is incorrect. Confronted with this evidence, my five-year old cannot offer an alternative source of trouble, or a solution to the problem. His model is so oversimplified as to be worthless. My ten-year old, with his advanced model, is capable of offering, say, five more reasons why the car may be stalled. This makes his model immensely more workable. I, finally, may offer five additional causes. As a last act of desperation I may take the car to a garage. The mechanic on duty has a greatly more complicated model. In fact, using this model of his, he will put my car back into running condition.

Lest I be misunderstood, let me hasten to say that complexity of an economic model is not in and of itself a guarantee of its workability. A model may be as complicated as you please, yet be dead wrong. What I am saying is that a certain minimum complexity is required. This minimum complexity plus a correct assembly of the model will enable us to monitor many important variables. If the economy is stalled, a complicated model opens up many more potential trouble sources than does a simple model. As a result, the range of solutions is greatly increased.

Introductory macroeconomic models, for example, oftentimes have no government sector in them. As a pedagogical device, such a model is not, perhaps, totally without merit. But in a real economy such as ours, where the government spends 20% of our GNP and where government actions are deliberately instituted to move the economy in one direction or another, a model without a government sector is about as useful as my five-year old's gasoline-steering wheel model on automotive propulsion.

Having spent more than a page apologizing for its complexity, let me delay the introduction of the model itself a little longer. An overview of our model, a look at the forest before we lose ourselves in the trees, may give the reader a sense of the direction in which we are headed. Let us begin with a model that we are all very familiar with, namely the simple supply and demand model from microeconomic theory. Such a model is shown in Figure 5–1, using apples as the relevant good.

Given the apple-demand curve *D* and the apple-supply curve *S*, we know from microeconomic theory that Point *A* in Figure 5–1 represents an equilibrium position in the sense that the market-clearing price and output are co-determined at \$.50 and 100 units. Suppose, now, that the demand for apples suddenly decreases as shown by the dashed line *D'*. Such a decrease in demand may reflect shifting preferences of the buyers, for example. The new

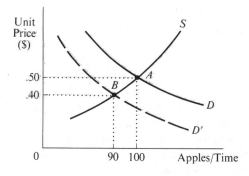

Figure 5–1   *Supply and Demand*

equilibrium position after the downward shift in demand will be at Point *B*,
where the price and the output of apples have fallen. If you are in the apple-
growing industry, you are faced by a shrinking output. This means, of course,
that some of the productive resources previously used in that industry are
now being idled. As an apple grower you will tend to regard Point *A* as a norm
and you will complain that the insufficient demand for apples is at the root of
your problem. Translate the model in Figure 5–1 into aggregative terms and
you have in essence our macroeconomic model, as shown in Figure 5–2.

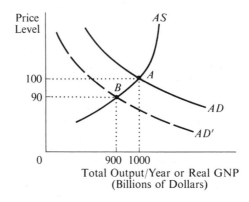

Figure 5–2   *Aggregate Supply and Demand*

Instead of measuring apples on the abscissa, we use all the goods and
services that are produced in a given year, i.e., the nation's real GNP, and
express it in constant dollars. Similarly, instead of the price of apples, we use
the average price of all goods and services, as approximated by the price level,
on the ordinate. What we are really interested in is real national wealth or its
flow equivalent, namely real national income. But we have previously agreed
that we will be no worse off by using the real GNP instead of the theoretically
preferable national income.

In comparing the supply curve in Figure 5–1 with the *AS* curve in Figure
5–2, it will be noted that the *AS* curve is characterized by a rapidly rising slope
beyond the full-employment equilibrium position designated by Point *A*. In
fact, the *AS* curve reaches an absolute maximum beyond which the nation is
incapable of raising its GNP. As we will see in Chapter 6, this is a reflection
of the fact that a nation, at any given point in time, is subject to very definite
limits in the utilization of its factors of production (resources, capital stock,
labor force, to name a few). Using all productive factors at its disposal, the
nation can only produce so much. The concept of the production-possibility
frontier makes its appearance.

Coming back to our *AS-AD* system in Figure 5–2, let us suppose that the *AD* curve is shifted downward. As we will see later, such a shift may be induced by the expectation that bad times are just around the corner. The dashed *AD'* curve now intersects the *AS* curve at Point *B*. At that point the price level has fallen to 90 and the real total output has been reduced by $100 billion. If Point *A* represented a full-employment equilibrium position in the sense that all productive resources, especially capital and labor, were employed, then Point *B* must be a less-than-full employment position. Our economy is experiencing a recession. That is, some capital and some labor must be idle when the real output rate shrinks from $1000 billion to $900 billion.

The dashed *AD'* curve, then, represents a case of insufficient *AD*. The economy can be returned to its full-employment level at Point *A* by the simple expedient of stimulating *AD*. This fundamental idea was first formally developed by J. M. Keynes in his *General Theory*. Significantly, this influential book was written in the aftermath of the Great Depression when insufficient *AD* was indeed the prime cause of the prevailing economic troubles.

Let us stipulate that in Figure 5–2 the *AD* is increased rather than decreased. Though this is not shown in the figure, the reader will have no trouble in seeing that such an increase in *AD* will be inflationary. A sudden increase in *AD* may be the result of changing expectations; for example, if people fear that a war is imminent they may rush into the market and buy up durable and nonperishable nondurable consumer goods. Such a move would, in fact, set up inflationary pressures by shifting the *AD* curve upward.

So far we have concentrated our attention on the demand side of the macroeconomic model. As we will see later, there is a good reason for this somewhat one-sided approach. For one thing, the *AD* side has historically received more attention than the *AS* curve ever since Keynes wrote his *General Theory*. For another thing, all monetary and fiscal policy actions work through the *AD* side, and this, perhaps more than any other factor, has centered the attention of policy makers and economists alike on the *AD* side. After all, that is the side where the action is.

Rediscovery of the *AS* side as an integral part of the economy is relatively recent. It was brought about by the realization that monetary and fiscal policies do not always offer satisfactory solutions to economic problems. Just as the *AD* curve may be subject to shifts, so may the *AS* curve. For example, an upward shift of the *AS* curve indicates a reduction in *AS*. In Figure 5–3, this may be expressed in one of two ways. First, we may say that the prices of all goods (the price index) rise for any given GNP when a nation's aggregate supply is reduced. And second, we may say that for any given price level a reduction in *AS* will cause a reduction of the GNP the nation is willing to produce. The student should be able to verbalize the opposite case of an increase in *AS*. With the aid of Figure 5–3, let us briefly discuss the effects of a shifting *AS* curve.

Again we start with a full-employment equilibrium position at Point *A*, where the real GNP is one trillion dollars and the price level is 100. If the *AS* is reduced, as it might be, for example, by a move from a predominantly com-

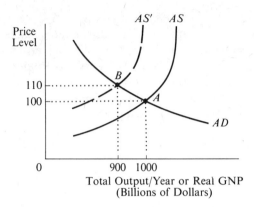

Figure 5–3   **Shifts in Aggregate Supply**

petitive market form to a monopolistic or a cartel form, the real GNP is reduced while the price level rises, Point *B*. Such a move away from a competitive market structure is one possible cause of a reflation. Alternatively, if the
AS curve is shifted down, i.e., the *AS* is increased, say through technological
progress, the real GNP will rise and the price level will tend to fall. All of these
possibilities will be discussed in more detail after we have developed our
model.

  Unfortunately, while the above discussion correctly describes the results
of our model, the approach is too simplistic to be of much use. As a policy tool,
the model shown in Figures 5–2 and 5–3 is about as useful as my five-year-
old's model on automotive propulsion. Suppose we are at Point *B* in Figure
5–2; that is, we agree that our economy is in the grip of a recession. Clearly,
all we need to do is to stimulate the *AD*. But how? Our model does not tell
us. We need to know something about the components of *AD*. Maybe we can
concentrate our policy efforts on just one such component. By stimulating it,
we may stimulate the *AD*. But suppose this component depends on several
variables. Which of these variables are we going to attack? And what are the
effects on the other variables? And suppose we succeed in stimulating this
component of *AD*, will the other components be positively reinforced or
negatively affected by such policy actions? The whole set of underlying and
interdependent forces must be reckoned with before we can dare attack the
recession. None of these forces, none of the many variables that make up the
economy, are revealed by our simple model. To lay bare at least the major
variables and to learn their effect on our economy is the purpose of the model
we are about to build. In doing this, we will greatly facilitate our task by investigating separately the *AS* side and the *AD* side of our model. The *AS* side
is by far the least complicated of the two. For this reason we will attack it
first, in Chapter 6. Chapters 7 and 8 will then be devoted to the *AD* side of the
model.

Problems

1. Suppose the economy is in a position as shown by Point *B* in Figure 5–3: The price level has risen and the real GNP has declined. The implication of this statement is that unemployment exists in the land. Why? If the government is committed to a policy of full employment, how can it get the GNP back to 1000 billion real dollars' worth? Suppose the government can only effectively work through the *AD* curve, i.e., stimulate or destimulate *AD*, what is the inevitable result of reestablishing full employment?

2. Suppose our economy is in a position of full employment as shown by Point *A* in Figure 5–3. What will be the result of an unexpected increase in *AD*?

3. One way of interpreting the *AS* curve is to look upon it as reflecting the cost to the buyers (expressed in terms of an index number) of this nation's total output. The *AS'* curve in Figure 5–3, for example, may thus be viewed as reflecting a greater cost of our GNP at every output level, relative to the *AS* curve. What do you think might cause this cost curve to be shifted up? Try to anticipate the problems that are involved in shifting the curve back to its previous equilibrium level.

4. When an economist speaks of technological progress, he means that an economy can produce any output at a lower cost than heretofore. In terms of our *AD–AS* system, what does this mean? What is the implication of technological progress?

Suggested Readings

C. L. Schultze, "Recent Inflation in the United States" (Study Paper No. 1; Joint Economic Committee), *Study of Employment, Growth, and Price Levels,* 1959, pp. 4–16.

F. Machlup, "Another View of Cost-Push and Demand-Pull Inflation," *Review of Economics and Statistics,* XLII (1960), 125–139.

A. P. Lerner, "An Analysis and a Suggestion for Dealing with Inflationary Depression," printed in Subcommittee on Antitrust and Monopoly of the Committee on the Judiciary, U.S. Senate, *Administered Prices: A Compendium on Public Policy* (Washington, D.C.: Government Printing Office, 1963), pp. 196–212.

6 *The Aggregate Supply Curve*

From our preview in the preceding chapter we know that the *AS* curve is positively sloped over most of its range, i.e., that a price-level rise will cause the GNP supply to increase and vice versa. Why this is so and what variables play a leading role in shaping the *AS* curve is the topic of this chapter.

The total output of a nation is determined in part by strictly technical factors and in part by economic factors. These two factors are, of course, interdependent. An example may clarify this. One determinant of a nation's output is its resource endowment. But whether an existing raw material is a resource depends among other things on its price. No one will question that crude oil is a very important raw material in the production of energy. But the untold reserves of crude oil locked into oil shales in the United States is not presently a resource simply because it cannot be produced profitably. At some time in the future, unless some other raw material, like the atom, has replaced crude oil in the process of energy production, the dwindling of world oil reserves may push the price of oil up to the point where the shale oil can be commercially tapped, and it will then have become a resource to this country. Thus, the definition of a nation's resource endowments encompasses more than mere physical presence, since it takes into consideration such economic factors as the price of the resource.

The strictly technical part of our nation's total output is summarized in the aggregate production function, which defines the maximum possible output of a nation, given its labor force, capital stock, and resource endowment. This total output or real GNP implicitly depends upon several additional variables that are part of the aggregate production function. Of these the two most important are:

1. Technology. Obviously, the more advanced the technology of a country, given its labor force, capital stock, and resource endowment, the greater this country's total output. Similarly, technological progress implies greater total output with a given productive resource base.
2. Labor skill. All other things being equal, total output is not simply a function of the number of workers. The training and professional skill of the labor force play an important role, as does managerial competence.[1]

A nation's labor force, its capital stock, and its resource endowment, then, are the primary determinants of its total output or GNP supply. Thus, the aggregate production function may be written as follows:

$$GNP = f(L,K,Re),\qquad\qquad 6\text{-}1$$

where GNP = total real output, expressed in constant dollars,
L = labor force,
K = capital stock,
Re = resource base.

Equation 6–1 assumes that certain other variables, in particular technology and labor skill, are not subject to change. For our model, which is essentially a short-run model, this is a reasonable assumption.

This brings up a problem that we have slighted so far, namely the problem of the relevant time period of our model. We might begin by stating emphatically that ours is not a long-run growth model. What we are primarily interested in is the short-run maximization of aggregate wealth, called national income. Employment, total output, and price level are the primary variables we will be monitoring in this endeavor. To put our objective differently, we wish to build a model that will help us to understand and ultimately to pre-

---

[1] It may come as a surprise to see managers included in the labor force. As far as total output is concerned, managers like labor are production-oriented human input. Only when it comes to determining the claims on total output, i.e., when the problem of income distribution arises, are managers and workers in opposing camps; the managers, at least in this country, predominantly give their loyalty to the resource owners. This, of course, gives rise to the widely publicized labor-management conflict.

vent violent business-cycle fluctuations. Ideally, the repression of recessions and inflationary periods is our goal. Specifically, what length of period is relevant in this task is no easy question to answer. It may be very short, on the order of two to three months, or longer, say two to three years, certainly not more than that. Our assumption of a given level of technology and labor skill is not unreasonable, because neither is very likely to undergo great changes, if we consider the relevant short-run time period to be, say, one year. Similarly, if an exact definition is required, the long-run time period may be considered for our model to be not less than five years.

Our aggregate production function given by equation 6–1 states that a nation's total output depends on three independent variables. A geometric presentation of equation 6–1, therefore, requires a four-dimensional graph, which has always given me great trouble to draw on a two-dimensional plane. Let us simplify things by stipulating that in our relevant one-year time period the resource base of this country is essentially constant. That is, we do not allow for a sudden discovery of gold in California, or for extreme price increases in crude oil that would add the U.S. shale-oil reserves to this country's resource endowment. Our aggregate production function then simplifies to the following equation:

$$GNP = f(L,K). \qquad\qquad 6–2$$

Equation 6–2 can be presented geometrically as in Figure 6–1: The aggregate production function describes a surface, the height of which depends on the labor-capital input and represents the relevant real GNP. The meaning of Point A, for example, is that a labor force of ten million people using a capital stock worth $20 billion will produce a GNP of $60 billion. Remember that the production surface of Figure 6–1 assumes a constant technology, labor skill, and resource endowment. If any of these were to improve, a new production surface would result that would be everywhere higher than the old surface, except along the zero-GNP borders.

Suppose a nation has a labor-capital combination corresponding to that of Point *A*. If that nation wishes to increase its total output, it can do this by increasing its capital stock, its labor force, or both. An increase in capital stock, while holding the labor force constant, corresponds to a move toward Point *C* in Figure 6–1. As we can see in this figure, the constant labor force of ten million people will increase the GNP from $60 billion to $80 billion by using a capital stock of $30 billion rather than $20 billion. Similarly, a move from Point *A* to Point *B* in Figure 6–1 will also result in a $20 billion increase in GNP. Such a move is accomplished by holding the capital stock of the nation constant while increasing the labor force.

Our model is primarily concerned with business-cycle fluctuations. This makes it a short-run model in which substantial changes in capital stock are not very likely to occur. For our model, let us assume that the capital stock re-

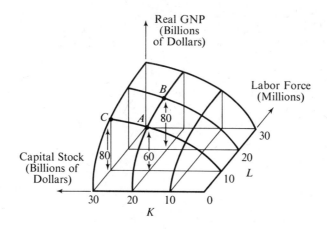

*Figure 6–1   The Aggregate Production
Function (Variable Capital Stock)*

mains constant and let us derive the analytical consequences of such an assumption.

Suppose a nation, at a given point in time, has a capital stock of $20 billion. Suppose further that our nation's level of technology, labor skill, and resource endowment are such that its production surface is as shown in Figure 6–1. If we add the limiting assumption that this nation's capital stock does not change in the short run, its GNP can be changed only by increasing or decreasing the labor force. In equation form, the aggregate production function given by equation 6–2 would be simplified as follows:

$$GNP = f(L, \bar{K}).$$ 6–3

Translated, the GNP depends on the input of labor only, given the existing capital stock. The bar over the K in equation 6–3 serves to remind us that the capital stock is a parameter not subject to change.

Equation 6–3 can be given a geometric interpretation by Figure 6–1. Given our previous assumption of a constant capital stock worth $20 billion, a variable labor force means that our economy is limited in its moves to the arch that is defined by Points A and B. This arch can be presented in a two-dimensional graph as shown in Figure 6–2.

Points A and B have been reproduced in Figure 6–2 as they originally appeared in Figure 6–1. The aggregate production curve for $\bar{K}$ = $20 billion, as shown in Figure 6–2, has two characteristics. First, it goes through the origin. This property, of course, is derived from the way the original production

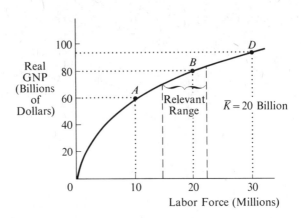

Figure 6–2   The Aggregate Production
Function (Constant Capital Stock)

surface was drawn. No particular practical importance is attached to this characteristic of the aggregate production curve, for a reason that is easy to see. Suppose our economy normally operates at Point *B* in Figure 6–2. Then the maximum range over which the labor force may fluctuate is on the order of 15 to 22.5 million people. The lower limit is based on the worst depression the United States has experienced this century, when unemployment was as high as 25%. The upper limit is based on a 12% increase of the U.S. labor force during World War II, when all available productive resources were put to work, including people past normal retirement age and housewives.

The second characteristic of the aggregate production curve in Figure 6–2 is that it is convex from above over its entire range. Again, in a practical sense, this matters only in the relevant range, i.e., for a labor force between 15 and 22.5 million people. This convexity of the aggregate production function reflects the well-known principle of the diminishing marginal product. In essence, this principle states that an increase in the use of any productive input, in our case labor, while holding all other inputs (capital) constant, results in an increase in total output, but the rate of increase diminishes as more of the variable input is used. We will have more to say on this subject when we come to the labor market.

Equation 6–3 and its geometric counterpart in Figure 6–2 describe our aggregate *production* function. This function tells us what a nation's real output will be, given a constant capital structure, if a certain size of labor force is employed in producing it. What we are after, however, is the aggregate *supply* function: We wish to know how the real GNP is affected by changes in the price level. If we can determine a nation's employed labor force at given price levels, then we can determine its real GNP at those price levels with the aid of our aggregate production function, equation 6–3. To do this, let us turn our attention to the labor market.

The Labor Market

Since no one in our society can be compelled to take a job or to offer a job, the labor force is what it is because a balance has been struck between those seeking a job and those offering one. We have a supply and demand system that determines the labor market equilibrium.

The worker—and as we have pointed out, this term includes the professor of economics—through his willingness to work (or the lack of it) makes up the supply side of the labor market. We will not delve into the derivation of the labor-supply curve, available in any good textbook on microeconomic theory. Let us simply state that the supply of labor is a function of real wages:[2] As real wages rise so does the number of laborers willing to work. Intuitively, this is what we would expect. An increase in real wages may cause housewives to seek part-time or even full-time jobs; it may cause middle-aged executives to abandon early retirement plans; it may even lure some people out of retirement, or off the welfare rolls for that matter.

While the supply of labor is determined by the willingness of labor to work, the demand for labor is determined by the willingness of management to hire. That is, the demand for labor originates wholly with the firms. In theory, a firm will pay a worker what he is worth, no more and no less. If the firm paid more, it would lose money in employing the man in question. If the firm paid less or, what is the same thing, if the laborer brought in a revenue greater than his own cost, the firm would want to hire more people, until the additional revenue brought by the last man is equal to that man's cost. This, in essence, is the theory of the value of the marginal product of labor. The value of the marginal product curve, in fact, constitutes a firm's demand-for-labor curve in a competitive market. (Again, refer to any good textbook in microeconomic theory.[3])

The supply-and-demand apparatus for the labor market is shown in Figure 6–3. Point A in this figure designates the equilibrium position, where the real wage of labor w_0 is such that exactly the same number of laborers are offering their services (L_S) as firms are willing to take on (L_D). At a real wage higher than

---

[2] This derivation is based on a utility analysis using leisure as one good and the composite of all other goods as the other good. The amount of leisure, and by difference the amount of work, that a laborer opts for is then derived by varying the wage rate. See, for example, C. E. Ferguson, *Microeconomic Theory*, Revised Edition (Homewood, Ill.: Richard D. Irwin, Inc., 1969), pp. 371 and 372.

[3] For example, C. E. Ferguson, *op. cit.*, pp. 360–370.

w_o—for example, w' in Figure 6–3—more workers wish to work than firms will want to hire: We have unemployment. At a real wage lower than w_o, such as w'', a labor shortage results. Neither case is stable in free markets, since wage adjustments tend to equilibrate supply and demand.[4] Wages are expressed in real terms, since it is not the dollar figure on the paycheck that motivates people to work, but the goods and services represented by this dollar figure. This has been discussed in Part 1 and needs no elaboration.

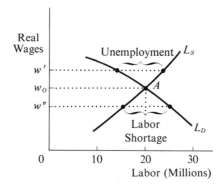

Figure 6–3   The Labor Market

In the real world, however, wages are paid in money terms. This makes them vulnerable to price-level changes. Any person who has been on a fixed money income over the last two or three years will testify to that. The rising price level has been chipping away at that person's real income; i.e., the constant monetary income has been buying fewer and fewer goods and services in the market. The relation between the price level and real wages for given monetary wages is defined by a rectangular hyperbola as shown in Figure 6–4.

Suppose you draw a monthly paycheck of $1000. At a price level of 100, Point A, this check commands a given market basket of goods and services. This market basket is defined to have a value of 1000 real dollars. If the price level doubles, Point B, your money wage of $1000 commands only half a market basket. This we express by saying that your real wage has been cut in half, from 1000 to 500 real dollars. Conversely, Point C defines the real value of a $1000 check after the price level has been cut in half. In this instance, your given paycheck will buy two market baskets, meaning that your real wage has doubled.

This completes our discussion of the individual pieces that go into the *AS* model. We will remember that Figure 6–2 represents our aggregate production

---

[4]This ignores the issue of sticky wages which we will take up in a moment.

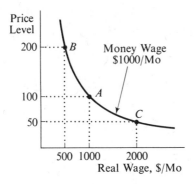

Figure 6–4   **Real Wages — Money Wages**

function. Mathematically, this figure was translated to say that at any given point in time the GNP of a nation depends on that nation's labor force and on its constant capital stock. The size of the labor force was found to be dependent on real wages, Figure 6–3. And, of course, real wages are affected by price level changes, Figure 6–4. Let us now put the whole puzzle together to derive our *AS* curve.[5]

Aggregate Supply

Suppose we are viewing an economy in equilibrium: All productive resources are employed and the price level is 100. This initial equilibrium position is depicted by Points *A* in Figure 6–5. In particular, starting at the price level axis labeled P and moving to the left, a money wage of $1000 per month and a price level of 100 correspond to a real wage of $1000 per month. Figure 6–5 has been deliberately drawn in such a way that the labor-demand and labor-supply curves intersect at Point *A* in Quadrant III. This point corresponds to full employment in the labor market. The size of the labor force may be read from the vertical axis labeled *L*. Using this labor force, the economy produces a total output of, say, 900 billion real dollars. In Quadrant I, this output occurs at a price level of 100. Point *A* in this quadrant is the first point on our aggregate supply curve.

---

[5] In doing this we will borrow an analytical format that was first developed, I believe, by Pesek and Saving. But note that our simplified model ignores the real-wealth effect on the labor-supply curve. See B. P. Pesek and T. R. Saving, *The Foundations of Money and Banking* (New York: The Macmillan Company, 1968), Chapter 21.

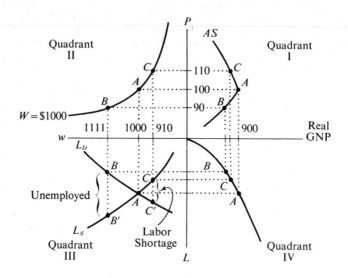

Figure 6–5   The Aggregate Supply Curve
(Constant Money Wages)

Now let us assume that the price level in our economy falls to 90 and let us investigate the effect of such a price-level fall on the aggregate supply. The money wage of $1000 per month is raised to a real wage of $1111 per month. But at a monthly real wage of $1111, the existing labor force no longer produces the value of its marginal product. To see this, suppose for a moment that the firms will continue to employ the same labor force. This means that the total output will remain the same in real terms. In monetary terms, however, this same output will bring only 90% of what it used to bring. Contrast this with the constant nominal factor payments we have assumed and the picture of the profit squeeze is complete.

One way for the firms to increase the value of labor's marginal product and thus to bring it to equality with their increased real wages is to employ fewer people while using the existing capital stock to the fullest extent possible. This will increase the capital-labor ratio and, therefore, labor's productivity. In terms of Figure 6–5, Quadrant III, the firms will want to move from Point *A* to Point *B* along the labor-demand curve, where the new real wage of $1111 per month creates a disequilibrium position. Moving along the labor-demand curve L_D (i.e., labor's value marginal product curve), the firms now wish to employ the number of workers represented by Point *B*. The laborers, of course, are more eager to go to work at the new and higher real wage. They would like to move along the labor-supply curve L_S to Point *B'*. This is where the significance of a previous statement comes into focus. The fact that labor cannot force itself onto the firms causes the labor-demand curve, which originates with the firms, to be the determinant of the labor force at real wages of $1000 and above. As a result, a state of unemployment exists at the real wage of $1111 per month. The extent of this unemployment is given by the distance between Points B' and B. This distance is the geometric equivalent of the difference between the number of people seeking work and the number of people finding work.

Point B in Quadrant III corresponds to Point B in Quadrant IV. Given the labor input in Quadrant IV, the total real output can be read off the abscissa labeled real GNP. Connecting this new GNP with the relevant price level (90) gives Point B on the aggregate supply curve. A derivation similar to the one described above could be made for several different price levels below 100. This would yield the positively sloped section AB of the AS curve.

Before we move on to section AC of our AS curve, let us summarize the meaning of our geometric exercise. A fall in the price level in the face of given money wages sets up a profit squeeze for firms. This squeeze is met by letting a part of the labor force go. This has two effects on the economy: (1) a state of unemployment is created, and (2) the total output or real GNP is reduced.

The whole chain of events is predicated upon the assumption that firms will not reduce money wages when the price level falls. That is, the firms, when faced by the option of reducing wages and thereby reestablishing the full-employment equilibrium at Point A, or else of reducing the labor force, will take the latter alternative. Obviously, the empirical validity of this assumption is very important to the validity of the model itself. However, the record is exceedingly clear. Unemployment is one of the most closely watched economic indicators precisely because the firms vary the size of the labor force in response to economic conditions. Across-the-board reductions in wages, on the other hand, are still rare enough in this country that any such occurrence in a major firm makes the headlines in financial papers.

Let us now turn our attention to the negatively sloped section AC of our AS curve in Figure 6–5. Starting again in Quadrant II, a 10% increase in the price level will reduce the money wage of $1000 per month to a real value of $910. At that lower real wage, of course, the firms are eager to employ more people. To see this point, assume for a moment that the firms could convince the entire labor force to stay on at the given money wage, i.e., at the lower real wage. If that happened, the firms would produce the same total output corresponding to Point A in Quadrant I, and their nominal factor payments would remain the same. But that output would bring 10% more than it did before, since the price level rose by 10%. This would be a good thing for the firms— such a good thing, in fact, that the profit-maximizing firms would want more of the same—via an increase in employment to Point C' in Quadrant III, Figure 6–5.

However, to reason that there will be an increase in employment is to reckon without the laborers. Just as the laborers cannot force themselves onto the firms, so the firms cannot force the laborers to work for them. In fact, the reduction in real wages associated with an increase in the price level will cause the laborers to work less. In the labor market in Figure 6–5, the quantity of labor supplied at a real wage of $910 is given by Point C, while the firms are willing to hire the number of people corresponding to Point C'. The distance between Points C' and C, then, corresponds to the difference between people wanted and people willing to work. Since more people are wanted than are available, we have a labor shortage: At the going money wage of $1000 per month and a price level of 110, the firms are unable to get the people they wish to employ.

According to Point C in Quadrant III, the labor force is reduced by the price-level increase. Working with the constant capital stock in the country, this reduced labor force will produce a total output of real GNP as shown by Point C on the aggregate production function, Quadrant IV of Figure 6–5. Connecting this output with the relevant price level gives us the negatively sloped section AC of the AS curve.

Let us again summarize the meaning of our geometric exercise. An increase in the price level in the face of given money wages reduces labor's real wages. This causes some workers to withdraw from the labor force with a twofold effect: (1) A labor shortage results, and (2) the total output or real GNP is reduced.

A negatively sloped AS curve is a suspicious character calling for closer scrutiny. Since the negative slope was the result of our constant-money-wage assumption, let us begin by asking if such an assumption is warranted. We have already discussed the stickiness of wages in a downward direction, so we need not repeat ourselves here. But what about the constancy of money wages when price levels rise? The peculiar thing about this case, illustrated by Points C in Figure 6–5, is that the workers produce more revenue than they cost the firms. As a result the firms are very eager to put more people to work. At the going real wage of $910 per month, however, they can't find these people. What, precisely, keeps the firms from bidding up money wages? Nothing, really, and this is what is going to happen. This is illustrated in Figure 6–6.

The positively sloped section AB from Figure 6–5 is exactly the same in Figure 6–6. That is, Figure 6–5 correctly describes the chain of events that is induced by a fall in the price level. However, things are different in the case of a price-level increase. The dashed curve in Quadrant II of Figure 6–6 indicates the 10% increase in money wages that firms are willing to pay when the price level rises by 10%. This means, of course, that money wages rise from $1000 per month to $1100 per month. The real wage, as a result, remains the same, and so does the labor force. That labor force, using the nation's given capital stock, will produce a total output designated by Point C on the aggregate production curve shown in Quadrant IV. Point C in this Quadrant coincides with Point A, and what holds true for one arbitrarily selected price-level rise holds true for all: Starting with a full-employment equilibrium position and assuming wages to be flexible in an upward direction, an increase in the price level will induce higher money wages, while the nation's real output remains constant. In Quadrant I, Figure 6–6, the AS curve is vertical for price levels above 100.

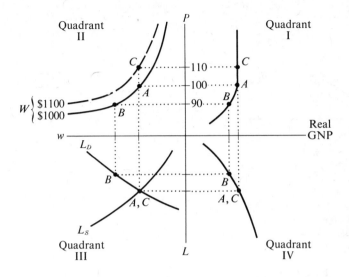

*Figure 6–6   The Aggregate Supply Curve
(Money Wages Flexible Upward)*

This terminates our derivation of the aggregate supply curve. But before we abandon the subject, let us ask ourselves how the AS curve is affected if the competitive market structure underlying it is removed. In particular, let us take a look at both management and labor cartels. A schematic graph for both cases is given in Figure 6–7.

A monopsony may be a legitimate, bone fide corporation dominating the labor market, usually due to an accident of geography. The coal mine in a remote region is an example of such a situation if everyone or nearly everyone in that region depends on the mine for a living. Employee hands-off agreements may serve as an example of a not-so-legitimate management cartel. Because laborers cannot force themselves onto a firm, the demand for labor, i.e., the willingness to hire people, originates wholly with the firms. Thus, any move by firms toward a cartelization in input markets will affect the labor-demand curve: It will be reduced. In Panel A of Figure 6–7, the L_D curve is shifted toward the origin, L'_D. This can be interpreted in two ways: First, for a given size of labor force the firms will be paying less; and second, for a given real wage, fewer laborers will find employment. In short, our firms no longer pay their laborers the value of their marginal product. The new point of intersection of the L'_D curve with the L_S curve determines both the reduced labor force and the reduced real wage. The latter, i.e., the reduced real wage, corresponds to a lower nominal wage at the given price level of 100. This reduced nominal wage is shown by the dashed curve in Quadrant II, labeled $W = \$900$. The

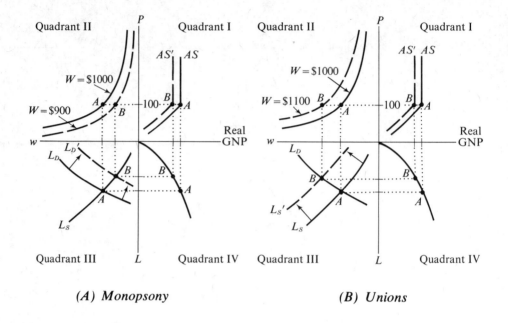

(A) Monopsony   (B) Unions

Figure 6–7   Cartels and the AS curve

reduced labor force, working with the existing capital structure, will produce fewer goods and services. In Quadrant I, this is illustrated by a reduction in *AS* or, geometrically, by a leftward shift of the *AS* curve. To be noted is the fact that the labor market is in equilibrium at Point *B:* given the reduced demand for labor, all laborers seeking employment at the lower real wage are finding it. In Quadrant I, the implication is that the vertical section of the *AS* curve is moved to the left: The nation's production possibility frontier is retracted.

In the case of unions, Panel B of Figure 6–7, higher money wages at given price levels cause higher real wages. Contrary to the monopsony case, changes in the labor market now originate with the labor-supply curve. This curve is shifted to the left, indicating that higher real wages are now required to maintain a given labor force at work. The now-too-expensive labor force is partially let go and as a result the total output again declines. Thus, as in the preceding case, the *AS* curve is shifted to the left. Again, we have a reduced full-employment equilibrium position, causing the production possibility frontier to be reduced.

The two cartels we have considered so far are concerned with noncompetitive conditions in the input markets. What about similar conditions in the output market? The effect of a shift from competitive to monopolistic markets, for example, again causes the *AS* to be reduced, but for a different reason. Monopolies have the power to set their own prices. While it is true that monopolies do not always have greater-than-normal rates of return (after all, even railroads have been known to go broke), monopolies will tend to maximize their profits or minimize their losses by appropriate pricing-output combinations. For the economy as a whole, if the majority of the monopolists achieve their raison d'être, namely a greater-than-normal rate of return, the cost to the purchasers of any given size GNP will be increased, i.e., the *AS* will be reduced.

The effect in the labor market is not clear. Monopolies pay to the laborers not the value of their marginal product, but the marginal revenue product. That is, monopolies take into consideration the fact that an increase in factor usage causes the total output to rise; but in order for this increased output to be sold, prices have to be cut. Nevertheless, if the labor market is competitive, wages may not be affected. For example, consider an economy where each good is produced by a monopolist, but where the monopolists compete among themselves for the input of labor. Given the competitive nature of the labor market, wage levels may not be affected. And given the lack of competition in the output market, prices will rise. If we assume that wages are not affected by a move towards monopolistic output markets, the equilibrium labor force will not be affected. In this case the reduction in *AS*, strictly speaking, takes the form of an upward shift of the *AS* curve. As a result, the nation's production-possibility frontier remains the same in physical output, but the charge to buyers of that full-employment GNP will rise. This is illustrated by Figure 6–8.

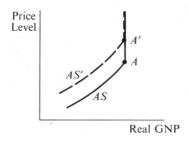

Figure 6–8   Monopolies

The overall result, then, is as follows: No matter where the imperfections manifest themselves, in the input market or in the output market, a shift from competitive to noncompetitive market structures causes a decline in *AS*. We will have a great deal to say on this subject when we get to our monetary and fiscal policy discussions in Part 3.

In our discussion of market imperfections, we have used the *AS* curve as we derived it in Figure 6–6. The vertical section of that curve, as we men-

tioned earlier, designates the nation's maximum possible output. In microeconomic theory, this is comparable to the concept of the production-possibility frontier. The output mix of this maximum GNP may be subject to change,
but the existence of a maximum output at any given point in time is a well-
established economic concept. See any good micro book for a discussion of
the production-possibility frontier.[6]

In Chapter 4, we discussed the problem of a maximum acceptable level of
unemployment. We mentioned at that point that a precise definition of that
level presents certain difficulties. Let us assume, for the sake of the argument,
that an unemployment rate of 4% has been designated as the maximum level
of unemployment. In other words, no remedial policies will be implemented
so long as the nation stays within a 4% level of unemployment. For our *AS*
curve, this establishes a new norm to the left of Point *A*, i.e., at a GNP somewhat smaller in magnitude than the zero-unemployment GNP designated by
Point *A*. This new benchmark is normally referred to as the "full-employment"
GNP. The term full employment as used here does not mean zero unemployment; rather, it means the maximum employment level we may reasonably
expect in the nation. Geometrically, our adjusted *AS* curve now looks as shown
in Figure 6–9.

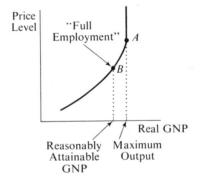

Figure 6–9   *The Final* AS *Curve*

The one difference between the *AS* curve in Figure 6–9 and that in Figure
6–6 that has not been discussed is the disappearance of the kink at Point *A*.
It is doubtful that such a kink exists in a nation's aggregate supply curve. We
have introduced it into the discussion to focus attention on the two distinctly
different sections of that curve. This allowed us to discuss first the one, then
the other section as though they were separate entities. In real life, most

---

[6] For example, A. A. Alchian and W. R. Allen, *Exchange and Production, Theory in Use,*
(Belmont, California: Wadsworth Publishing Company, Inc., 1969), Chapter 1.

economists would probably agree that the transition from a greater-than-zero-unemployment economy to a zero-unemployment economy is gradual, i.e., that the transition at Point A is smooth. The AS curve as shown in Figure 6–9, then, will be the basis of all further discussions.

This terminates our discussion of the AS curve. What an economy is willing to produce at given price levels may or may not be what that same economy is willing to absorb. Both AD and AS must be taken into consideration in discussing the national economy. Let us, therefore, in Chapter 7 and 8, develop a nation's AD curve.

Problems

1. "The discovery of huge oil reserves has solved Lybia's economic problems. Proximity to the European markets assures steady sales of oil. As a result, Lybia's wealth is firmly established." From our model, we would agree that this is true in the short run. However, in the long run, this might not hold at all. Why not?
2. Write down the aggregate production function that is part of our AS model. What variables that are not explicitly shown are nevertheless present and assumed constant? Why is the assumption concerning this constancy not unreasonable?
3. On the AS side of our model, we have an aggregate production function and an aggregate supply function. What is the difference between the two? List the relevant variables of the aggregate production function, including those that are assumed to be constant.
4. Our aggregate supply model does not admit technological progress. If it did, how would it affect the production function and, through it, the supply function?
5. One important sector in the aggregate supply model is the labor market. What is its significance? What determines the demand for labor and the supply of labor?
6. "The firms have the upper hand in dealing with labor. They hire and fire according to their current needs, regardless of the laborer's welfare." Leaving aside the union problem (i.e., organized labor), do you agree with this statement? (Hint: Draw up the geometric equivalent of the labor market before answering this question).
7. If nominal wages are held constant, a disequilibrium position may prevail in the labor market. Explain with the aid of a geometric presentation of our model.
8. Geometrically present the four-quadrant model of our AS side. Starting

at the zero-unemployment position, explain in detail why the *AS* declines as the price level falls.

9. Geometrically present the four-quadrant model of our *AS* side. Starting at the zero-unemployment position, explain in detail why the *AS* curve is vertical at price levels greater than 100.

10. Draw up (do not derive) the full-fledged four-quadrant geometric model of our aggregate supply curve. Suppose now that the economy is undergoing a slow change in its market structure towards monopsonistic markets. What are monopsonistic markets? Show on your geometric model, and explain in words, how this affects the aggregate supply curve.

11. Draw up (do not derive) the full-fledged four-quadrant geometric model of our aggregate supply curve. Suppose now that the economy is undergoing a slow change towards labor cartelization. Show on your geometric model, and explain in words, how this affects the aggregate supply curve.

Suggested Readings

On the production function:

E. Kuh, "Unemployment, Production Functions, and Effective Demand," *Journal of Political Economy,* LXXIV (1966), 238–246.

R. M. Solow, "Technical Change and the Aggregate Production Function," *Review of Economics and Statistics,* XXXIX (1957), 312–320.

On the labor market:

E. J. Mishan, "The Demand for Labor in a Classical and Keynesian Framework," *Journal of Political Economy,* LXXII (1964), 610–616.

J. Tobin, "Money Wage Rates and Employment," in S. E. Harris, ed., *The New Economics,* (New York; Alfred A. Knopf, Inc., 1950), Chapter 40.

D. Patinkin, "Price Flexibility and Full Employment," *The American Economic Review,* 38 (September 1948), 543–564.

For a different view of AS and AD, see:

P. Wells, "Output and the Demand for Capital in the Short Run," *The Southern Economic Journal,* XXXII (October 1965), 146–152.

7 Components of Aggregate Demand

In the preceding chapter we derived the *AS* curve. Somewhat loosely, we used the term GNP and we spoke of the size of the GNP that would be forthcoming at given price levels. Our imprecision was for convenience of expression; a more precise term would have been GNP supply, since this would have made clear that only one side of a two-sided coin was being investigated.

Equilibrium in any market, including the aggregate output market of an economy, is determined by the interplay of supply and demand forces. Producers or sellers cannot simply bring so many units of a given good to the market. They have to take into consideration the number of goods the buyers are willing to take off their hands at posted prices. Similarly, the buyers or demanders cannot simply go to the market wishing to purchase so many goods at desired prices. They have to make allowance for the fact that the suppliers may not be able to produce the desired quantities at the hoped-for prices. A market-clearing price and quantity must, therefore, be reached by a consensus of the suppliers and demanders. What the suppliers' market reactions are was the topic of Chapter 6. Chapters 7 and 8 deal with the demand side of our economy, i.e., its *AD*. Again, we will mostly be speaking in terms of GNP, but it is clear that what we have in mind is the GNP demand. Basically, the question is how many goods and services the people of this nation wish to buy at given price levels.

From our discussion in Part 1 we know that this country's GNP is subdivided into four major categories: consumer purchases, investment, government expenditures, and net exports. We will retain this subdivision of the GNP in building our *AD* curve, with one exception—net exports. There are two reasons for not including it in our model. First, net exports are of relatively insignificant size in our GNP—in 1969, for example, less than one half of one percent (see Table 3–1).[1] Second, the inclusion of foreign trade at this point would unduly complicate our discussion. Thus we will consider our economy to be what professionals call a closed economy—that is, one which does not engage in foreign trade. Such an assumption will focus our attention on domestic problems. Later in the game, in particular in Part 4, we will open up our discussion to include international repercussions of domestic problems and domestic repercussions of international problems. To whet your appetite, let us give an example of each: One of the things we will talk about is the international repercussions of a domestically induced change in the Federal Reserve discount rate; another topic will be the domestic repercussions of a consistently negative balance of payments.

Our model, then, will incorporate a GNP consisting of consumer spending, investment, and government spending. And since it is the GNP-demand or *AD* that we are considering here, a more precise definition of its components would be consumption demand, investment demand, and government demand. Moreover, as we will see shortly, consumption demand will at times be subdivided into demand for durable goods and demand for nondurables and services. This division will not be formally introduced into the model, but it will be verbalized on occasion.

Obviously, there exists an infinite number of ways in which we could have subdivided our GNP demand. Why pick consumers, investors, and government as the relevant buyers in the commodity market? The reason is simple enough: If we wish to make sweeping generalizations about the spending decisions of various units in our economy, we must be reasonably sure that these decisions are subject to fairly similar motivations. By and large, the decision processes in buying a loaf of bread, legal advice, or a car, are pretty much the same. The buyers of such items fall into a very distinct class, called consumers, who are assumed to be utility maximizers, subject to their individual budgetary constraints.

Analogously, all investors can be assumed to be motivated by similar thought processes. But investment spending is not based on the same criteria as is consumption spending. Finally, the government, and in particular the federal government, is motivated by still other criteria. If we can define the reasons why the various units in our economy wish to spend their funds, we can arrive at some conclusion about the individual sector demands and, through them, about our *AD* curve. In other words, we are after the independent variables determining consumption spending, investment spending, and government spending. Knowing these variables we will know the individual sector demands, which can then be aggregated. What is more, by knowing the in-

---

[1] Nevertheless, net exports are a very important part of our GNP, since they determine our balance of trade with other nations. They also affect very significantly our balance of payments.

dependent variables of the individual sector demands, we can make at least qualitative statements about the effects of changes in these variables. This will allow us, for example, to study and to predict the impact of certain government policies on total output, employment, and price levels, and ultimately on this nation's aggregate wealth.

The commodity market, as we will see later, is not the only relevant market in our economy. We will include two more markets in our model, the money market and the credit market. Money and credit, as we all know, play singularly important roles in the U.S. economy. If we left them out, we would be guilty of mutilating the U.S. economy beyond recognition, and that is the last thing in the world we want to do. Since the commodity market is the easiest to understand, let us discuss it first.

The Commodity Market

By commodities we mean the total output of goods and services of the economy. There are, as we have seen, three claimants on this total output: the consumers, the investors, and the government. For our model we will assume that the consumption decisions are made exclusively by individuals in the so-called household sector, whereas investment spending originates solely with the business sector. As we know from our discussion of the national income accounts, this is not an unreasonable assumption. The government buys both consumption and investment goods. Wheat, for example, is an intermediate good, but to the extent that it is exported by the government, it is a consumption good that gives rise to income in this country. Printing presses run by the government are examples of what normally would be investment goods. Moreover, there are goods, such as tanks, that escape our neat two-way classification. What matters here, however, is not the type of good that is purchased by the governments, federal, state, or local, but the criteria used in deciding upon these purchases.

Consumption Spending

Let us begin our discussion by taking a close look at the determinants of consumption spending. We will stipulate that the people's consumption expenditures are primarily determined by the following variables: their net incomes, their accumulated stock of wealth, the rate of interest, and their expectations. Symbolically, this can be expressed by the following consumption function.

$$C = c\{(y-t), A, r, E\}, \qquad 7\text{--}1$$

where C = real consumption,

$\quad c$ = functional relationship,

$\quad y$ = aggregate income, a flow variable,

$\quad t$ = taxes,

$\quad A$ = accumulated wealth, a stock variable,

$\quad r$ = rate of interest, and

$\quad E$ = expectations.

Two points in equation 7–1 deserve special mention. First, the terms $(y-t)$ and A are part of the people's aggregate wealth. In fact, the term $(y-t)$ describes the income equivalent of their wealth, i.e., their after-tax revenue that flows from their labor services or from their possession of productive assets. The term A, on the other hand, is the stock equivalent of their wealth, their holdings of real assets; these are composed of their accumulated durable consumption goods such as homes, cars, boats, etc., and of their real money holdings. Thus, the people's real assets A can be expressed in equation form as follows:

$$A = D + \frac{M}{P}, \qquad 7\text{--}2$$

where D = accumulated durable consumption goods,

$\quad M$ = nominal money holdings,

$\quad P$ = price level.

The second point that deserves mention in equation 7–1 is the variable E, denoting the expectations of the people. Unlike the other variables in equation 7–1, E has no dimensions and is nonquantifiable. Mathematically speaking, therefore, E is not strictly a variable and does not belong in equation 7–1. But we do not claim mathematical rigor in this discussion, and, indeed, this and all other equations are not intended to represent exact mathematical relations, but are, rather, a convenient shorthand description, no more. This approach allows us to include the people's expectations, which are a very important determinant of consumption expenditures, especially in times of economic instability. Combining equations 7–1 and 7–2, we obtain the following aggregate consumption function.

$$C = c\{(y-t), \left(D + \frac{M}{P}\right), r, E\}. \qquad 7\text{--}3$$

One more variable is needed in the aggregate consumption function, namely the capital gain or loss on financial assets. Typically, but not exclusively, such gains or losses are incurred daily as a result of speculative pressures in the major stock markets. In fact, the Great Depression was launched into being by the collapse of the stock market that had been subject to overheating, i.e., to undue speculative buying. The Great Depression turned out to be an expensive lesson, but a lesson it was. As we will see in Part 4, it was the cause of legislation designed to curb speculative pressures in the stock markets and thus to prevent another collapse of the stock market on the gigantic scale of Black Tuesday, October 29, 1929.

Still, the stock market by its very nature is a speculative market: Though speculative forces may be reduced by legislation, such as the setting of margin requirements on stock purchases, they cannot be eliminated. The existence of speculative forces is reflected in sometimes unusual rates of return. Actually, rather than the concept of a rate of return, the common measure used in the stock market is the price-earnings ratio, which is simply the inverse of the fractional rate of return. For example, a price-earnings ratio of 40 is not at all unusual in the stock market. This corresponds to a rate of return of 2.5%, low by any standard outside the stock market. Why would anyone want to buy a share yielding 2.5%, when any bond or savings account can do better than that? The answer is growth or capital gain. If a given firm has exhibited the ability to grow, if its shares have been subject to substantial and repeated increases in value, the investor, letting past performance be his guide, will be willing to pay a higher price for the growth stock than for a bond that, by definition, cannot appreciate in value, at least not if it is purchased when initially floated and is held to maturity.

Equation 7–3 does not contain the capital gains (or losses) that have been obtained in the past. Suppose, for example, that I buy a $100-share at a price-earnings ratio of twenty, i.e., a share yielding a return of 5%. That return, in the form of dividends, is included in the variable y in equation 7–3. Suppose now that my share doubles in value, perhaps because other highly knowledgeable investors besides myself have discovered the growth potential of that firm. This increase in the value of the share does not affect the dividends paid by the firm. These continue to be $5 per share per year. But the share itself is now worth $200. The new yield on the share, for anyone considering its purchase after the increase in value, is $5 per year on an investment (price) of $200, i.e., a return of 2.5%. This, as we have seen, corresponds to a price-earnings ratio of 40.

The dividends, we said, are included in the term y in equation 7–3. What about the capital gain of $100? It is nowhere in the aggregate consumption function. Since we have opted to label $A(= D + M/P)$ the people's accumulation of real assets, the increase in their real wealth due to capital gains on financial assets does not properly belong in this category. We will simply label such capital gains CG and introduce this variable separately into the aggregate consumption function as follows:

$$C = c\{(y - t), CG, \left(D + \frac{M}{P}\right), r, E\}. \qquad 7\text{–}4$$

Equation 7–4, then, is our final aggregate consumption function; it will be the basis of our subsequent discussions. Let us take each variable in the equation and determine its effect on consumption spending.

a. $y =$ aggregate income. The higher the people's aggregate income, all other variables remaining the same, the more they will want to consume, i.e., the greater their consumption spending. This is conveniently expressed by the following shorthand formula:[2]

$$\frac{\Delta C}{\Delta y} > 0.$$

b. $t =$ tax payments. The higher the people's tax payments, the lower their net income and, therefore, the smaller their demand for consumer goods. Thus,

$$\frac{\Delta C}{\Delta t} < 0.$$

c. $y - t =$ net or disposable income. This variable is positively related to consumption spending, i.e.,

$$\frac{\Delta C}{\Delta (y - t)} > 0.$$

d. $CG =$ real capital gain. This is in the nature of a windfall profit on a financial asset. The greater this profit, the wealthier the owner and the greater his demand for consumption goods, i.e.,

$$\frac{\Delta C}{\Delta CG} > 0.$$

As are all variables in equation 7–4, the capital gain CG has been adjusted for price-level changes. That is, CG as used here does not

---

[2] Strictly speaking, the fraction $\Delta C / \Delta y$ is the partial derivative of C with respect to y, $(\partial C / \partial y)$. See Appendix B for elaboration.

reflect changing price levels; it is solely the result of speculative market forces.

e. A = accumulated wealth. Obviously, the wealthier the people, the greater their consumption expenditures. Thus:

$$\frac{\Delta C}{\Delta A} > 0.$$

But since $A = D + \dfrac{M}{P}$, it follows that

$$\frac{\Delta C}{\Delta D} > 0, \quad \frac{\Delta C}{\Delta M} > 0, \quad \text{and} \quad \frac{\Delta C}{\Delta P} < 0.$$

In regard to the first inequality, the more cars, for example, there are in the nation, the more funds will be spent on gasoline and tires. Similarly, the more homes there are, the greater the demand for seed and fertilizer and lawn mowers. Generally, the greater the amount of durable goods held in a nation, the greater are that nation's consumption expenditures.

The second inequality says that the more money people have, the more they spend on consumer goods. However, if the price level rises, the nominal money holdings M lose value and people will cut down consumption spending. This is the meaning of the third inequality, which describes what has been called the real wealth effect.

f. r = rate of interest. The rate of interest is the price of credit. The higher the interest rate, the more expensive is the credit and therefore the good that is purchased on credit. Thus, an increase in the rate of interest will reduce consumption.

$$\frac{\Delta C}{\Delta r} < 0.$$

The preceding relationship typically but not exclusively applies to durable consumer goods such as cars, homes, refrigerators, etc., since a great proportion of these goods is bought on credit.

g. E = expectations. Nothing can be said about changes in consumption spending induced by changes in expectations. Depending on the particular situation, a change in expectations may stimulate or dampen consumption spending. For example, at the outset of the Korean conflict, people's expectations of a forthcoming shortage of durable consumer goods caused them to rush into the market and buy up all such goods. This is one documented instance where consumption spending was increased as a result of a change in expectations. The exact opposite of this behavior may occur at the outset of a depression. People see nothing but rainy days ahead, and in expectation of the forthcoming lean months or years they tighten their belts, i.e., cut down consumption expenditures. (Incidentally, when they do this, they unknowingly aggravate the problem and hasten the advent of the depression.)

Both variables E and CG reflect speculative forces, but they are not the same thing. Their difference rests with their time orientation. The variable E, as we have seen, is oriented towards the future: People increase their purchases of consumer goods because of certain anticipated events. The variable CG, on the other hand, reflects capital gains that have been accumulated in the past, due to past speculation.

Let us return to our aggregate consumption function, equation 7–4 and, graphically, in Figure 7–1. It will be noted in this figure, that the real GNP is

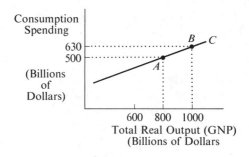

Figure 7–1   The Consumption Function

used on the abscissa, rather than the national income y. From our preceding discussion we know that aggregate consumption spending is positively related to real national income. But we also know from Part 1 that the national income is for all practical purposes a constant fraction of the GNP. Therefore, if y is increased, so is the GNP, and $\Delta C/\Delta y > 0$ implies that $\Delta C/\Delta GNP > 0$. In other words, aggregate consumption spending is also positively related to this nation's GNP, as can be seen on Figure 7–1, where consumption spending is plotted on the ordinate.

Point *A* on the aggregate consumption function of Figure 7–1 has the following meaning: Given a total output or GNP of 800 billion real dollars, the people in that nation will consume goods and services worth $500 billion. If the GNP rises to $1000 billion, aggregate consumption is increased to $630 billion. The reason why an increase in GNP gives rise to an increase in aggregate consumption is easy to see. As the GNP rises, the income stream that is derived from the production of goods and services will also rise. And as the people's income rises, so will their demand for consumption goods. This has been discussed in connection with equation 7–4 and needs no elaboration here. Suffice it to say that the slope of curve *C* in Figure 7–1 is approximately 0.6 in the United States.

Suppose, now, that a variable other than the GNP, and with it *y*, is subject to change. How does this affect aggregate consumption spending? Let us discuss this case in terms of an increase in the rate of interest, presented in Figure 7–2.

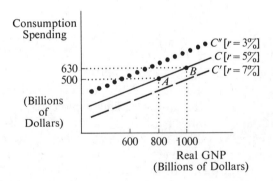

Figure 7–2   Parametric Shifts of the Consumption Function

Suppose we start at Point *A*. Our economy has produced a GNP worth 800 billion real dollars. In producing these goods and services, an income stream was generated that produced enough purchasing power among the people to want to purchase consumer goods worth 500 billion real dollars. All variables, other than income, shown in equation 7–4 are assumed to be constant along the aggregate consumption function shown in Figure 7–2. In particular, since we will be investigating the effect of a change in the rate of interest, we will assume that that rate is 5% everywhere along curve *C*. This is specifically indicated in Figure 7–2.

Now let us assume that the rate of interest rises, say, to 7%. As we know from our previous discussion, an increase in the rate of interest makes goods purchased on credit more expensive; as a result, fewer will be purchased. For a given GNP, this means that fewer consumption goods are now purchased, i.e., the aggregate consumption function C is shifted downward. In Figure 7-2, this is indicated by the dashed C' curve, which is characterized by a rate of interest of 7%.

Suppose, however, the rate of interest remains constant and another one of the variables is changed. This will induce similar parametric shifts. The direction of these shifts is indicated by the inequality signs of our preceding discussion. For example, the reduction in aggregate consumption spending as shown in Figure 7-2 could equally well have been the result of the following changes:

1. an increase in the price level,
2. an increase in taxes,
3. a fall in accumulated durable consumption goods holdings,
4. a fall in money holdings,
5. incurring of capital losses, i.e., a depressed stock market,
6. a change in expectations.

Suppose, now, that we are again at Point A in Figure 7-2, and that the rate of interest falls. This will encourage credit purchases and the aggregate consumption curve will be shifted upwards. This is indicated by the dotted curve C'' in Figure 7-2. Such an upward shift, of course, could also have been produced by changes in variables other than the rate of interest. The student should consider each variable in equation 7-4 and determine for himself how it would cause an upward shift of the C curve in Figure 7-2.

This terminates our discussion of aggregate consumption. As the reader will remember, we have disaggregated our nation's total spending into consumption spending, investment spending, and government spending. Let us now turn our discussion to the investment sector. Having discussed this topic, we will study government expenditures at the end of this chapter. In Chapter 8, then, we will take up the money and credit markets which are needed to complete the building of our aggregate demand curve or GNP-demand curve.

Investment Spending

As we have pointed out before, investment spending is assumed to originate exclusively with firms. Since our firms are held to be profit maximizers, they will be governed in their investment decisions by the difference between the prevailing rate of interest and their internal rates of return, especially in times of economic stability. During times of galloping inflation or of unemployment, another variable asserts itself, namely the firms' expectations, especially but not exclusively in regard to price levels. In equation form, then, investment spending can be expressed as follows:

$$I = i(r,R,E) \qquad 7\text{--}5$$

where I = real investment,
     i = functional relationship,
     r = rate of interest,
     R = internal rate of return,
     E = expectations.

Let us put aside for the moment the variable E and focus our discussion on the rate of interest and the rate of return and their effect on investment spending. A profit maximizing firm will invest its funds into the most attractive ventures. Suppose, for example, that a firm is considering two investment projects A and B, and let these projects have a risk-free pre-tax rate of return as shown in Table 7–1.

Table 7–1
Investment Opportunities

Project	Rate of Return
A	10%
B	6%

Suppose further that the current rate of interest on risk-free bonds, say government bonds, is 5%. Clearly, under these conditions, the firm will undertake both projects A and B, since the alternative use of corporate funds, namely the purchase of government bonds, yields a lower return. But what will happen if the market rate of interest rises to 7%? In that case, project B is no longer attractive, since our firm can buy a government bond at 7%, rather than engage in project B at 6%. The economist calls the rate of interest, as shown in the present case, the firm's opportunity cost. If, after the rate of interest has risen to 7%, our firm still wishes to implement project B yielding 6%, its opportunity cost of 7% would be greater than its rate of return, and our firm would incur an economic loss of 1% on this venture.

While this is not, strictly speaking, the current topic, let us expand the concept of the opportunity cost to the personal level, because the concept is of the greatest importance in economic theory. Suppose an employee makes a monthly salary of $1000. Let this employee have the opportunity to go into business for himself, selling Pizza Pastrami à la Helmut Merklein, an honorable endeavor that will provide him an assured income of $1500 per month. Now suppose our employee's wife talks him out of the deal. Our man continues on his job. So long as the Pizza-Pastrami-à-la-Helmut-Merklein opportunity continues to be open to him, our man can truthfully say that it costs him $500 a month to work for his firm. In fact, he probably *will* say it, not to his firm, of course, but to his wife, and more than once. The cost he is referring to is the difference between his current income and his opportunity cost, i.e., the additional income he could receive in the pizza business.

Coming back to the effect of changes in the rate of interest on investment spending, Table 7–1 and the discussion following it show that the two are inversely related. As the rate of interest rises from 5% to 7%, our firm abandons project B and buys government bonds instead. This strategy yields a higher rate of return. Conversely, a fall in the rate of interest will stimulate investment. Suppose, for example, that the president of our firm, on his way to the stockbroker, hears a news bulletin to the effect that the rate of interest has fallen from its temporary 7% level back to 5%. If our man is the profit maximizer we and his stockholders want him to be, he will never complete his trip. Rather than buying the bonds, he will reactivate project B. Using our now-familiar shorthand expression, the effect of the rate of interest can be presented as follows:

$$\frac{\Delta I}{\Delta r} < 0.$$

This inequality assumes that all other variables remain constant. But as we have seen, it is not the absolute level of the rate of interest that determines investment spending. Rather it is the market rate of interest, relative to our firm's internal rate of return. That is, an increase in the market rate of interest while our firm's rate of return on various projects remains the same induces a cutback in investment. Suppose now that the market rate of interest remains the same while the firm's internal rate of return is increased. This will stimulate investment spending, and for the following reason.

In Table 7–1 we have listed two investment projects, and we have discussed a firm's investment decisions given the market rate of interest and the calculated rates of return on the projects. But these two projects do not just happen to be there. They have been developed, at a cost, by our firm. Now, if a firm's rate of return on existing projects rises relative to the market rate of interest, the firm will develop new investment opportunities. This is typically done through market studies, technical feasibility studies, and various other methods, which will result in the development and subsequent implementation of new investment projects. This is why we say that a firm's investment spending is positively related to its internal rate of return.

One way of increasing a firm's internal rate of return is by way of granting tax breaks. The investment tax credit or an increase in depreciation rates are examples of such tax breaks that are designed to increase the business sector's internal rates of return. The government grants these breaks precisely because they stimulate investment spending and through it aggregate demand. This is one way of turning a lagging economy around, if the cause of the recession is insufficient aggregate demand.

Let us summarize in our shorthand fashion the effect of the firm's rate of return, and of taxes, on investment spending.

$$\frac{\Delta I}{\Delta R} > 0; \qquad \frac{\Delta I}{\Delta t} < 0.$$

A graphic presentation of the aggregate investment function is given in Figure 7–3. The peculiar thing about gross investment, which is the dependent variable in this figure, is that it is not related to total output. Yet, gross investment has consistently risen with GNP, as Figure 4–2 has demonstrated. Thus, the question may well be asked how our model explains this relation between gross investment and total output. The answer is simple enough: That is the wrong question. Ours is a short-run model. It attempts to explain the peaks and valleys on the long-run investment curve shown in Figure 4–2, because these fluctuations are closely linked to the business cycles we are attempting to suppress. In the long run, i.e., outside of our model, it may well be that other forces are operative in shaping aggregate investment spending. In fact, it is entirely possible that the GNP itself is the overriding force. Little is really known about these long-term forces. Suffice it to say that our short-run model does not attempt to deal with the problem and that, as a result, the aggregate investment function in Figure 7–3 is independent of total output, i.e., is a horizontal line.

Also shown in Figure 7–3 is the dashed I' curve. This curve is the result of a parametric upward shift of the I curve. Such a shift may be induced by a number of reasons:

1. the rate of interest may have fallen,
2. a tax break may have been given the business sector,
3. managers' expectations regarding future sales or prices may have turned from cautious to confident.

This completes our discussion of the investment function. The one sector we have not yet discussed is the government sector and the determinants of government spending.

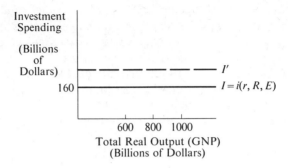

Figure 7–3   The Investment Function

Government Spending

As Figure 4–5 has shown, government expenditures are about equally divided between the federal government on the one hand and state and local governments on the other hand. Taken together, which is what we will do in our model, government expenditures are positively related to the GNP. In fact, as we pointed out in Chapter 4, they have run at about 20% of the GNP over the past fifteen years. Still, there is a very strong autonomous element in government spending, due to the federal government's involvement in economic policy matters. The federal government can, and sometimes does, increase or decrease its expenditures at will. The spending peaks during World War II and the Korean conflict are clear, if somewhat extreme, examples of this ability (Figure 4–5).

For our model, we will assume that government spending is autonomous. Its level is determined by policy decisions rather than by the GNP, tax receipts, or some other variable. The reason for this is easy to see. Suppose the government believes that the economy is headed for a recession: The real GNP is declining, tax receipts are falling, and unemployment is growing – in short, the nation's wealth is deteriorating. If government spending were positively related to the GNP or to its tax receipts, then its expenditures, too, would decline, thereby aggravating the recession problem. Instead, what the government is very likely to do is to attempt a reversal of the current economic trend by increasing its expenditures. This will increase the nation's aggregate demand and may stimulate the economy to return to its full-employment level.

A graphic presentation of aggregate government spending would result in a horizontal straight line similar to the investment function in Figure 7–3. Nothing is to be gained in presenting such a curve separately. Instead, let us combine the three sector spending curves of this chapter in one graph and let us look into the problem of equilibrium in the commodity market.

Equilibrium in the Commodity Market

So far, the topic in this chapter has been aggregate consumption spending, aggregate gross investment spending, and government spending. For the sake of convenience, let us list once more the equations for each sector.
Consumption spending:

$$C = c\{(y - t), CG, \left(D + \frac{M}{P}\right), r, E\} \qquad 7\text{-}6$$

Gross investment:

$$I = i(r, R, E) \qquad 7\text{-}7$$

Government spending:

$$G = g \qquad 7\text{-}8$$

The three individual sector curves and their summation, called total spending, are presented in Figure 7–4.

The curves labeled C, I, and G are the consumption function, the investment function, and the government-expenditure curve, respectively. The curve labeled TS is the total spending curve, which was obtained by a vertical summation of the three sector spending curves. As we have discussed earlier, on the abscissa of Figure 7–4 we have total real output. But the people did not produce this output for nothing. They derived their incomes by producing it: wages, profits, interest payments, rentals, etc. Furthermore, since gross investment is included in the total output, the income stream that is derived from its production includes the income to firms called capital consumption allowance.

On the ordinate we have the nation's total expenditures. Expressed in physical units, this means the goods and services that people, firms, and governmental units wish to buy in the market. The qualifying phrase "wish" to buy serves to remind us that we are in the process of developing the nation's

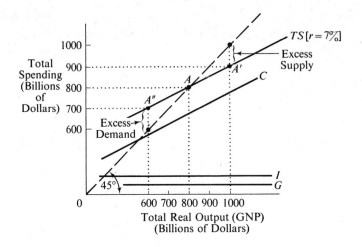

Figure 7–4   Total Spending

AD curve reflecting the people's ability and willingness to absorb the nation's total output. As we can see in Figure 7–4, the nation's level of total spending depends, among other things, on its total output. The unit of measurement on both axes of Figure 7–4 is real dollars, i.e., instead of physical units as units of measurement, their real value is used.

With these definitions in mind, what is the meaning of Point *A* on the *TS* curve in Figure 7–4? At Point *A,* reading off the abscissa, people are receiving an income of $800 billion. Again, this income is paid in return for the production of goods and services worth $800 billion. Thus, our economy is confronted by an output stream of goods and services (GNP) worth $800 billion per year.

Reading off the ordinate, people wish to absorb goods and services at the rate of $800 billion per year. That is, the total spending level is exactly equal to the total income, or *TS = TI*. Geometrically, this is indicated by the fact that Point *A* is located on the dashed 45-degree line which is the locus of all points where *TS = TI*. There is no inventory build-up at Point *A,* since the total output is exactly absorbed by the combined demands of households, industry, and the government. Alternatively, the income that is received for the production of a nation's total output is exactly spent in purchasing this output.

Now let us engage in a hypothetical experiment: Let us stipulate that the economy is at Point *A'*. Aggregate income at *A'* is $1000 billion; it is the result of the production of goods and services worth $1000 billion (abscissa). But our *TS* curve shows that if people receive $1000 billion per year, they are willing to absorb goods and services worth only $900 billion. Thus the total output of goods and services worth $1000 billion is only partially absorbed. There will remain goods worth $100 billion which no one is willing to claim: We have a build-up of inventories or excess supply of $100 billion. Alternatively, of their total annual income of $1000 billion, people wish to spend only $900 billion.

Now let us look at Point A''. Total income at this point, and total output giving rise to this income, are equal to $600 billion. Total desired spending at A'' is $700 billion. Thus, at A'' the people's desired spending is greater than their total income. We have excess demand for goods and services. This, too, is a disequilibrium position, because it implies a reduction of inventories which cannot be maintained quarter after quarter. Point A, then, in Figure 7–4 represents the only equilibrium position on the TS curve in the sense that $TS = TI$. This equality of spending and income implies that the total output of goods and services is exactly taken off the market. Points A' and A'', on the other hand, are disequilibrium positions.

One of the variables that interests us greatly in macroeconomic theory is the rate of interest, r. Let us investigate the effect of changes in the rate of interest on total spending, TS. In particular, let us see if such a change will alter the equilibrium position A in Figure 7–4. If so, a plot of equilibrium TS versus the rate of interest will help us in putting the model together when the money and credit markets are brought in.

Suppose that the rate of interest is reduced from 7% to 5%. The result of this change is twofold: Investment spending and consumption spending are stimulated as loans become cheaper. The overall result is an upward shift of the TS curve, indicated by the dashed TS' curve in Figure 7–5. Equilibrium in the commodity market is established at Point B, where $TS = TI$, since B falls on the 45-degree line going through the origin.

In Figure 7–5, Point A represents an equilibrium position, in the sense that $TS = TI$, when the rate of interest is 7%. At a 5% rate of interest, the equilibrium position is shifted to Point B. Let us reword these sentences a bit. Given all the variables that go into equations 7–6, 7–7, and 7–8, and assuming

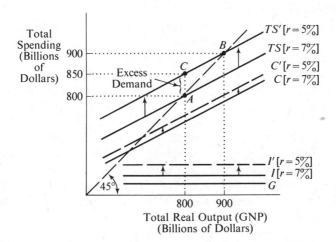

Figure 7–5   Shifts in Total Spending

a rate of interest of 7%, people will absorb the economy's total output if, and only if, this output equals $800 billion. Should the rate of interest fall to 5%, the people's *TS* will be stimulated. At the old total income of $800 billion, the people now wish to absorb goods and services worth $850 billion, Point *C*. That is more than what is available. Thus, the economy must expand its output. But as it does, the income that is generated by the increase in output causes the *TS* to rise further. Since the incremental rise in *TS* is less than the increase in total income, the excess demand at Point *C* will eventually be eliminated as the *TI* rises. In Figure 7–5, equilibrium will be reached at Point *B,* where the total spending level is such that the total output of goods and services worth $900 billion is exactly taken off the market.

If we crossplot the equilibrium total income streams as represented by Points *A* and *B* and similar points versus the rate of interest we will have a commodity-market equilibrium curve, historically called the *IS* curve, because along this curve investment, *I*, and saving, *S*, are equal. To see this, let us assume that we can do only three things with the income we receive: pay taxes, consume, and not consume, or save. If the government is assumed to have a balanced budget, the tax payments are exactly absorbed by government expenditures; consumption expenditures, on the other hand, use up only a part of the people's after-tax incomes; the other part, savings, is made available for investment. That is, incomes that the people do not spend themselves, the business sector of the economy will spend for them. This takes place through financial intermediaries such as banks, savings and loan associations, etc. Now, if the savings provided by the people are exactly equal to the investment requirements of the firms, i.e., if $S = I$, our commodity market is said to be in equilibrium or on the *IS* curve, since the total income received is being spent in the market. Points *A* and *B* in Figure 7–5 are examples of such equilibrium positions. Figure 7–6 shows the *IS* curve as it was derived from Figure 7–5. Point *A* in Figure 7–6, for example, shows that the equilibrium spending level of 800 billion dollars is attained at a rate of interest of 7%.

Generally speaking, the *IS* curve represents a condition in which the economy's total spending is just sufficient to take the total output off the market. What about points off the *IS* curve? For example, Point *A′* in Figure 7–4 represents excess supply. Where on Figure 7–6 will this excess supply be? The rate of interest along the *TS* curve in Figure 7–4, we remember, is equal to 7%. The income received, including depreciation, at Point *A′* is $1000 billion, while total desired spending is only $900 billion. Thus, in Figure 7–6, the excess supply falls between the Points *A′A′*, i.e., to the right side of, or above, the *IS* curve. This fact can now be generalized: The area above the *IS* curve is a disequilibrium region in the sense that $TI > TS$: the excess-supply region.

Conversely, the area below the *IS* curve is the excess-demand region. For example, at an interest rate of 7% and a total income of $600 billion, Figure 7–4 shows that the total desired spending level is $700 billion, i.e., $TS > TI$, illustrated by Points *A″A″* in Figure 7–6.

Before we abandon the commodity market, let us investigate how the commodity-market equilibrium curve or *IS* curve is affected by independent

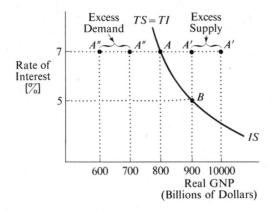

*Figure 7–6   The Commodity-Market
Equilibrium Curve (IS Curve)*

variables other than the rate of interest. Obviously, since the *IS* curve shows
an economy's equilibrium GNP as a function of the interest rate, any change
in that rate causes a move *along* the *IS* curve. Conversely, a change in any
other variable causes a parametric shift *of* the *IS* curve. The question is, a
shift in what direction? Actually, from our previous discussion, we already
know the answer; we just didn't bother to state it.

Suppose, in Figure 7–4, that our economy is operating at an equilibrium
GNP of $800 billion, while the rate of interest equals 7%. Now, for some un-
explained reason, let the people's desired consumption spending rise at that
rate of interest. This will shift up the nation's total spending curve, thus creating an excess-demand condition. But we already know from our discussion of
Figure 7–6, that the left side of any *IS* curve is the excess-demand side. Hence
the newly created excess-demand condition must be on the left side of our new
IS' curve, i.e., the new *IS'* curve must lie to the right of or above the old *IS*
curve. This can be generalized as follows: A change in any independent variable, other than the rate of interest, that will stimulate (shift up) an economy's
total spending curve will cause a parametric upward shift of the *IS* curve.
Conversely—and the reader should reason this out—a change in any independent variable, other than the rate of interest, that will reduce (shift down)
an economy's total spending curve, will cause a parametric downward shift
of the *IS* curve.

As we will see in Part 3, all fiscal and monetary policy tools affect aggre-
gate spending. Thus, in part at least, these policies work through the *IS* curve.
Let us, therefore, give an example of such a parametric shift of the *IS* curve.
Suppose, again for some unexplained reason, that the price level falls in the

economy, while all other independent variables remain the same. How will
this affect aggregate spending and in what direction will it shift the *IS* curve?
From our consumption function, equation 7–6, we know that a fall in the price
level will increase the people's real money holdings. That is, the nation's given
stock of nominal money will buy more goods in the market. Everything else
remaining the same, the people are wealthier as the result of a fall in the price
level, and because they are wealthier, their level of consumption spending
rises. This phenomenon has been called the real-wealth effect.[3]

In our commodity market, an increase in consumption spending corresponds to an upward shift of the consumption function. Since neither investment nor government spending is directly affected, the total spending curve
will be shifted up by an equivalent distance. This is shown in Figure 7–7.

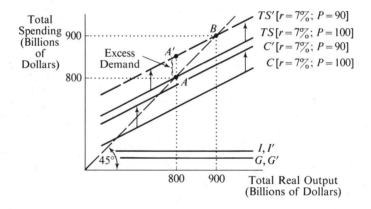

*Figure 7–7   Price-Level Changes and
Total Spending*

Starting at the initial equilibrium Point *A* in Figure 7–7, our economy is
characterized by an interest rate of 7% and a price level of 100. Now let the
price level fall to 90 while the interest rate remains the same. Our initial *TS*
curve is shifted upward to *TS'* for the reasons we have discussed previously.
The new equilibrium position is found to be at Point *B*, where the dashed *TS'*
curve intersects the 45-degree line. This means, of course, that *TS = TI* at
Point *B*, i.e., that the equilibrium GNP for *P = 90* is equal to $900 billion.
Figure 7–8 shows the initial *IS* curve going through Point *A*; this point

[3] On the real-wealth effect, see, for example, Don Patinkin, *Money, Interest and Prices,* 2nd
edition (New York: Harper and Row, 1965), Chapter 9.

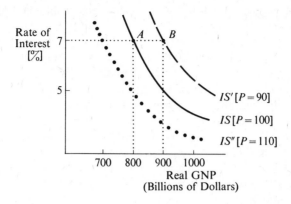

*Figure 7–8   Price-Level Changes
and the IS Curve*

corresponds to Point A in Figure 7–7. As we have seen, a fall in the price level, at an interest rate of 7%, results in an equilibrium GNP of \$900 billion; this Point B is also shown in Figure 7–8. The higher GNP that is attained at the given rate of interest of 7% causes Point B to lie to the right of Point A. Since any point on the initial IS curve could have been chosen for this experiment, it follows that all points on the IS curve are shifted to the right, i.e., the entire curve is shifted to the right. Also shown in Figure 7–8 is the IS'' curve that re-sults from a price-level rise. The student should be able to develop this curve on his own.

If people could dispose of their incomes only by consuming, paying taxes, and saving, *any* point on the IS curve would be an equilibrium position in the sense that total spending is just sufficient to take the total output off the market. But people can do one more thing with their incomes: They can hoard or dis-hoard money; that is, they can add to or reduce their average money holdings. To see how this affects our economy, let us discuss the money market in Chap-ter 8.

Problems

1. Why and how does the rate of interest affect consumption spending? Of the many variables, which one is by far the most important determinant of consumption spending? Write down the consumption function and indi-

cate the change in consumption spending (ΔC) induced by a change of every relevant variable.

2. In our model, what are the determinants of investment spending and why? Write down the investment function and indicate the change in investment spending (ΔI) induced by a change of every variable.
3. Briefly explain the concept of the opportunity cost.
4. Geometrically present the commodity market. Show the consumption function, the investment function, and government spending.
5. When it comes to making business investments, managers (unlike consumers) are not likely to be impulsive buyers. Hence, any attempt to stimulate aggregate demand via fiscal policies had better be directed toward the consumer. Do you agree? Why or why not? Can you list examples of business-oriented fiscal stimulants?
6. Write down the aggregate spending function. Two variables in this function are subject to direct control by governmental authorities. Which variables? And in which direction do increases in these variables shift the total spending curve? One variable in this function can be indirectly affected by policy action. Which one? And in which direction does an increase in this variable shift the function? How do changes in the price level affect total spending?
7. Equilibrium in the commodity market means that total spending on commodities = total income derived from the production of commodities. Explain. Plot the three sector spending curves and the total spending curve. From this plot, derive the *IS* curve. What is its meaning? Relative to the *IS* curve, where is the excess-supply region?
8. Geometrically derive an *IS* curve from the commodity market and explain your derivation. Suppose the price level falls from 100 to 90, how does this shift your *IS* curve? Why? Why does equilibrium in the commodity market not assure equilibrium aggregate demand?
9. Suppose you are told that your derivation of the commodity-market equilibrium curve is wrong, because it assumes implicitly that the 45-degree line you used in the derivation is an *AS* curve, whereas elsewhere you have developed a different *AS* curve. How would you counter that argument?

Suggested Readings

On consumption spending:

J. S. Duesenberry, "Income-Consumption Relations and Their Implications," in *Income, Employment, and Public Policy,* Essays in Honor of Alvin H. Hansen (New York: W. W. Norton & Company, Inc., 1948), pp. 54–81.

M. J. Farrell, "The New Theories of the Consumption Function," *The Economic Journal,* 69 (December 1959), 678–696.

M. Friedman, "The Permanent Income Hypothesis," in *A Theory of the Consumption Function* (Princeton: Princeton University Press for the National Bureau of Economic Research, 1957), pp. 220–224.

S. H. Hymans, "The Cyclical Behavior of Consumers' Income and Spending: 1921–1961," *The Southern Economic Journal,* XXXII (July 1965), 23–34.

On investment spending:

A. P. Lerner, "On Some Recent Developments in Capital Theory," *The American Economic Review: Papers and Proceedings,* LV (1965), 284–295.

W. H. White, "Interest Inelasticity of Investment Demand—The Case from Business Attitude Surveys Re-examined," *The American Economic Review,* 46 (September 1956), 565–587.

On commodity-market equilibrium:

W. L. Smith, "A Graphical Exposition of the Complete Keynesian System," *The Southern Economic Journal,* XXIII (October 1956), 115–125.

8 *Money, Credit, Aggregate Demand*

Before we proceed with our derivation of an economy's *AD* curve, let us pause to take our bearings. We started our discussion in Part 2 by presenting, in Figure 5-2, the completed model, or at least that part of it which is easily visible. As we pointed out in Chapter 5, this model is too simplistic to be of much use in understanding the inner workings of an economy. Different forces assert themselves in the making of the *AD* and *AS* curves. Unless we can get at these forces; unless we understand the main variables affecting *AD* and *AS;* unless we know something about the interdependencies of these variables; our grasp of the economy is dangerously incomplete.

Because we want to do better than talk about the economy in superficial generalities, we proceeded to take a separate look at *AS* and *AD*. In Chapter 6, devoted to the *AS* curve, we showed that the main forces behind this curve are a country's resource base, its level of technology, the size and skill of its labor force, and the size of its capital stock. For a given price level, these are the primary variables that determine the GNP a country is capable of producing.

Capability of production, however, is only half the story. No matter how much a country can produce, it cannot sustain its output rate unless the goods and services it produces find takers in the market. If they do not, our country will bury itself under a growing mountain of inventories. The *AD* curve was taken up in Chapter 7, where we looked at the main components of total spending: consumption, investment, and government spending. Assuming that the total income can go either to pay taxes, to finance consumption expenditures, or to finance the business sector's investment expenditures, we developed a commodity-market equilibrium curve along which total spending is equal to total income, the *IS* curve. But there is one more alternative way for people to use their after-tax incomes: They can add to or deduct from their money holdings. How this affects our economy's *AD* is the main topic of this chapter. But before we discuss this issue, let us turn our attention once more to the *IS*, or commodity-market equilibrium, curve.

The *IS* curve was developed by varying the interest rate in an economy and finding the corresponding equilibrium total spending rate. The relevant question in this derivation was: How does a change in the interest rate affect our economy's level of equilibrium spending, in the sense that the new level of income, which is the result of our nation's total output, is just sufficient in magnitude to induce a level of spending that will take the total output off the market? It may well be asked why we are so concerned about the rate of interest. After all, we could have developed and plotted a commodity-market equilibrium curve as a function of any one of the variables in equations 7–6 to 7–8. There are two reasons for this: First, the rate of interest in and of itself is a very important determinant of both consumption and investment demand; and second, governmental attempts to stimulate or dampen a nation's *AD*, the so-called monetary or fiscal policies, all affect the rate of interest, and through it, at least in part, the level of spending. This will become clear in Part 3, where we will discuss monetary and fiscal policies.

The Money Market

As we have pointed out before, *if* people could dispose of their incomes only by consuming, paying taxes, and saving, *any* point on the *IS* curve would be an equilibrium position. That is, the spending level would always be just sufficient to take the total output off the market, provided that investment is equal to saving. Now let us introduce the fact that people have one more alternative in the use of their incomes: They can add to or reduce their money holdings. The question then arises: At what level of total output is the currently existing money stock such that people do not wish to hold more or less money? Let us discuss the role of money in the income-spending stream of an economy with the aid of a schematic diagram, Figure 8–1.

The circular flow pattern of the income and spending streams in an economy is shown in Figure 8–1. This schematic diagram can be interpreted as follows. Let us start at the top of the diagram, labeled *TI* for total income, which is defined as wages, net interest payments, proprietors' income, pre-tax profits, etc. Since the term *TI* includes the income to firms called depreciation, it corresponds to the GNP of our national income accounts. Out of this total income, *TI,* the government takes its tax receipts, leaving an income stream to the private sector, shown as after-tax income in Figure 8–1. Both consump-

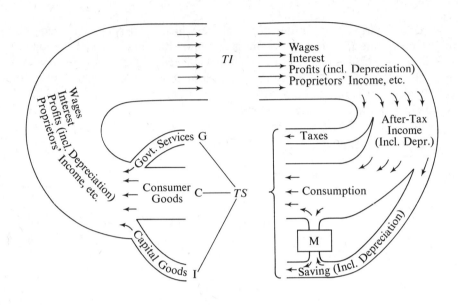

Figure 8–1   The Income-Spending Stream

tion and saving are funded by this after-tax income. Leaving aside the money
problem for a moment, the diagram makes clear that saving is nonconsumption.

Now let us introduce money. Unlike all the other variables in Figure 8–1,
money is not a flow variable. At any given point in time, there exists in the
economy a given stock of money which has been supplied by the Federal Reserve System, an autonomous agency of the government. But, depending on
various circumstances, people (including the government) may wish to hold
more or less money than the amount supplied by the Federal Reserve System.
In our diagram, the amount of money people wish to hold is shown as *M* and
placed between the consumption and savings streams. If the people wish to
hold more money, they can do so by reducing their savings stream, their consumption stream, or both. To say that an increase in desired money holdings
has to come out of saving ignores the possibility that it might come out of consumption; or to say that it has to come out of consumption ignores the possibility that it might come out of saving. We do not know whether people increase their desired money holdings by switching out of consumption or out
of saving (financial assets), nor whether they reduce them by switching into
consumption or into financial assets. But one thing is clear: An increase in the
people's desired money holdings, regardless of its source, comes out of the
nation's after-tax income.[1]

---

[1] But again, an increase in the *supply* of money comes as the result of policy actions on the
part of the Federal Reserve System. The matching of the people's demand for money and the
Federal-Reserve-supplied money will be discussed later in this chapter.

To complete the income-spending stream of Figure 8–1, tax receipts are taken in by the government in return for its services, consumption spending buys consumer goods, and saving (including business saving called depreciation) gives rise to the purchase of capital goods. The production of these goods and services gives rise to various kinds of incomes (wages, profits, interest payments, etc.) and the circle is complete.

Let us discuss the problem of a nation's money holdings in terms of the *IS* curve in Figure 7–6 (page 95). Point *A*, for example, lies on the *IS* curve in that figure. The meaning of this point is this: At a 7% interest rate, if the people produce a GNP of $800 billion, they will derive an income from this total output that is just right to take this total output off the market. There will be neither a build-up nor a reduction of inventories. Alternatively, the income that is received from the production of a nation's GNP is exactly spent in purchasing that GNP. The question we have neglected so far is: Given this equilibrium GNP of $800 billion and the interest rate of 7%, is the existing money stock the correct size to support this GNP? Suppose the existing money stock is too large for a GNP of $800 billion. In that case, maybe Point *B* in Figure 7–6 is consistent with the existing money stock. That is, if the interest rate fell and our equilibrium GNP rose to $900 billion, maybe then the existing money stock would be correct in size, in that people neither wish to add to nor reduce their money holdings, while their aggregate income is just sufficient to take this total output of $900 billion off the market. Clearly, what we need to know is whether or not there is such a point on the *IS* curve where the existing money stock is of the correct size: where the demand for money is equal to the supply of money. If such a point exists, the problem remains to locate it. To do this, let us discuss the money market and then incorporate it into our model.

Demand for Money   People use money because it pays for them to do so. The alternative to a money economy, a barter economy, is completely impracticable in the twentieth century. The cost of such a system in lost production is prohibitive. Suppose a bootmaker wishes to obtain two shirts for a pair of boots that he just made; to carry out such a deal on barter terms, there must exist what has been called a double coincidence of wants. That is, if our bootmaker wants to trade a pair of boots for two shirts, he has to locate a tailor who presently wants a pair of boots and who is willing to give up two shirts in return. By the time our two craftsmen locate each other they could have produced another pair of boots and two shirts, respectively. The economy as a whole has lost one pair of boots and two shirts in the deal: These are the goods that could have been, but have not been, produced because our craftsmen wasted so much time trying to locate each other.

In a money economy, our bootmaker can sell his boots to anybody in return for money and go directly to any tailor and, using this money, buy his shirts. Time spent in this transaction would be minimal; our economy would not lose a pair of boots and two shirts as a result of this transaction and, thus, the GNP would be increased by these goods solely through the existence and use of money. Money, as it turns out, is productive and that, of course, is the only reason for having it.

But how much money should a person have? What are the variables that determine the demand for money? Who, in an aggregate economy, holds money? And what, precisely, is the difference between money and income?

Money, as we will discuss in some detail in Part 4, consists essentially of two things: currency, i.e., dollar bills and coins, on the one hand, and checking accounts on the other hand. Either can be used to settle outstanding debts or to purchase goods; in fact, by far the greatest portion, almost 80%, of this nation's money is in the form of checking accounts, or demand deposits as these accounts are called in financial circles.

One constant source of confusion is the fact that incomes are ordinarily paid in monetary units. The popular notion that people make money applies, strictly speaking, only to counterfeiters. People don't make money; they receive an income in return for their services. That income is a flow variable, $1000 per month, for example, or, which is the same thing, $12,000 per year. By contrast, money is a stock variable. There is just so much money in an economy at any given point in time. Each individual in that economy, and each firm, for that matter, holds a given amount of money. They have to hold money for reasons of liquidity. When you purchase a loaf of bread in a supermarket, it will do you no good to tell the manager that your income is, say, $1000 a month. He wants to see money. Knowing this, you keep a sufficient amount at your disposal, as cash on hand or as deposits in your checking account, to facilitate your daily purchases. Your money holdings, then, are your source of liquidity. In fact, the greater a person's income, the more he will ordinarily buy, and the greater is the amount of money he needs to facilitate these purchases. This is called the transactions demand for money.

Suppose you receive a monthly paycheck (after taxes) in the amount of $1000. Let us assume that you wish to spend only $800 of it. This $800 you put into a checking account and the remaining $200 into a savings account. As we mentioned earlier, the $800 in your checking account continues to be classified as money. The $200 in your savings account is not money. This should not concern you too much now; you are asked simply to accept this proposition on faith until, in Part 4, we will clarify the matter.

Suppose the balance in your checking account at the end of each month is $300. On the first of the month, then, you deposit an additional $800, so that you start the month with a checking account worth $1100. Suppose, now, that you spend your $800 evenly over the month so that the last of the month finds you again with $300. Your average money holdings for the month, in this case, will be $700, i.e., $(1100 + 300)/2.

If you get a raise, you will save more than before, but you will also spend more. Suppose you now spend $900 a month; that is, you put this amount into your checking account at the beginning of each month, and by the end of the month you have spent it all. Your average money holdings, i.e., the average size of your checking account, are now $750, assuming a close-out balance of $300 at the end of each month. Thus, your demand for average money balances, your demand for money, is positively related to your expenditures. This holds true for the economy at large: Holding all other factors constant, the greater a nation's real GNP, the greater is its demand for real money. In our shorthand form,

$$\frac{\Delta m_d}{\Delta \text{GNP}} > 0,$$

where m_d = demand for real money.

We have chosen to use real money in this discussion to make the money market consistent with our commodity market, which we have expressed in terms of real GNP.

In addition to the transactions demand for money, another variable affects our average money holdings: the cost of holding it, determined by the opportunity foregone in holding idle money balances. Suppose, for example, that the average balance of your checking account is $1000. That money brings you no return. If you had put that money into a savings account at a rate of interest of 5%, you would draw an annual income of $50 from it. Your money holdings of $1000 deprive you of that income, i.e., it costs you $50 a year to hold $1000 in the form of money. (This, by the way, is another application of the concept of opportunity costs.)

Suppose, now, that the interest rate rises to 10%. This would raise your opportunity cost, i.e., the cost of holding money, from $50 to $100 per year. But we know that the quantity demanded of any good, including money, falls if its cost rises. Thus, at a 10 percent interest rate, you will want to reduce your average money holdings. This holds true for the economy at large: The demand for money is negatively related to the rate of interest. In our shorthand form,

$$\frac{\Delta m_d}{\Delta r} < 0.$$

While the theoretical relevance of the interest rate as a major determinant of the demand for money is fairly well accepted, the empirical validity of this postulate is sometimes questioned. After all, interest rates typically move in fractions of one percent. And, surely, an increase in the interest rate from, say, 5% to 5½% will not induce the average individual (you or me, for example) to adjust his average money holdings. But the point is, all the individuals taken together, i.e., the household sector of our economy, hold only about one third of this nation's checking-account money, which makes up almost 80% of the total money supply.[2] The remaining demand deposits are held predominantly

---

[2] *Federal Reserve Bulletin*, June 1971, p. 457.

by business and financial enterprises, i.e., by people who are sensitive to changing interest rates. Corporate treasurers respond to such changes by adjusting the composition of their corporate portfolios that normally include money, bonds, and equity instruments. In large firms having a high degree of financial sophistication, money holdings have been known to respond to changes in foreign interest rates.

In equation form, then, the demand for real money is defined as follows:

$$m_d = \frac{M_d}{P} = m(GNP,r). \qquad\qquad 8-1$$

A plot of equation 8–1, using the interest rate as the independent variable and the GNP as a parameter, is shown in Figure 8–2.

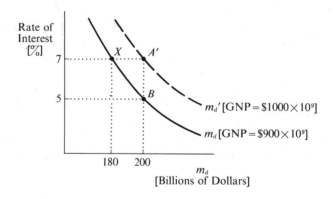

Figure 8–2   The Demand for Money

The curve labeled m_d and going through Points X and B is the money-demand curve for an economy having a GNP of $900 billion. For example, at an interest rate of 5%, this economy is characterized by a money demand of $200 billion. If the rate of interest (the cost of holding money) rises to 7%, the money demand is reduced to $180 billion.

Suppose our economy is operating at Point X; i.e., to facilitate a real GNP of $900 billion at a rate of interest of 7%, the U.S. economy requires a stock of money in the amount of $180 billion. Now suppose that our GNP is increased to $1000 billion. This greater GNP requires a larger stock of money; i.e., the money-demand curve is shifted to the right as indicated by the dashed curve

m'_d. Point A' on this curve, for example, signifies that an increase in the real GNP from \$900 billion to \$1000 billion requires an increase in the money stock from \$180 billion to \$200 billion, if the rate of interest, i.e., the cost of holding money, is held constant at 7%. In other words, the higher GNP has pushed the money demand to \$200 billion at the given rate of interest.

Supply of Money and the LM *Curve*   At any given point in time, the supply of money is autonomously determined by an independent governmental agency called the Federal Reserve System, which has the power to increase or decrease the money supply. How this is accomplished will be the main topic of Part 4; suffice it to say here that any action that is undertaken by the public or by foreign central banks and that tends to affect the money supply in this country can be offset by appropriate measures of the Federal Reserve System — or the Fed, as this agency is frequently called. Thus, when we say that the money supply is determined autonomously by the Fed, we do not ignore outside effects. Indeed, we will devote a good part of our discussion in Part 4 to these outside effects on the money supply. We merely say that the Fed can neutralize these effects — and this is why, for all practical purposes, the money supply is what the Fed wants it to be.

In equation form, the real money supply is given as follows:

$$m_s = m_s. \qquad\qquad\qquad 8\text{-}2$$

Since the money supply is expressed in real dollars, it is inversely related to the price level; i.e., $m_s = M_s/P$. We will take up this issue in a little while. Let us first derive a money-market equilibrium curve for a given price level. Such a curve is called an *LM* curve, since it reflects a state of equilibrium between what historically has been called the Liquidity-preference function (our money-demand function in equation 8-1) and the Money-supply function, equation 8-2. To derive this equilibrium curve, let us redraw Figure 8-2 with the addition of a constant money supply of \$200 billion. This money-supply curve will be a straight vertical line located at $m = \$200$ billion, as shown in Figure 8-3.

At any given point in time, the money supply is given by policy of the Fed. Thus, in the absence of policy actions by the Fed, movements of our system are limited along the m_s curve. Changes in GNP, then, and the resulting changes in the transactions demand for money will be reflected by changes in the equilibrium rate of interest. Suppose, for example, our economy is initially operating at Point A': Its GNP is \$1000 billion and the interest rate is 7%. At that interest rate, the supply of and demand for money are equal; i.e., the size of the GNP and the cost of holding money are such that the aggregate money requirements are exactly matched by the amount of money that is being supplied by the Fed. Our money market is said to be in equilibrium and Point A' is one point on the *LM*, or money-market equilibrium, curve.

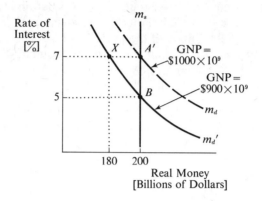

Figure 8-3   *The Money Market*

Suppose now that the GNP falls to $900 billion. The smaller GNP causes the demand for money to fall; i.e., we have a leftward shift of the money-demand curve. At the old interest rate of 7%, Point X, we have a disequilibrium position. The money supply, of course, has not changed. But the transactions demand for money has fallen: At the lower GNP of $900 billion and the old interest rate of 7%, people (including corporate treasurers) no longer wish to hold average money balances equal to $200 billion, i.e., the amount of money that is being supplied by the Fed is no longer required with the lower GNP. People do not mind holding $200 billion at a lower GNP, provided the cost of holding money is reduced. In fact, in Figure 8-3, if this cost, i.e., the rate of interest, were reduced to 5%, people would again want to hold $200 billion. Thus, at Point B we have a new equilibrium position in the sense that $m_d = m_s$. Let us transfer the two equilibrium positions in Figure 8-3, Points A' and B, onto an LM curve, plotting the GNP on the abscissa and the relevant equilibrium rate of interest on the ordinate. The result of such a crossplot is shown in Figure 8-4.

The question now arises: Where in Figure 8-4 is Point X, which in Figure 8-3 designates a position of excess money supply? That point corresponds to $r = 7\%$ and a GNP of $900 billion; thus, it falls to the left of or above the LM curve in Figure 8-4. Again we generalize: Any point above the LM curve falls within the region of excess money supply. Conversely, any point below the LM curve falls within the region of excess money demand.

To find a position of equilibrium aggregate demand for the economy as a whole, all we have to do is to superimpose the IS and LM curves. At their intersection, both the commodity market (IS) and the money market (LM) are in equilibrium, in that total spending is just sufficient to take the total output off the market, while at the same time the exact money stock required to facilitate this total output is being supplied by the Federal Reserve System.

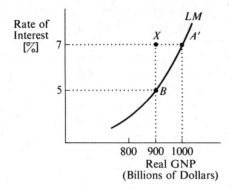

Figure 8-4   *The Money-Market Equilibrium*
                 Curve (**LM** *Curve*)

That is, without wanting to add to or reduce their money holdings, people spend all of their incomes on commodities which are exactly taken off the market. Not the same people, of course: Some people do save (nonconsume), but others spend over and above their incomes (invest) the exact amount that our first group of people saves. Let us now superimpose in Figure 8-5 the *IS* and *LM* curves of Figures 7-6 and 8-4.

The *IS* and *LM* curves have been derived by varying the rate of interest while holding all other independent variables, including the price level, constant. Let us assume, then, that the *IS* and *LM* curves in Figure 8-5 are those that are relevant for a price level of 100, indicated by the brackets in Figure 8-5. Under these conditions, the meaning of Figure 8-5 is this: Given a price level of $P = 100$, the *AD* in our economy will be in equilibrium when the real

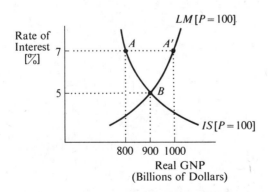

Figure 8-5   Equilibrium Aggregate Demand

GNP is equal to $900 billion and the interest rate is 5%, Point *B*. That is, at Point *B* the spending level is such that the total output is exactly taken off the market; there will not be a build-up or a depletion of inventories (*IS* curve). At the same time, the GNP-interest rate combination is such that the required amount of money (the aggregate money balances that people are willing to hold) is, in fact, being supplied by the Federal Reserve System (*LM* curve). Point *B*, then, is one point on the nation's *AD* curve.

Point *A'* in Figure 8–5 is not an equilibrium position, and for the following reason: The GNP-interest rate combination is correct for equilibrium in the money market, but Point *A'* falls to the right of the *IS* curve. Therefore, the commodity market at Point *A'* is characterized by an excess supply, i.e., a build-up of inventories, which cannot be maintained for very long.

Conversely, Point *A* is not an equilibrium position. This point reflects equilibrium in the commodity market, but the interest rate (the cost of holding money) of 7% is too high for the indicated GNP of $800 billion. That is, the people prefer to hold less money than the amount being supplied by the Fed. We have the case of an excess supply of money.

Lest we forget, what we are after in this chapter is the derivation of an economy's *AD* curve. This curve relates the total output demanded in the market (the GNP-demand) to the price level. In our discussion of the commodity market, we brought out the effect of a price-level change on the *IS* curve. The effect of price-level changes on the *LM* curve is the last piece of evidence we need to put together our theory of *AD*.

Consider the sequence of Figures 8–6 and 8–7. Suppose we assume that the money market in Figure 8–6 is in the initial equilibrium position indicated

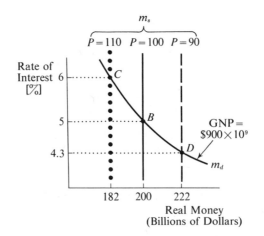

Figure 8–6   *Price-Level Changes in the Money Market*

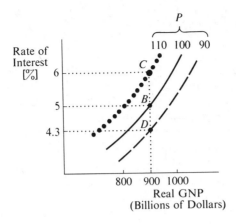

Figure 8–7   Shifts of the **LM** *Curve*

by Point *B*, where the money supply is $200 billion and the prevailing price level is 100. The solid *LM* curve in Figure 8–7 was derived from Figure 8–6 by the method discussed previously. Now suppose the price level falls to 90. Since our money demand and the relevant GNPs are expressed in real dollars, the effect on the demand for money is nil. However, a change in the price level does affect the supply of money—for the simple reason that money is being supplied by the Fed in nominal, not real, terms, while our model deals in real, not nominal, money.

Suppose, for example, the nominal money stock in an economy is $200 billion. At a price level of 100, this corresponds to a real money stock of the same amount. If the price level falls to 90, the constant nominal money stock of $200 billion will be worth more in purchasing power; in fact, it will be equal to 222 billion real dollars (200/.90). In Figure 8–6, what does that do to the rate of interest? With the given GNP of 900 billion real dollars, the people wished to use the exact quantity of money that was supplied by the Fed, so long as the interest rate was 5%. Now, due to a fall in the price level, people have more real money than before; in fact, for the given real GNP of $900 billion, they think they have too much. The only way to persuade them to hold this kind of money, namely 222 billion real dollars, is to lower the cost of holding it. In Figure 8–6, in fact, equilibrium with the higher money stock is reestablished at an interest rate of 4.3%, Point *D*. Transferring Point *D* (GNP = $900 billion and *r* = 4.3%) to Figure 8–7, produces the following result. A fall in the price level will shift the *LM*, or money-market equilibrium, curve to the right. Conversely—and the student should reason this out by himself—an increase in the price level will induce a leftward shift of the *LM* curve.

The Aggregate Demand Curve

We have essentially come to the end of our road. In Chapter 7, we discussed the commodity market, developed a commodity-market equilibrium curve, and established the direction of parametric shifts of this *IS* curve caused by price-level changes. This derivation culminated in Figure 7–8, where these shifts are illustrated. The present chapter has been devoted to the money market. Again, a money-market equilibrium curve was found as well as the direction of parametric shifts of this *LM* curve caused by price-level changes (illustrated in Figure 8–7). Let us now, in Figure 8–8, superimpose a set of *IS* and *LM* curves similar to those derived previously. With the aid of this figure the *AD* curve can be derived. It is plotted in Figure 8–9.

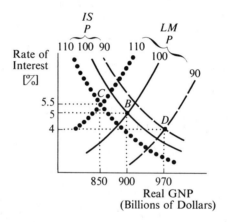

Figure 8–8   Deriving the AD Curve

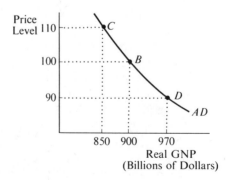

Figure 8–9   The Aggregate Demand Curve

Let us assume that our economy's initial equilibrium condition is at Point *B* in Figure 8–8. The meaning of Point *B,* again, is this: At a price level of 100, an interest rate of 5%, and a real GNP of $900 billion, the commodity and money markets are both in equilibrium, since Point *B* is the point of intersection of the relevant *IS* and *LM* curves. At Point *B,* then, the spending level is just sufficient to take the total output off the market (*IS*), while the people wish to use the exact money stock that is being supplied by the Federal Reserve System (*LM*). Thus, Point *B* is one point on our *AD* curve of Figure 8–9: At a price level of 100, the *AD* is equal to $900 billion.

Suppose, now, that the price level rises: From our previous discussion we know that this will cause a leftward shift of both the *IS* and *LM* curves. This is shown in Figure 8–8, where Point *C* is now the new equilibrium position for the higher price level.[3] At Point *C* the equilibrium *AD* is $850 billion. Similarly, a fall in the price level causes a rightward shift of both the *IS* and *LM* curves, with a concurrent fall in the interest rate. The resulting equilibrium *AD* is equal to $970 billion. Points *C* and *D* from Figure 8–8 have been transferred to Figure 8–9. Similar changes in the price level could be assumed and the resulting *AD* derived and plotted onto Figure 8–9. Connecting these points gives us the long-awaited *AD* curve.

The Credit Market

In deriving our *AD* curve we stipulated, but did not prove, that the interest rate rises and falls with the price level. In Figure 8–8, this means that the *LM* curve is subject to greater shifts than the corresponding *IS* curve when the price level changes. In Figure 8–9 it means that the rate of interest varies along the *AD* curve. For example, at Point *B* this interest rate is lower than at Point *C,* but it is higher at Point *B* than at Point *D.* This in itself is a worthwhile discovery that we could not have gotten from our simplistic model, such as the one in Figure 5–2.

To show why the interest rate falls and rises with the price level, we have to take a look at one more market, the credit market. This market is implied in the model we have developed, so all we have to do is to bring it out and discuss it explicitly. We have said earlier, in discussing the equilibrium position denoted by Point *B* in Figure 8–8, that the GNP of $900 billion and the interest rate of 5% are just right, such that all products find buyers in the market (*IS*), while people wish to hold the exact amount of money that is being supplied by the Fed (*LM*). As we pointed out, this implies that the total income

---

[3] Note that the rate of interest at Point C is higher than at Point B. Since we do not wish to interrupt the thrust of our argument, the student is asked to accept this on faith for the moment. The reason that *r* is increased as the price level rises will become clear at the end of this chapter, when we discuss the credit market.

that is derived from producing an economy's goods and services is exactly spent in purchasing these same goods and services. But we were careful to point out that this need not hold true for the individual members in an economy: Some people spend less than they receive, i.e., they save, while other economic units, mostly firms and government units, spend over and above their incomes (borrow) the exact amount that our first group of people saves. The savers are said to be suppliers of credit and the borrowers are demanders of credit.

The institutional aspects and the magnitude of the credit market will be discussed in Part 4. We will simply point out here that one may get a rough idea of the importance of the credit market if he considers that the total credit volume is approximately thirteen times the volume of money outstanding. The total money supply as of December 1969 was $205 billion, while the total credit outstanding was in the amount of $2.7 trillion, roughly three times that year's GNP. How is it possible for the volume of credit outstanding to be a multiple of the money supply? The answer is that a given loan may give rise to a whole chain of derivative loans. Suppose, for example, that I wish to buy a home and I go to a savings and loan association for the required loan. Where does the association's money come from? It borrows the funds from the public for the specific purpose of loaning them out again. Thus, it is the savings and loan association's credit it receives from the public that enables it to extend credit to me. This is one instance of a derivative loan: The savings and loan association merely acts as a collector and redistributor of available funds; i.e., it is a financial intermediary.

As we will discover when we discuss the flow-of-funds matrix, the primary net suppliers of credit are households, while business firms and the federal government are the chief net demanders of credit. The most important credit instruments used in the market are corporate and government bonds. For that reason, the credit market is often called the bond market, and credit is discussed in terms of bonds.[4]

If the public is the primary supplier of credit, what, then, determines the supply of credit? Saving (supplying credit), as we have pointed out before, is nonconsumption. The determinants of consumption are also the determinants of nonconsumption; that is, saving is closely linked to the consumption function in the commodity market. Symbolically, the savings function or credit-supply function may be written as follows:

$$S = Cr_s = cr\left\{(y - t), CG, \left(D + \frac{M}{P}\right), r, E\right\},\qquad\text{8-3}$$

where S = saving,
         Cr_s = supply of credit.

---

[4] But note that this concept reverses our relationships: A firm is a demander of credit, i.e., a supplier of bonds. Conversely, the public is a net supplier of credit, i.e., a net demander of bonds. This must be kept in mind in reading texts that refer to the bond market rather than the credit market.

With the exception of the interest rate, and possibly of expectations in equation 8–3, the partial derivatives of the consumption and savings functions have the same sign: An increase in income, for example, will raise both consumption and saving, as will an increase in the money supply. An increase in taxes will reduce both consumption and saving, because it reduces disposable income. Suppose, however, the interest rate rises. That rate determines the trade-off between present and future consumption, i.e., between consumption and saving. For example, at an interest rate of 5%, if I refrain from consuming a $100 suit today, I may buy a $105 suit next year. If the interest rate rises to 10%, I may buy the $105 suit plus a peppered steak. For a given sacrifice today, a higher rate of interest yields a greater return next year, i.e., the future goods are cheaper than present goods. Thus, everything else being the same, an increase in the interest rate will cause me to demand more future goods, i.e., to save more (consume less in the present). This is why the interest rate is a trade-off between present and future goods. From our consumption function we know that:

$$\frac{\Delta C}{\Delta r} < 0.$$

Conversely, since saving is the same as supplying credit:

$$\frac{\Delta Cr_s}{\Delta r} > 0.$$

The preceding inequality means that the supply of credit is positively related to the interest rate.

What about the demand for credit? We have said that this demand originates primarily with the business sector and the federal government. The credit demand of the government, like its expenditures, is wholly autonomous; it is set as a matter of policy, subject, among other things, to political considerations. In fact, the government's ability to obtain credit is what makes deficit spending a workable macroeconomic policy tool. We will discuss this issue in Part 3. Let us, therefore, focus our attention here on the business sector's demand for credit.

We have seen that the credit-supply, or savings, function, equation 8–3, has its counterpart in the commodity market, namely the consumption function. Similarly, the credit-demand function has its counterpart, namely what in the commodity market has been called the investment function. Because a firm's net investment in plants, machinery, or inventories is frequently financed through credit, the determinants of investment demand are, again, also the determinants of a firm's demand for credit. Symbolically,

$$Cr_d = cr(r,R,E), \qquad\qquad 8\text{--}4$$

where Cr_d = demand for credit.

   As we have seen before, an increase in the interest rate, for a firm's given internal rate of return will reduce its investment demand and, therefore, its demand for credit. That is, an increase in the market rate of interest will cause our firm to cut back on some of the less attractive projected ventures. In shorthand form,

$$\frac{\Delta\ Cr_d}{\Delta r} < 0.$$

   Graphically, the preceding inequality means that the demand for credit is inversely related to the rate of interest, i.e., the credit-demand function is negatively sloped. Conversely, the credit-supply function has been shown to be positively sloped. Let us bring the two functions together in one graph, Figure 8–10. It should be noted in that figure that all the other determinants of

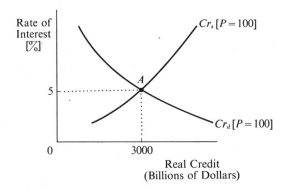

Figure 8–10   *Supply of and Demand for Credit*

the supply of and demand for credit are held constant. In particular, the price level is assumed to be equal to 100 along these curves, as is indicated by the brackets. A change in any one of the variables other than the interest rate will bring about a parametric shift of the relevant curves. Since we are interested in AD, let us increase the price level and see how this affects our credit curves. In particular, we want to see how our present equilibrium position A (credit =

$3 trillion and $r = 5\%$) is affected by these shifts. To bring out the tie to the commodity market, we will investigate these shifts in both the commodity and credit markets, Figures 8–11 and 8–12.

Because an increase in the price level, as we have seen previously, makes people worse off, they wish to reduce their consumption expenditures, as shown by the dashed C' curve in Figure 8–11. At the same time, however, they wish to cut back their savings. In Figure 8–12, this means that the credit-supply curve is shifted to the left. This is shown by the dashed Cr'_s curve.

An increase in the price level, on the other hand, does not affect the busi-

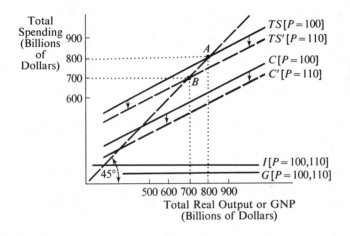

Figure 8–11   *Price-Level Changes in the Commodity Market*

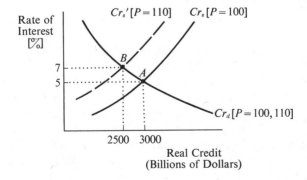

Figure 8–12   *Price-Level Changes in the Credit Market*

ness sector's level of investment spending. In our commodity market, Figure 8–11, this means that the investment curve is not shifted up or down as a result of a change in the price level. In our credit market, Figure 8–12, it means that the demand for credit also remains the same.

What we have set out to show now emerges from Figure 8–12: An increase in the price level will raise the rate of interest, Point *B*. Conversely—and the reader should convince himself of this—a fall in the price level will reduce the rate of interest. Moreover, rising price levels cause the equilibrium volume of credit to be reduced, and vice versa. The overall result, then, is as follows: Rising price levels bring about tight credit conditions, since the unaltered demand for credit is accompanied by a reduction in the supply of credit.

Just as we have derived a commodity-market equilibrium (*IS*) curve and a money-market equilibrium (*LM*) curve, we can derive a credit-market equilibrium (*CC*) curve and observe its shifts due to price-level changes. However, the presentation is a bit messy and not worth the effort. Indeed, the entire credit market could be left out of the explicit discussion of our model for one simple reason. In our three-market model, if our economy is in equilibrium, a two-market equilibrium implies that the third market is necessarily also in equilibrium. In Figure 8–5 (page 109), Point *B* denotes a position of equilibrium *AD:* People take off the market their entire output, while the money supply exactly matches their needs. If we stipulated that *B* denotes an equilibrium position, then it follows that the aggregate demand for and supply of credit are also matched at that point.

This terminates the construction of our model. Admittedly, it was not always simple, but then, neither is the U.S. economy. Part 3, then, will go to the heart of our subject matter, fiscal and monetary policy discussions.

Problems

1. Geometrically derive the money-market equilibrium curve (*LM* curve) and explain your derivation. What is the significance of the *LM* curve? Besides equilibrium in the money market, what other condition must be fulfilled to produce equilibrium aggregate demand?
2. Suppose the economy is in a depression due to insufficient *AD*. One way to stimulate the *AD* is by having the Federal Reserve System inject money into the economy. What does such a policy do to the *LM* curve?
3. When the *AD* curve is derived for an economy, the money market must be considered. Why? Why does equilibrium in the commodity market not guarantee overall equilibrium-aggregate-demand? Write down the money-demand function and plot it for two levels of income (do not derive the *LM* curve).

4. Geometrically derive a nation's *AD* curve.
5. We have mentioned repeatedly that people can dispose of their incomes not only by consuming, paying taxes, and saving, but also by adding to their money holdings. Suppose you are told that saving must have a peculiar definition if it is not equal to after-tax income minus consumption. Take issue.
6. In discussing the credit market we said that, at a given level of income, when the price level goes up both consumption and saving go down. Suppose you are told that this is definitionally impossible, since an increase in consumption, at a given income level, necessarily implies a reduction in saving. Take issue with this assertion.

Suggested Readings

On the money market:

M. Bronfenbrenner and T. Mayer, "Liquidity Functions in the American Economy," *Econometrica,* 28 (October 1960), 810–834.

K. Brunner, "Some Major Problems in Monetary Theory," *The American Economic Review,* LI (May 1961), 47–56.

H. R. Heller, "The Demand for Money: The Evidence from the Short-Run Data," *Quarterly Journal of Economics,* LXXIX (May 1965), 291–303.

L. S. Ritter, "The Role of Money in Keynesian Theory" in D. Carson, ed., *Banking and Monetary Studies* (Homewood, Ill.: Richard D. Irwin, Inc., 1963), pp. 134–150.

On aggregate demand and aggregate income:

J. R. Hicks, "Mr. Keynes and the 'Classics'; A Suggested Interpretation," *Econometrica,* 5 (April 1937), 147–159.

R. A. Mundell, "A Fallacy in the Interpretation of Macroeconomic Equilibrium," *Journal of Political Economy,* LXXIII (1965), 61–66.

B. P. Pesek and T. R. Saving, *The Foundations of Money and Banking* (New York: The Macmillan Company, 1968), Chapter 22.

Part Three
Income Stabilization Policies

9 The Depressed Economy

In Part 1 we dealt with the problem of measuring the performance of an economy in terms of the people's well-being. The objective was to capture the meaning of a nation's wealth or well-being and to express this wealth quantitatively. The concept of the gross national product and of national income was introduced. This allows us to evaluate a nation's economic development over time, and facilitates a comparison of the wealth of two different nations at a given point in time.

Conceptually, the measure of wealth we decided to use was national income, a flow variable. Analytically, its use as a measure of a nation's wealth has much to commend itself: It is easily understood, it fits readily into a geometric or mathematical model, it is not overly difficult to quantify statistically, and it is subject to empirical verification. Real national income is an acceptable reflection of real per capita national income, because we are primarily concerned with short-term fluctuations, which rule out significant changes in population.

In Part 2 a macroeconomic model was developed. It was shown that the aggregate supply of a nation depends on that nation's resource endowment, the skill of its labor force, the state of technology, and the utilization of productive resources, including labor. A cutback in output was shown to affect employment first and foremost. To the manager, labor (and that includes professors of economics) is a variable input, i.e., wage payments are a variable cost and, therefore, subject to cutbacks in cost-reduction programs.

The aggregate demand of a nation was shown to depend on a great many variables. In particular, aggregate spending was disaggregated into consumer spending, investment spending, and government spending. Both the commodity and money markets had to be taken into consideration in developing the aggregate demand curve.

One of the objectives of economic policy makers is to keep a nation's economy producing at or near capacity, thereby assuring full employment. This is by no means the only policy objective; long-term economic growth and price-level stability are other very important goals of policy planners. In this book, we will concentrate our attention on short-run economic disturbances and on the policy actions by which these disturbances can be alleviated. Capacity production and full employment at stable price levels are the primary objectives of such short-run policies.

A number of policy actions are possible to stimulate a lagging economy. Almost all of them work through the aggregate demand side. We will discuss the most important policies one by one, but first let us develop a disequilibrium condition in our economy that calls for policy action.

Consider the sequence of Figures 9–1 to 9–4. Figure 9–1 illustrates an equilibrium position in the commodity market at Point *A*. Assuming an in-

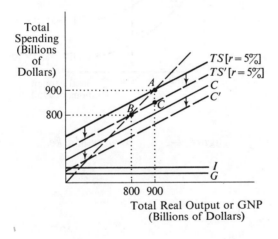

Figure 9–1   Commodity Market

terest rate of 5%, the total spending level for goods and services at Point *A* is just sufficient to take the total output of 900 billion dollars' worth of goods and services off the market. To put this concept into a different context, at Point *A* the total income received in the amount of $900 billion is *all* spent for the purchase of commodities, most of it by the household units, some by the business sector and some by the government. Using the procedure outlined in Part 2, let us suppose that the solid commodity-market equilibrium curve, or *IS* curve, in Figure 9–3 was derived from the commodity market shown in Figure 9–1. This *IS* curve must, of course, go through Point *A*.

Now let us consider the money market in Figure 9–2. Suppose that the amount of money supplied by the Federal Reserve System is $200 billion and that the money-demand curves are as shown in this figure. Again, Point *A* was chosen to correspond to a total GNP of $900 billion and a rate of interest of 5%. That is, given a total GNP of $900 billion and an interest rate of 5%, people, including corporate treasurers, wish to hold a money stock of $200 billion, the exact amount that is being supplied by the Fed.

Again, let us assume that we have used the derivation of Chapter 8 to obtain the money-market equilibrium, or *LM*, curve shown in Figure 9–3. If

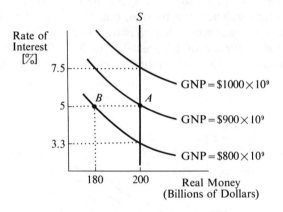

Figure 9–2   Money Market

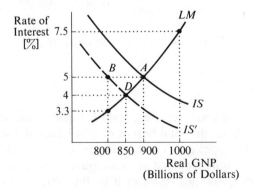

Figure 9–3   IS and LM Curves

we assume further that both the *IS* and *LM* curves have been derived for a price level of $P = 100$, we can plot the equivalent of Point *A* in Figure 9–3 onto Figure 9–4, again labeled Point *A*. This is one point on our *AD* curve; other points may be obtained by varying the price level in both the commodity and money markets, by observing the resulting shifts in the *IS* and *LM* curves, and by transferring the newly obtained points of intersection onto Figure 9–4. Since this technique has been discussed earlier, we will simply

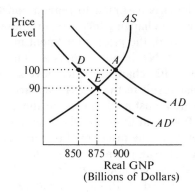

Figure 9–4   Aggregate Demand and Supply

stipulate here that the solid *AD* curve in Figure 9–4 was derived in this manner.

Furthermore, let us assert that the *AS* curve in Figure 9–4 was derived in accordance with the model of Chapter 6. Since the *AS* curve of Figure 9–4 intersects the *AD* curve at Point *A*, this point designates our initial equilibrium condition for the economy, where all resources are fully employed. The term "fully employed" is, of course, subject to the reservations made earlier concerning an acceptable level of unemployment on the order of 4%, more or less. Moreover, Points *A* in Figures 9–1 to 9–3 correspond to Point *A* in Figure 9–4; they represent equilibrium conditions in the commodity market, the money market, and, by implication, in the credit market. In short, Point *A* in Figure 9–4 designates a full-employment equilibrium position for the economy as a whole. Thus Points *A* will serve as a benchmark on all subsequent graphs — the goal, if you wish, that our monetary or fiscal policies will attempt to reach.

Having established our equilibrium positions *A* in Figure 9–1 to 9–4, let us now create a disequilibrium position that we can use in our policy discussions as a starting point toward full employment. In particular, let us assume that consumption spending suddenly declines, due, say, to the expectation on the part of consumers that bad times are just around the corner. This will induce consumers to increase savings for the rainy days ahead, at the going interest rate of 5% and the current price level $P = 100$. Such behavior by the consumers causes the consumption function in the commodity market to shift downward to C'. Since the TS curve in this market is made up in part by the consumption function, it will be shifted downward to TS' by the same distance: See the dashed curves in Figure 9–1. In the $IS–LM$ apparatus in Figure 9–3, the reduction in aggregate consumption spending will induce a downward shift of the IS curve. This can be explained in two ways, either with an income-adjustment model or with a price-adjustment model. With the income-adjustment model, the price level is assumed to remain constant and the economy responds to disturbances by changing incomes, or, more precisely in our case, by changes in the GNP. With the price-adjustment model, on the other hand, a given aggregate income, GNP in our case, is assumed, and the economy responds to disturbances with changing price levels. Whichever adjustment process is used, the final result in the $AD-AS$ apparatus in Figure 9–4 is the same. Because the income-adjustment model has the advantage of being easier to state and understand, we will limit our discussion to it.

Let us assume, then, that the price level remains constant throughout the adjustment process. As consumption spending declines, we know from our previous discussion that our economy will at first be operating at the disequilibrium position designated by Point C in Figure 9–1. Of the total output being produced at the rate of $900 billion per year, only a part is taken off the market. The result is a build-up of inventories due to an insufficient level of total spending. The rate of production of goods and services worth $900 billion gives rise to an income (including depreciation) of $900 billion per year. Of that amount, people are willing to spend only a part. It makes no difference whether you think of inventory build-ups or of reduced income to producers as people spend less in the commodity market: The two concepts are manifestations of the same phenomenon, overproduction. Given our assumption of a fixed price level and interest rate, the only alternative to producers is to cut back production. This they will do until equilibrium is reestablished in the commodity market at Point B, where the total spending level exactly matches the total income. Transferring Point B from the commodity market in Figure 9–1 to the $IS-LM$ apparatus in Figure 9–3, we see that the given interest rate of 5% and the reduced equilibrium level of spending in the amount of $800 billion have caused the IS curve to shift downward to the dashed IS' curve.

What are the repercussions in the money market of a reduction in consumer spending? Again, these can be explained by an income-adjustment model or by a price-adjustment model; and again, the price-adjustment model is a bit more intricate. For this reason, and also because empirical evidence points toward relatively inflexible prices in a downward direction, we will limit our discussion to the income-adjustment model. That is, we will assume that prices remain constant.

In the income-adjustment model, then, what are the repercussions of a reduction in consumer spending in the money market? The supply of money, as we have seen, is determined exogenously by the Federal Reserve System;

i.e., the money supply remains the same, given the constant price level. In Figure 9–2, this means that the money-supply curve does not shift. The demand for money, as we have seen in Chapter 8, is a function of the real GNP and the rate of interest. This is indicated in Figure 9–2 by the three negatively sloped money-demand curves.

We have already discussed that a shift of the money-market equilibrium, or *LM*, curve can come about only by a change in the real money supply. Such a change may be the result of one of two developments, which may come about separately or in combination: Either the supply of money has been changed by policy action of the Fed while the price level remained the same, or the price level has changed, thereby changing the real money supply, given a constant nominal supply of money. Neither of these two changes has taken place. In fact, the only change we have admitted so far was the original decline in aggregate consumption spending. The money-supply curve, therefore, does not shift. As a result, the money-market equilibrium, or *LM*, curve in Figure 9–3 does not shift either.

Our *IS-LM* apparatus allows us to determine the new equilibrium aggregate demand curve. We know from our previous discussion that both the commodity market and the money market are in equilibrium where the *IS* and *LM* curves intersect. In Figure 9–3, the new equilibrium-demand position is at Point *D*. Again, at that point the total output is exactly taken off the market (*IS*), while people do not wish to add to or reduce their money holdings (*LM*). The result of our stipulated reduction in consumer spending, then, has been to reduce the aggregate demand and the rate of interest.

It should come as no surprise that the aggregate demand declines if one of its components is reduced. But what about the rate of interest? Why does it decline? A rigorous answer to that question requires the formal introduction of the credit market. At the risk of disappointing the more ambitious student, let us answer that question verbally, without formally incorporating the credit market into our model.

When people decide to consume less, i.e., to save more at the going rate of interest, the equilibrium GNP in the commodity market is reduced. In our example, Figure 9–1, the new equilibrium point is *B* which corresponds to a total income (including depreciation) of $800 billion. Transferring Point *B* to the money market, we see that we are faced with an excess-money-supply situation: At the lower total income of $800 billion and the initial interest rate of 5%, the demand for money is less than the supply of money, by a total of $20 billion (the distance between *A-B* in Figure 9–2).

Let us analyze the situation by means of Figure 9–3. Point *B* is located on the *IS'* curve, where the commodity market is in equilibrium. But Point *B* falls above the *LM* curve, i.e., into the excess-money-supply region. From the *IS'* curve we know that the total income received is being spent in the commodity market. But we also know from the *LM* curve that people think they are holding too much money. That is, at an interest rate of 5%, the given money supply of $200 billion is too much for the reduced equilibrium GNP of $800 billion. How can that excess money be absorbed? The consumers do not want to use it; they have just opted to reduce spending. Thus, their transactions demand for money has been reduced. The government does not want to use that extra $20 billion; it had nothing to do with the creation of the excess supply of money. Nor does the business sector want to use the money for investment purposes; it *would* use it if the rate of interest were lower, but not at the going rate of 5%. At a lower rate of interest, the business sector's investment spending would be stimulated and this, in turn, would induce the firms to absorb the excess money. In other words, a lower rate of interest would stimulate the business sector's demand for money. And, for that matter, the consumers, too, would consider using some of the money, if the rate of interest were lowered. After all, if they could obtain low-cost loans, they would increase consumption spending.

What would it take to get the government to absorb some of the excess money? As a matter of policy action, the government might do something about that excess $20 billion, but not as the result of a built-in reaction to any variable. Government spending is an exogenous variable, and not directly affected by forces in the market.

In short, at Point *B* in Figure 9–3 there are 20 billion uncommitted dollars seeking an outlet. Something has to give, and that something is the rate of interest. As we will see in Chapter 11, an excess supply of money will tend to reduce the rate of interest. But this is not the only force at work.

The whole chain of events was brought about by people's lack of confidence in the economy: They reduced their spending level out of their current incomes in order to build up reserves for the expected rainy days; they wished to consume less and to save more. This option was discussed at the end of Chapter 8, where it was shown that both the rate of interest and the expectations of people may cause consumption to vary at the expense of saving, whereas all other variables affected desired consumption spending and saving in the same direction. The present case is one of changing expectations. Thus, as people consume less, they increase their savings rate, i.e., they supply more credit. This increase in the supply of credit, in the face of an unchanged demand for credit, creates a condition of excess credit at the initial rate of interest of 5%: Loanable funds seeking an outlet cannot find one, because the rate of interest is too high. Again, something has to give, and again, that something is the rate of interest.

The downward pressure on the rate of interest thus emanates from both the money and credit markets. Too much money and too much credit, at any given real GNP, will reduce the rate of interest. As it falls, both the business and household sectors increase spending and, as a result, they absorb some of the excess money. In Figure 9–3, the economy moves along the *IS'* curve, from Point *B* to Point *D*, where the *IS'* curve and the *LM* curve intersect. At that point, the equilibrium rate of interest is 4% and the real GNP is $850 billion.

At Point *D* in Figure 9–3, the excess supply of money has disappeared. Part of the excess money is used for transactions, i.e., to facilitate an additional 50 billion dollars worth of output, relative to Point *B*. This is illustrated in

Figure 9–5. The reduction of the interest rate due to the existence of excess money and credit caused the investment and consumption curves to shift upward. As a result, the *TS'* curve in the commodity market also shifted up. This new *TS"* curve intersects the 45-degree equilibrium line at a real GNP of $850 billion. That is, given the depressed interest rate of 4%, total income equals total spending in the commodity market, when the GNP is $850 billion.

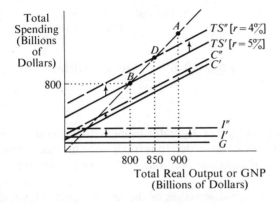

Figure 9–5   *Commodity Market*

What happened to that part of the excess money supply that was not absorbed by additional transactions? The demand for money, we remember, is a function of the GNP of an economy and of the rate of interest, i.e., the cost of holding money. As the interest rate fell from 5% to 4%, total spending was stimulated and so was the transactions demand for money. But at the same time, given the reduction in the cost of holding money, people wish to hold more for any given GNP. The overall result is illustrated in Figure 9–6. At Point *B* in that figure, the economy is confronted with an excess supply of money: More money is available than wanted. As the rate of interest falls, the economy is willing to hold more money for the given GNP of $800 billion. This is illustrated in Figure 9–6 by a move from Point *B* to Point *F*. At that point, given a GNP of $800 billion, a money stock of $190 billion is required.

At the same time, however, the increase in aggregate spending that is induced by the falling rate of interest also causes the transactions demand for money to rise. This is shown by the dashed money-demand curve in Figure 9–6. Final equilibrium in the money market is obtained at Point *D*. The move from Point *F* to Point *D*, then, is strictly a case of an increase in the transactions demand for money; i.e., for the given interest rate of 4%, the greater

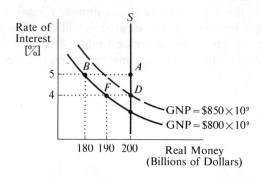

Figure 9–6   Money Market

GNP ($850 billion) requires a greater money stock. You may wish to refer to Figure 8–1 at this point in order to refresh your memory about the convertibility of money into consumption and saving (i.e., ultimately into investment spending).

Before we turn to a discussion of the resulting price-level effects and total output, let us summarize the chain of events up to this point. The decision by the household sector to consume less caused the level of total spending to be reduced. At the same time it became apparent that less money would be needed to accommodate the reduced total output. Thus, money was freed and began to seek an outlet. Of the potential users of money, the government was unwilling to employ it under any condition; the business and household sectors were willing to use some of it, if the rate of interest were reduced. This downward pressure on the rate of interest was reinforced by conditions in the credit market. Responding to the market pressure, the interest rate did fall, with two effects: (1) A portion of the excess money was absorbed into private and corporate average cash balances, due to the lower cost of holding money. (2) The reduced rate of interest stimulated aggregate spending, although not back to the original equilibrium level. Thus, the remainder of the excess money was now needed to facilitate the additional transactions.

For the *AD-AS* apparatus of Figure 9–4, what does all of this mean? Transferring Point *D* from Figure 9–3 to Figure 9–4, we see that the *AD* curve is shifted downward to *AD'*. Point *D,* in this figure, corresponds to a price level of 100 (since we assumed a constant price level throughout) and an equilibrium aggregate demand of $850 billion. At that price level, however, the *AS* equals $900 billion. We have an excess supply of $50 billion. Clearly, this is a disequilibrium position. But is it stable? The stability of position *D* in Figure 9–4 depends on the rigidity of the price level.

Let us first assume that the price level is flexible downward. In that case the excess supply of goods and services will cause the sellers to reduce prices. As prices fall, the quantity demanded of goods and services is increased. That is, purchasers react by moving downward along the AD' curve (Figure 9–4). At the same time the quantity supplied of goods and services is reduced, since the less efficient producers are squeezed out of the market by falling prices: Suppliers move along the AS curve. Equilibrium is established at Point E, where $AD = AS$ and the price level is 90. The national income (including depreciation) at that point is $875 billion.

Point E, we just said, represents an equilibrium position. That is true, of course, in the sense that $AD = AS$. But in a larger sense, E is *not* an equilibrium position. Total output at Point E is less than the preceding equilibrium output, designated by Point A in Figure 9–4, by $25 billion. Some resources had to be idled to reduce this output, and as always, the variable factor labor suffers most. Thus, while $AD = AS$ at Point E, we are nevertheless faced with an unemployment situation.

What happens to total output if the price level is rigid? In Figure 9–4, the total quantity demanded will be $850 billion dollars' worth of goods and services. Producers are willing to supply goods and services worth $900 billion. Price-level adjustment, the normal equalizing mechanism, has by assumption been removed from the market. Since the sellers cannot force their goods on the buyers, total output will be what the buyers are willing to take off the market: $850 billion. Thus, in the case of inflexible prices, we have an even greater undercapacity output than we did with flexible prices: $50 billion vs. $25 billion.

Let us once more summarize our results. A reduction in consumer spending brings about a disequilibrium position in the economy, and unemployment results; more unemployment if prices are inflexible downward, less unemployment if they are not. Thus, whether prices are flexible or not, a lagging economy due to inadequate AD can be stimulated by stimulating AD. The direction of the required policy action is clear. What is not clear is the intensity.

If the price level is rigid, the economy will produce below capacity by a total of $50 billion. If the price level is flexible, undercapacity production will be on the order of $25 billion. Clearly, in the first case a more drastic stimulation of AD is called for. But how does the price level behave in real life? We will assume, for our model, that it is rigid downward, though this is not exactly correct. The price level has been known to decline, but the last time this happened in this country to any appreciable extent was in the period 1930 to 1933. Thus, it took the Great Depression and large-scale unemployment, on the order of 20 to 25% of the work force, to bring about a decline in the price level. Empirically, then, the price level more nearly approximates rigidity than it does the complete flexibility of Point E in Figure 9–4.

If you are apprehensive about this assumption of rigid prices, you may think of a flexible or semiflexible price level; the policy recommendations that follow will be exactly the same; only the magnitudes of the recommended measures differ. But in this book we are not overly concerned with magnitudes. We will content ourselves with cause-and-effect relationships of macroeconomic theory, leaving the quantification of our policy recommendations to presidential advisers, Treasury officials, Federal Reserve economists, and other more qualified experts. These people have cause to be apprehensive; they know what kind of medicine to prescribe, but being a bit unclear about its curative powers, they do not always know how much to prescribe.

We have now accomplished what we set out to do in this chapter. We have defined a disequilibrium condition in our economy, where unemployment prevails due to insufficient aggregate demand. In the case at hand, a decline in consumer spending was the culprit, but the result would have been the same had the reduction in spending originated in the business or government sector.

Assuming that prices are inflexible in a downward direction, we have derived a disequilibrium condition in the geometric model and labeled it Point D in the various figures of this chapter; similarly, the initial full-employment position has been labeled A throughout. Thus, the stage has been set for the introduction of policy actions that are designed to stimulate our lagging economy. The objective of these policies will be to move the economy from the

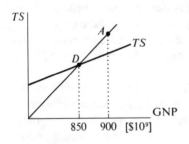

Figure 9–7
Commodity Market

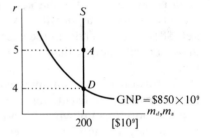

Figure 9–8
Money Market

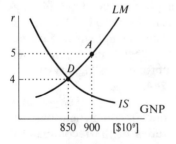

Figure 9–9
IS and LM Curves

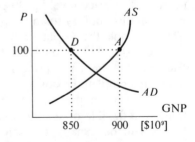

Figure 9–10
AD and AS Curves

unemployment Point *D* back to full employment at Point *A*. This is summarized geometrically in Figures 9–7 to 9–10, which will serve as a basis for all subsequent policy discussions.

A word may be in order at this point concerning our methodology. The model we developed in Part 2 is fundamentally static; i.e., it does not explicitly include time as a variable. Most macroeconomic models do not, since the inclusion of time severely complicates them. Instead, like most models, ours assumes a static position as a starting point and then moves to another static position that is brought about by policy or other changes. No formal discussion is offered concerning the path our economy follows in moving from the first to the second position, or the time it takes to get there. That is, our model is incapable of formally analyzing the dynamic changes taking place in the economy. This is why our model is limited in its application to the short run, where the population stays essentially the same, capital equipment does not change appreciably, technology is constant, etc. But being locked into a short-run model is no great handicap in the discussion of monetary and fiscal policies, since these too are short-run policies. We will have a lot more to say on this subject in the final chapter of the book.

Problems

1. Suppose a nation is going through a genuine recession: The price level falls and the total output is reduced. Could this or could this not be the result of insufficient aggregate demand? Explain with the aid of a simple *AS-AD* model. Suppose insufficient *AD* is indeed the culprit, how can the current situation be rectified?
2. Rather than using the simple *AS-AD* model, explain the recession of problem 1 with the aid of our full-fledged model, showing the major repercussions in the commodity and money markets.

Suggested Readings

Since Chapter 9 is an elaborate application of Chapters 7 and 8, see these two chapters for references.

10 Fiscal Policies

We have come a long way in the development of our model. We have learned to measure an economy's performance (to use a somewhat ill-defined but frequently used term). We have made clear the meaning of the term, a nation's aggregate wealth, which we have used as a proxy for well-being. We have developed a model that will allow us to roughly understand the inner workings of an economy. Finally, in the preceding chapter, we have set up and defined a disequilibrium position in which unemployment prevails.

We are now ready to deal with fiscal and monetary policies: Everything we have done up to this point has been preparatory. Having developed the required tools, let us now proceed to use them.

As was pointed out in the preceding chapter, we will base all of our subsequent discussions on the disequilibrium condition of Figures 9–7 to 9–10. In particular, Points D in all of our graphs will show our economy in disequilibrium. Points A are the full-employment equilibrium points, the targets we are attempting to hit by our policy applications. In this chapter we will take up the subject of fiscal policies; in the next chapter, monetary policies.

Fiscal policies may be defined as policies affecting the level of government expenditures or receipts. Government expenditures, in our model, are defined by the exogenous variable G. In the event of a recession, when resources are unemployed and undercapacity production is the order of the day, one way to alleviate the problem would be for the government to increase its expenditures—either in a direct manner, by putting unemployed people on federal, state, or local government payrolls, or indirectly, by letting out government contracts for large projects, such as the Interstate Highway System, development of the SST, or NASA. Though these projects are not begun or discontinued for fiscal policy reasons, the pace at which such existing projects are pursued can be accelerated or reduced through appropriate changes in government spending. In many ways, the indirect method of government spending is to be preferred. It is more flexible, because it does not commit the government to put a large labor force on its payroll where it is likely to remain even after the recession. And most researchers seem to agree that the effect on the economy is greater if employment is generated in the private sector.

There are other possibilities in the application of government funds. The variable G can be increased in the area of military spending. Certainly, we do not ordinarily think of defense expenditures as being a fiscal policy tool, but, again, policy planners cannot afford to ignore, and do not ignore, the effect of military spending on the performance of the economy. The anti-ballistic missile controversy (ABM) of the late 1960s may serve as an example of a military-fiscal debate. Finally, government funds can be spent on durables other than defense items or on nondurables, as well as on increased transfer payments to the unemployed. The curative effects of the various types of government expenditures vary in intensity. Attempts have been made to quantify these effects, but the results are questionable. For this reason, and also because we are primarily interested in cause-and-effect relationships, we will not pursue the quantification of policy actions any further.

Increases in government spending have to be funded. In principle, three sources of funds are open to the government: (1) increased tax receipts, (2) borrowing from the public by selling bonds, and (3) the printing of money. The first two sources will be analyzed in this chapter; the third will not be analyzed in this book, because, while important in many foreign countries, it is of little relevance in the United States, primarily because the administration does not also create money.

In addition to increasing its expenditures, the government can affect aggregate demand by stimulating consumer or investment spending through appropriate tax cuts. A fairly recent example is the 7% investment tax credit which has greatly encouraged investment, or the accelerated depreciation rate that was instituted by the Nixon administration in 1970. In the area of consumer spending, the imposition of a 10% income tax surcharge is an example of an attempt by the Johnson administration to reduce aggregate demand during inflationary periods.

If the government chooses to stimulate aggregate demand in a recession through a tax cut, this will reduce the government's tax receipts and induce a cutback in government spending. But if the government does not wish to reduce its expenditures, then it will incur a deficit. In order to hold spending at the pre-tax-cut level, the loss in tax revenue must be compensated by some means, and the government can do one of two things: (1) It can make up for the losses in tax revenue by borrowing from the public, i.e., by selling bonds; or (2) it can resort to the printing of money. Again, the printing of money will not be considered in this text.

For fiscal policies, then, the government has the following four anti-recession tools in its toolbox:

1. An increase in government spending financed by taxation.
2. An increase in government spending financed by borrowing.
3. Stimulation of investment spending by corporate tax cuts, while holding government spending constant, financed by borrowing.
4. Stimulation of consumer spending by reduced income taxes, while holding government spending constant, also financed by borrowing.

Let us discuss these fiscal policies one by one, in the indicated order.

A. Increase in Government Spending
Financed by Taxation

Broadly speaking, an increase in taxation may be directed primarily towards the business sector or the household sector. Let us discuss the latter choice; that is, the effects of an increase in personal income taxes. Such an increase has two effects: reduced consumer spending and reduced saving. Let us discuss these effects as shown in Figure 10-1.[1]

From the *IS* and *LM* curves we know that at Point *D* the total income received is being spent (*IS*), while the economy is using the exact amount of money that is being supplied by the Federal Reserve System (*LM*). For expository simplicity, let us at first ignore the money market and trace the sequence of events through the commodity and credit markets. The increased income tax will reduce disposable income and, therefore, consumption. But while people cut back consumption expenditures, they will also reduce saving, which, as we have seen, is also positively related to disposable income. Thus, a part of the tax burden falls on saving; i.e., the supply of credit is reduced.

The increase in personal income tax, however, does not immediately affect investment spending. Thus, with the same number of investment dollars sought after in the credit market and fewer dollars made available by savers for investment, investors will be forced to bid up the rate of interest in order to attract the scarce investment funds for their particular projects. But as the rate of interest rises, both consumption and investment spending are reduced. In fact, ignoring the money market, consumption and investment spending will

---

[1] In this and subsequent figures, the symbol ⇒ means "implies."

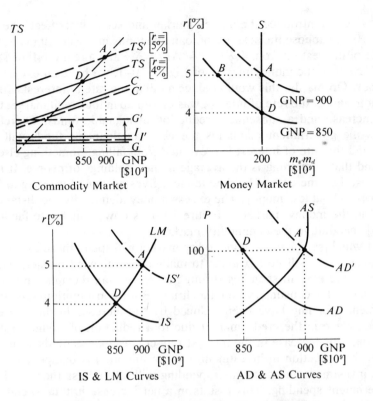

Figure 10–1   *Increase in Government*
Spending Financed by an Increase in
Income Taxes

Sequence of Events:

$G \uparrow$ through $t \uparrow \Rightarrow C \downarrow$ and $S \downarrow$, i.e., part of the tax burden falls on saving. But note that I spending is not immediately affected.

But: $S \downarrow$ while I spending remains the same $\Rightarrow r$ is bid up in credit market.

(1) Ignoring money market:
$r \uparrow \Rightarrow C \downarrow$ and $I \downarrow$ until $G \uparrow$ exactly offset by $C \downarrow$ and $I \downarrow$. No change in TS. Simple shifting of funds.

(2) With money market:
$r \uparrow \Rightarrow$ excess supply of money. These excess funds will stimulate C and I, causing them to be reduced by less than $G \uparrow$. Result: a net increase in TS due to funds made available in the money market, causing an increase in AD.

be reduced by the exact amount by which government spending is increased. That is, no new funds have been made available. There has only been a shifting of funds away from the private sector into the government sector, and the AD remains intact at the recession level as designated by Points D in Figure 10–1.

Now let us introduce the money market and see how it affects the *AD*. In Figure 10–1, suppose the scarcity of loanable funds in the credit market drives the rate of interest up from 4% to 5%. At $r = 5\%$ and a real GNP of $850 billion, Point *B* in the money market of Figure 10–1, we have an excess supply of money. Ordinarily, this would induce a fall in the rate of interest. But in the present instance, the rate of interest was driven up in the credit market through a tax increase and a subsequent reduction of loanable funds. Therefore, as long as the government maintains the new tax, loanable funds will remain scarce and the rate of interest is prevented from falling. Something else has to give, and that something is the average money holdings of people. If the rate of interest, i.e., the cost of holding money, gives no sign of wanting to fall, the answer is to hold less money. The excess money, defined by the distance from *A* to *B* in the money market of Figure 10–1, is now available to facilitate increased spending in the commodity market.

But which sector in the commodity market will spend these excess funds? The government will not: It plans to maintain a balanced budget; that is, to finance its increase in spending through increased tax receipts, and no more. That leaves the consumers and the firms. Both consumption spending and investment spending have been reduced by the increase in the interest rate that took place in the credit market due to a reduction of saving. But to the extent that this increase in the interest rate creates excess funds in the money market, the reduction in investment and consumption is dampened. In other words, investment and consumer spending will fall by less than the increase in government spending. This results in a net increase in total spending and, ultimately, in *AD*.[2]

The overall result in the commodity market, shown by the dashed lines in Figure 10–1, may be summarized as follows: Government expenditures rise; consumer spending falls as a result of the increase in income taxes. Moreover, the interest-rate-induced tendency for consumption and investment to fall is partially offset by the creation of additional funds in the money market. Overall, total spending rises and equilibrium will be established at Point *A* in the commodity market, corresponding to a total GNP of $900 billion. Until that point is reached, an excess supply of money will continue to facilitate increases in consumption and investment spending. This is so because the money market will only be in equilibrium, given the enforced 5% rate of interest, when the real GNP is equal to $900 billion. See the dashed money-demand curve.

In the *IS-LM* system, we are faced with an upward shift of the *IS* curve until it intersects the *LM* curve at the enforced 5% rate of interest and a GNP of $900 billion. Similarly the *AD* curve in the last panel of Figure 10–1 is shifted up to the original full-employment equilibrium position.

---

[2] It would be more correct analytically to describe the sequence of events as the exact converse of the sequence in Chapter 9. That is, the drying up of loanable funds drives *r* to some value greater than 5%, but the excess supply of money at that point induces a slight reduction in *r* back to 5%, thereby stimulating consumption and investment spending and creating a net increase in total spending. In the interest of reducing the complexity of the argument, a somewhat simplified approach was used in all fiscal policy applications.

A note may be in order about Figure 10-1 and all subsequent figures in this and the following chapter. The sequence of events induced by the policy action under discussion is summarized in abbreviated form below these figures. This is not meant to be a shortcut to wisdom; the reader is urged to give careful attention to the text, since it explains *why* the policies work, while the notes below the figure only say *how* they work. Having read and understood the text, you should find the notes helpful in reviewing policy actions.

B. Increase in Government Spending Financed by Borrowing

Suppose the government prefers to finance its increased anti-recession expenditures through borrowing, i.e., by selling bonds. There may be very good reasons for this policy: A tax increase has never been regarded with favor by the public, and one in the middle of a recession will be resented even more and might spell political death for those who enact it. This is one of the many areas where economic theory clashes with the realities of life, where a perfectly sensible economic policy is found unacceptable for political or other reasons. This is not a book on political science, and we will not pursue the subject further. We will simply stipulate that the government, for whatever reason, has decided to finance its increase in expenditures through borrowing.

The sequence of events of such a government policy is illustrated in Figure 10-2. We again start at the disequilibrium position D and attempt to reach the full-employment position A through our fiscal policy. In the absence of a money market that can be tapped for funds, the increase in government spending can be financed only by a reduction of consumer and investment spending. This would involve a shift of spending between sectors, rather than the desired net increase in spending.

But there is a money market, and it can be tapped for funds. In the case at hand, the sequence of events is almost exactly the same as in the income-tax case, where, we remember, the interest rate was driven up in the credit market because saving was reduced in the face of an unchanged level of investment. In the present case, where the government is borrowing the required funds, the business sector finds itself competing with the government for the existing loanable funds. As a result, the demand for credit is increased in the face of a given amount of savings or supply of credit. Something has to give, and that something is, again, the rate of interest.

As before, an increase in the rate of interest will create an excess supply of funds in the money market. With the government actively soliciting funds, people, including corporate treasurers, will invest their excess money in government bonds. Thus, to the extent that the excess funds from the money market are used by the government, the increase in government spending more than offsets the interest-rate-induced reduction in consumer and investment

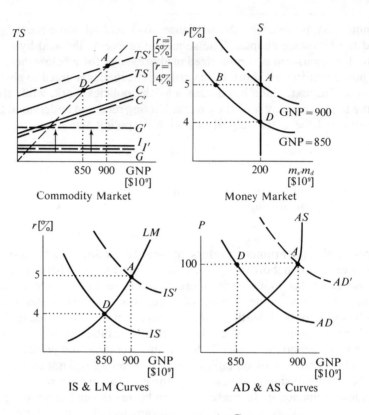

*Figure 10–2   Increase in Government
Spending Financed by Borrowing*

Sequence of Events:

$G \uparrow$ through borrowing $\Rightarrow r \uparrow$, causing $C \downarrow$ and $I \downarrow$.

(1) Ignoring the money market:
   $G \uparrow$ exactly offset by $C \downarrow + I \downarrow$, i.e., $G \uparrow$ is funded by non-consumption and non-investment. No change in TS; simple shifting of funds.

(2) With money market:
   Sale of government bonds while S remains the same $\Rightarrow r$ is bid up and held at new level. $r \uparrow \Rightarrow$ excess supply of money. With people holding excess money and the government seeking to borrow funds and offering increased interest rates in return, the excess funds will be invested into government bonds. Result: a net increase in TS due to funds made available in money market, causing an increase in AD.

spending. The net effect is an increase in total spending and, ultimately, in AD.

The overall result is indicated by the dashed lines in Figure 10–2. It may be summarized as follows: The increase in the interest rate causes investment and consumption spending to fall. Government spending increases, of course, since that was the event that triggered all the other reactions. To the extent that funds are made available in the money market, the increase in government spending will be greater than the decrease in consumer and investment spending.

The creation of new funds in the money market will cease as soon as the increase in GNP causes the money-demand curve to shift to equilibrium with the money supply at Point A. The IS curve and AD curves will be shifted up as in the preceding case, and full-employment equilibrium will be restored.

C. Stimulation of Private Spending by Cuts in Corporate or Income Taxes

Let us first consider the case of a corporate tax cut. The government, faced by unemployment in the land, wishes to stimulate investment spending while holding its own expenditures at the same level. One way to accomplish this is to give specific tax advantages to firms making commercial investments. Such investment tax credits reduce the cost of investing and make otherwise marginal ventures financially attractive. But like any tax concession, the investment tax credit reduces government receipts. If the government wishes to hold its expenditures at the same level, a deficit is created. One way to finance this deficit is by borrowing from the public, i.e., by selling bonds.

The sequence of events induced by the investment tax credit and financed by the selling of bonds is illustrated in Figure 10–3. The immediate impact of the tax credit is to raise the business sector's investment demand. At the same time, the government enters into competition with the business sector in seeking funds to make up for lost tax receipts. As before, since saving is not affected by the investment tax credit, the government, determined to maintain its spending level, must bid up the rate of interest to solicit the required savings from consumers.

If we ignore the money market, no additional funds can be made available in the commodity market. Thus, the increase in investment spending with government expenditures constant must be financed by an equivalent reduction of consumer spending. We have an interesting three-way rearrangement of funds in the commodity market: Through the investment tax credit, the government makes funds available to business for investment; but by selling bonds and raising the interest rate, it dampens the investment demand somewhat and at the same time taps the public for funds that it needs to maintain its level of spending. The result is, of course, a decline of consumer spending.

But, again, the money market does exist and can be used as a source of funds. Since the rate of interest is bid up, we again find that people are confronted with an excess supply of money. Having greater cash balances than they care to have, they either spend them directly in the commodity market or—and this is more likely, since the highly liquid money is held predominantly by corporations and financial institutions—they invest them in government and

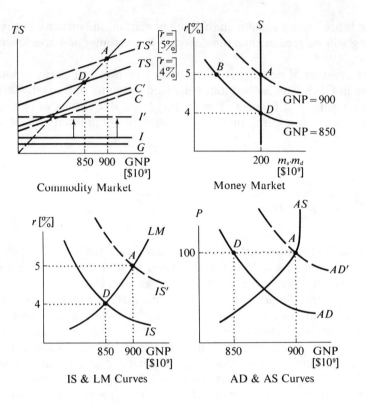

*Figure 10–3   The Investment Tax Credit
and Debt Financing*

Sequence of Events:

Investment tax credit $\Rightarrow I \uparrow$ and $G \downarrow$. Government borrowing $\Rightarrow G \uparrow$ to old level and $r \uparrow$.

(1) Ignoring money market:
    G remains the same; $I \uparrow$ at the expense of $C \downarrow$. No change in TS. Simple shifting of funds.

(2) With money market:
    $r \uparrow \Rightarrow$ excess supply of money. With people holding excess money and both the government and industry seeking to borrow funds, excess money will be invested in government and corporate bonds. As a result, $GNP \uparrow$ until $m_s = m_d$.

corporate bonds. The overall result, then, indicated by the dashed lines in Figure 10–3, is a substantial increase in investment and a small decline in consumption, while government spending remains the same. The creation of loanable funds in the money market stops as soon as the GNP has reached the level designated by Point *A,* where both the money and the commodity markets are in equilibrium. For the *IS-LM* graph and the *AD-AS* graph, this implies the familiar upward shift of the *IS* curve and the *AD* curve to full-employment equilibrium.

Instead of using the investment tax credit, the government could have directed its efforts toward consumption spending by lowering income taxes. This would have increased disposable income, which would have gone in part toward the purchase of consumer goods and in part toward increased saving. Since the increase in saving would be insufficient to cover the government's loss in tax revenue, additional selling of government bonds would have driven up the rate of interest and thus released funds in the money market. The overall result, then, would be as follows: Government spending remains constant; investment spending is reduced; consumer spending is increased so that a net increase in *AD* is obtained and full-employment equilibrium is reached.

A Final Note on Fiscal Policies

We have assumed in all of our policy discussions that the economy is taken back to the full-employment equilibrium position designated by Points *A* in the various graphs. That is, we have implied that the government knows exactly how severe the recession is and the exact magnitude of the required policy action. Nothing could be further from the truth. We will discuss later some of the practical difficulties in analyzing the current performance of an economy and in designing appropriate policy actions. For the time being, let us simply state that there is a great deal of trial and error in applying macroeconomic theory.

It should also be noted that the initial disequilibrium position was created by a fall in consumption spending as people expected bad times. If the government takes rigorous action to prevent a severe depression, and if as a result the GNP is returned to the full-employment level and held there, the people would eventually realize that they were mistaken in their somber prognosis and, accordingly, they would readjust their consumption spending upward. This would trigger inflationary pressures which would require the government to reverse the policy action that was originally undertaken. That is, Points *A* in the various graphs would eventually be at the same level of consumer, investment, and government spending where they had been in the pre-depression period.

There was one characteristic common to all recession-induced fiscal policies that is worth noting: Each fiscal policy had the effect of increasing the interest rate, which in turn created loanable funds in the money market. This gave a net increase in *AD* and, ultimately, in the GNP. The increase in the rate of interest and the subsequent creation of loanable funds, then, is the key to anti-recession *fiscal* policy actions.

Before we turn to the topic of monetary policies, let us briefly discuss some of the fiscal tools the government may use to fight inflation. We have mentioned the possibility of applying the recession-induced policies in reverse; let us see, case by case, what that means. We will limit our discussion to a summary of events for each case. The interested reader may wish to trace these events through our geometric model.

1. Let us consider first simultaneous cuts in government spending and in personal income taxes, such that the government maintains a balanced budget. As income taxes are reduced, consumption and saving rise. The increase in savings in the face of an unchanged level of investment spending will reduce the rate of interest in the credit market, thus stimulating both investment and consumption spending. Ignoring the money market for a moment, the increase in consumer and investment spending is exactly offset by the reduction in government spending. However, the money market does exist, and the fall in the interest rate creates an excess demand for money. As people wish to hold more money, available transaction funds are reduced. As a result, the increase in consumption and investment spending is dampened and the reduction in government spending predominates: the *TS* and, ultimately, the *AD* curves are shifted downward, reducing the GNP.

2. Elimination or reduction of deficit spending. Suppose the government is financing its deficit through borrowing and it wishes to make good a campaign promise to return to a balanced budget. With borrowed funds no longer available, government spending will be reduced. Since the government ceases to solicit funds, the rate of interest will decrease. While such a decrease of the interest rate will cause consumer and investment spending to rise, it will also cause a net withdrawal of funds from the commodity market, since people wish to hold more of the now cheaper money. As a result, the level of total spending will be reduced, causing an ultimate reduction in *AD*.

3. A tax increase. Suppose the government wishes to eliminate deficit spending while maintaining its current level of expenditures. A tax increase will do the job. Again, since the government no longer seeks funds through borrowing, the rate of interest will decrease. This will result in a net withdrawal of funds from the commodity market and the *AD* will be reduced.

The key to anti-inflationary fiscal policy actions is to effect a decrease in the rate of interest and a subsequent withdrawal of funds from the commodity market. The reduced availability of transactions money causes the *AD* to decline. If the culprit causing inflation was an excess *AD*, the decline in *AD* clearly is anti-inflationary.

Let us once more return to our depressed economy. On page 134 we listed four anti-recession fiscal policy tools that might be used if the recession is the result of insufficient AD. The first of these tools, an increase in government spending financed by taxation, we found to be politically unacceptable. The remaining three tools all involved deficit spending, that is, the government wished either to increase its expenditures while holding tax receipts constant, or to hold expenditures constant while granting tax concessions. The point is that to be effective a politically feasible anti-recession fiscal policy necessarily involves deficit spending. There is no escaping this basic fact. Yet, it is either not recognized or conveniently overlooked in legislative circles. It is not unusual, during a recession, to hear otherwise very conservative legislators who strongly believe in balanced government budgets clamor for tax cuts. These tax cuts, it is argued, will stimulate AD and get the economy moving again. Well, yes, they will, provided that they are accompanied by governmental deficit spending.

Similarly, during inflationary periods a cut-back in government spending is often demanded. But the variable to focus on is not government spending but deficit spending and, more precisely, changes in deficit spending. Moreover, as we will see shortly, changes in deficit spending are an effective fiscal policy tool only to the extent that the initial disturbance originates with the AD side. Unemployment, or inflation, or both, if they are the result of supply forces, cannot effectively be dealt with through fiscal policy tools, or monetary tools for that matter.

If there is confusion in the public debate on monetary and fiscal policies, this is in no small way due to the use of the ambiguous terms "inflationary" versus "expansionary" and "deflationary" versus "restrictive." A fiscal policy designed to stimulate AD will be labeled inflationary or expansionary, depending on the speaker's point of view. The first term, inflationary, carries with it the implied disapproval of the speaker; the opposite holds true for the term expansionary. Similar arguments apply to the terms deflationary and restrictive. The use of neutral, nonemotive terms would do much to clear the debate. A fiscal or monetary policy, for example, might be defined as stimulating or destimulating AD. The advantage of this or similar terminology is twofold: First, the term is neutral and the conclusion in regard to inflationary or expansionary (and deflationary or restrictive) effects is left to the audience, second, the term centers attention where it belongs, exclusively on the AD side.

Problems

1. With the aid of a geometric presentation and a minimum of words, explain in sufficient detail how an economy is stimulated by the following fiscal policy: investment tax credit granted to the business sector.

2. With the aid of a geometric presentation and a minimum of words, explain in sufficient detail how an economy is stimulated by the following fiscal policy: an increase in government spending financed by borrowing.

3. Analytically explain anti-recession fiscal policies through corporate tax cuts. In your discussion, take issue with the following statement from the text:

> Having greater cash balances than they care to have, people either spend them directly in the commodity market or, and this is more likely since the highly liquid money is predominantly held by corporations and financial institutions, they invest them in government and corporate bonds.

A geometric presentation, while not necessary for your answer, will help in formulating your thoughts.

4. In August 1971, when unemployment was running at near 6% of the labor force, and the price level was rising at about 6% per year, a leading politician (and potential presidential contender) proposed "the" answer to the economic dilemma: have the government provide more jobs — federal jobs, if necessary.

Oratory aside, what is this man really proposing? What *kind* of policy is he advocating? Analytically, using our model, what are the effects of such a policy?

Hint: If you can, verbalize the entire process, but it would help if you used the following geometric procedure.

a. Assume a pure recession due to insufficient aggregate demand. Make a reasonable and realistic assumption concerning the funding mechanism of the proposed policy. Then show the effect of this policy upon the final GNP. I am talking about the four-panel figure (commodity market, money market, *IS–LM, AD–AS*). Explain.

b. Having gone through the mechanics for a pure recession, redraw only the *AD–AS* graph (one figure) reflecting the. stipulated reflation. Superimpose the result of the proposed policy on that graph, and lay bare the real problem of the economic situation. Show the results of the proposed policy and discuss its feasibility, advantages, shortcomings.

Suggested Readings

A. P. Lerner, "Functional Finance and the Federal Debt," *Social Research,* 10 (February 1943), 38–51.

R. A. Musgrave, "Principles of Budget Determination," in *Federal Expenditure Policies for Economic Growth and Stability,* Joint Economic Committee, pp. 108–115.

A. Smithies, "The Balanced Budget," *The American Economic Review,* L (1960), 301–309.

D. J. Smith, "Built-in Flexibility of Taxation and Automatic Stabilization," *Journal of Political Economy,* LXXIV (1966), 396–400.

Council of Economic Advisors, "The Full-Employment Surplus," in *January 1962 Economic Report of the President,* pp. 77–84.

Council of Economic Advisors, "Fiscal Policy in Perspective," in *January 1963 Economic Report of the President,* pp. 66–83.

11 Monetary Policies

By definition, monetary policies affect the economy through changes in the money supply. In particular, an increase in the supply of money stimulates our nation's aggregate demand, while a decrease destimulates it. In the preceding chapter we saw that the government has at its disposal an impressive array of fiscal policy tools. Why then bother about monetary policy? Would it not be better to stick to one kind of remedy?

There are two important reasons for having and using monetary policies. The first has to do with the clumsiness of fiscal policies. Insofar as changes in taxes are concerned, fiscal policy actions are hopelessly slow: slow in being put into operation, since it literally takes an Act of Congress to change the tax structure, and slow in working themselves out in the economy once they are implemented.

Except for the fact that Congress has set a ceiling on the public debt, deficit spending or changes in its rate do not require an Act of Congress as do changes in tax rates. This in itself is an interesting phenomenon. It implies that the jealously guarded purse strings held by Congress are made of rubber: They give a little, if pulled. Since this is not a treatise on political science, no value judgment is expressed or implied. More will be said regarding the size of our public debt in Chapter 12. Another problem with deficit spending as a fiscal policy tool is that it is a residual factor: Its exact magnitude is not known until some time after the relevant period under consideration; thus, it has a built-in recognition lag.

Moreover, fiscal policy tools lack the discretion that is often needed for policy purposes. Suppose, for example, that the government wishes to stimulate business investment, and through it *AD,* by granting investment tax credits, coupled with an increase in deficit spending. While the proposed tax legislation is being discussed, the business sector will hold back investment pending the outcome of the legislative process, the exact opposite of what is deemed desirable by the administration. One way to partially offset this legislative "announcement effect" is to make the law retroactive to the date when such legislation was first proposed.

We said above that there are two reasons for wanting to have monetary policies, the first having to do with the clumsiness of fiscal policies; the second reason is, perhaps, more basic but nevertheless very important: Monetary policies are administered by an autonomous agency, the Federal Reserve System, which has been given extraordinary discretionary powers to achieve its stated goal of full employment, stable price levels, and assured economic growth. By being administered autonomously, monetary policy actions are removed from the political scene, that is, they are not motivated by political considerations.

A. Stimulating a Depressed Economy

The Federal Reserve System of the United States is empowered to increase or reduce this country's money supply. The methods whereby this may be accomplished, the mechanics of money, are a bit complicated. To introduce them at this point in the game would force us to unnecessarily digress and to confuse the reader with a number of institutional idiosyncrasies which are important, to be sure, but not required for an understanding of monetary policies within the framework of our model. Ultimately, the reader will need to know the mechanics of money; in fact, a great portion of Part 4 is devoted to the topic. For the time being, however, what needs to be known for a meaningful discussion of monetary policies is only the fact that the Fed can increase or decrease the money supply in this country. Since additional money is placed into the hands of the public through a series of credit transactions, an increase in the money supply is necessarily accompanied by an increase in the supply of credit. This also holds true in reverse; i.e., a decrease in the supply of money involves a decrease in credit supply. The reader will be asked to accept this proposition on faith until in Part 4 these and other institutional arrangements will be explained in some detail.

Suppose we are again confronted by a depressed economy as shown in Figure 11-1. As in the preceding chapter, let us assume that the economy is currently operating at Points *D,* where production is below capacity to the tune of $50 billion per year and unemployment is the order of the day. The recession in our economy, we will remember, was the result of a decline in *AD.* Suppose, now, that the Federal Reserve System wishes to bring the *AD* back to the full-employment level designated by Points *A.* The Fed will do this by

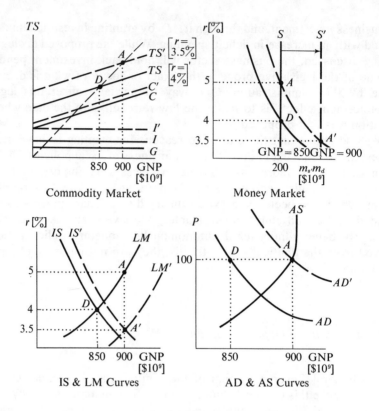

*Figure 11-1   Stimulating a Depressed
Economy by Monetary Policies*

Sequence of Events:

An increase in the supply of money $\Rightarrow C \uparrow$ and credit supply $\uparrow$.

Direct effect: $C \uparrow \Rightarrow TS \uparrow$.

Moreover, as supply of credit $\uparrow$, while demand for credit unchanged, $r \downarrow$.

Indirect effect through $r \downarrow : C \uparrow$ and $I \uparrow$.

Overall result: $m \uparrow \Rightarrow C \uparrow$ and $I \uparrow \Rightarrow TS \uparrow$ and $r \downarrow$ and,
ultimately, $AD \uparrow$.

increasing the supply of money. For simplicity we will assume that the Federal Reserve System miraculously knows the exact amount of additional money
required to produce full employment and that it increases the money stock in
this country by just this amount.

Figure 11–1 depicts the sequence of events induced by an increase in the
supply of money. This is shown in the money market by a rightward shift of the
exogenous money-supply curve to the dashed S' curve. The nation as a whole
is wealthier when its money stock is increased. As is true for any increase in
wealth, be it in the form of income or of a stock of accumulated wealth, an

increase in the money stock will stimulate consumer spending. See equation 7–4 on page 81 for a review of our previous discussion on the subject.

When a nation experiences an increase in wealth, it wishes to consume more of both present and future goods. As we have seen in Chapter 8, the consumption of future goods can be achieved by nonconsumption in the present, i.e., by saving or supplying credit. Thus, the increase of a nation's wealth due to an increase in the supply of money has two effects: It stimulates present consumption and increases the supply of credit, thereby reinforcing the previously mentioned increase in the supply of credit that is brought about by the institutional money-credit link. Thus, expansionary monetary policies, the so-called easy-money policies, work through a simultaneous expansion of money and credit. Again, this will be discussed in detail in Part 4.

The first effect of expansionary money policies, stimulation of consumer spending, has a direct bearing upon the level of increased total spending. The second effect, the increase in the supply of credit, will create an excess supply of loanable funds. In the first instance, the fact that more loanable funds are offered, in the money market and in the credit market, than are sought at the prevailing rate of interest will cause the rate of interest to fall; this in turn will stimulate both investment and consumer demand. The overall result, then, is as follows: An increase in the money supply by policy action on the part of the Fed will stimulate both consumption and investment and, therefore, the level of total spending; moreover, the rate of interest will be reduced.

In the money market in Figure 11–1, the new full-employment GNP of $900 billion causes the money-demand curve to shift to the right; i.e., for any given rate of interest, the greater the GNP the greater will be the nation's required money stock. Consistent with the previously mentioned fall in the rate of interest, the money-market equilibrium in Figure 11–1 is obtained at Point A'.

With our *IS* and *LM* analysis, the creation of additional money causes both the *IS* curve and the *LM* curve to be shifted to the right. The new point of intersection is characterized by a lower rate of interest, again due to the creation of additional loanable funds in both the money and credit markets. Point A' on the *IS* and *LM* graph corresponds to Point A in the last panel of Figure 11–1. At Point A, the *AD* has been shifted up. However, the original pre-recession rate of interest at full employment, which used to be 5% (Figure 9–1, page 121), has now been reduced to 3.5%. As always, that rate of interest changes with the price level along the AD' curve.

B. Anti-Inflationary Monetary Policy Actions

If inflation is plaguing the economy, monetary policies can be implemented to reduce *AD* and thereby to relieve the upward pressure on the price level—

the exact reverse of the stimulating policies described in the preceding section. Let us briefly describe the chain of events that will take place as a result of anti-inflationary monetary policy actions.

The strategy of such anti-inflationary policies aims at reducing the money supply, which will directly reduce consumption spending. Moreover, loanable funds now become scarce in both the money and credit markets and, as a result, they will command a premium: The rate of interest rises. This will further reduce consumption. At the same time, the increased rate of interest will discourage investment. With both consumption and investment expenditures reduced, total spending and, ultimately, AD will decline.

In the *IS* and *LM* analysis, we have a leftward shift of both the *IS* and *LM* curves, such that the new point of intersection corresponds to an increased rate of interest. This implies a downward shift of the *AD* curve in the *AD* and *AS* apparatus of our model.

A Practical Note on Monetary and Fiscal Policies

There is one question that an irreverent student occasionally asks a teacher in economics, and when he does the teacher is hard put to find the answer. The question is, of course: If you know so much about economics, how come you are not rich? At this point, you may wish to ask a similar question in regard to monetary and fiscal policies: If we know so much about how to regulate the economy, how come we still have inflations and recessions? How come we can have both an inflation and a recession at the same time?

The answer to this is twofold: Part of the trouble is that our knowledge is limited, that there *are* things that escape us, notably lags and the actual quantification of multipliers; and part of the trouble is that we know some of the reasons, but we are powerless to do anything about them through monetary or fiscal policy actions. Let us expand a bit on the lag problem we have previously touched on.

Lags

We will assume for the present discussion that the economy has been recognized as being in a recession: The administration, the Congress, the Federal Reserve System, the people at large, even the economists, agree that the current rate of unemployment is great enough to warrant corrective policy action, and that the recession was brought about by insufficient AD.[1] Such a unison of opinion is, in fact, a heroic assumption. The usual state of affairs is that a slight increase in unemployment will trigger a great debate among the experts. Some will contend that this is a temporary disequilibrium situation that will correct itself shortly, others will warn that this is the beginning of a severe recession. In such a case, what are the responsible authorities to do?

Suppose our authorities go along with the pessimistic economists. In that case, the authorities will undoubtedly initiate corrective policy actions, fiscal, monetary, or both. If the pessimistic economists were right in their assessment of the economy's performance, then the authorities will be successful in easing the unemployment situation. But suppose the pessimistic economists were wrong; that is, the decrease in unemployment was really a temporary phenomenon, and the economy was already on the road to recovery when the corrective policy action was implemented. In that case, the authorities will be guilty of overreacting: The well-intended policy action will stimulate the economy past the full-employment position smack into an inflation.

Rather than espousing the cause of the pessimistic economists, the responsible authorities might opt to lend credence to their optimistic colleagues. Believing that the disturbance is temporary and self-correcting, the authorities will refrain from taking any policy action. If this assessment of the current situation is correct, to have refrained from any policy action will be successful. But what if the assessment was wrong? In that case, failure to take corrective action might well further deteriorate employment and the nation may be plunged into a deep depression. Thus, the unpleasant alternatives in being wrong are either overreaction and inflation or an aggravated depression. Between these two extremes, the responsible authorities must try to find the middle road.

Let us go back to our initial assumption, namely that the economy is in a slight recession, that everybody agrees that a recession is, in fact, plaguing the land, and that corrective policy action becomes necessary. Suppose it has been decided to take such action. The question is then how much time will elapse until the effects of that policy action are felt in the economy. There are two different lags that come into play.

The first lag is the amount of time that passes between the decision to initiate corrective action and its implementation. In the case of fiscal policy actions, a change in tax rates may be deemed desirable by the administration. Since such a change in tax rates requires legislative sanction, implementation may be long in coming. In fact, it may never come, especially if a Republican President faces a predominantly Democratic Congress, or vice versa. Again, we are bumping up against political issues, but so is economic reality.

Suppose the administration chooses to stimulate the economy by increas-

---

[1]The public debate usually focuses on the rate of unemployment, rather than the more relevant GNP or National Income. Since an increase in unemployment implies a reduction in GNP or NI, the use of unemployment as a proxy for the nation's economic performance is not without merit.

ing government spending, and, further, that the government wishes to finance the resulting deficit by borrowing from the public (by selling bonds). Because this policy action falls within the discretionary powers of the administration, the delay before implementation is minimal. Similarly, Federal Reserve action can be quickly implemented if the need arises, since monetary policy measures can be taken at its discretion.

The second lag is the period of time between implementation of corrective measures and the point when the chain of economic reactions has run its course. Consider, for example, a cut in income taxes coupled with the sale of bonds such that government spending will be maintained. Suppose the law that enacted the tax cut instructs employers to reduce tax withholdings accordingly. This will increase the disposable income of people almost immediately, but whether it will also increase consumption spending right away is not clear. That depends on the people's expectations concerning the future. If people are apprehensive about the future, they may well prefer to save the greater part of the increase in disposable income, thereby negating the intent of the policy action. Thus, even though the increased income may be in the hands of the public in a reasonably short time, the hoped-for stimulation of *AD* may be slow in coming.

Bonds may be sold, on the other hand, without delay. But that is only half the story of deficit spending. If, as in the preceding case, the bonds are sold merely to make up for lost tax receipts, there is practically no delay in putting the loan to work. But suppose the bonds were sold in order to finance an increase in government spending. A considerable lag will occur until such a new spending program is implemented. If the government wishes to place additional employees on its payroll, a series of civil service examinations will retard new employment. If the government wishes to speed up military procurement, the letting, evaluation, and awarding of bids is time-consuming.

The Federal Reserve System can initiate monetary policies within hours if the need arises, but, as we will see in Part 4, expansion of the existing money stock requires many rounds of transactions throughout the economy, and that may take a considerable amount of time. If, on the other hand, the Fed wishes to reduce the money supply, the banks are under pressure to quickly contract their holdings of demand deposits by the required margin. Thus, a reduction in the supply of money can be achieved with relative speed.

Unfortunately, the two lags we have discussed up to this point are not the only ones in existence. In addition to the period of time that elapses between (1) recognition of the problem and implementation of corrective action and (2) implementation of corrective action and achievement of the hoped-for results, there exists the problem of first recognizing the existence of an economic disequilibrium position.

When an economy is headed into a recession, the course of events tends to gather momentum: As people begin to be laid off, the business community will be somewhat more reluctant to invest in new plants and equipment; investment spending will decline as firms take defensive measures. At the same time, those who remain employed will become apprehensive about their job security and will reduce consumption and increase savings for the rainy days ahead. But a reduction of consumption spending brings about a contraction in sales and a build-up of inventories. If such a state of affairs persists over some length of time, firms have no choice but to cut back production and investment even more, laying off more people in the process. This, in turn, will cause consumers to further tighten their belts, thereby starting an additional round of sales declines, etc., etc. We are faced with a vicious spiral which, if unchecked, will plunge the nation into a deep depression.

Obviously, the earlier a recession can be detected, the sooner can corrective measures be initiated: Fewer people will be unemployed and less output will be permanently lost to the economy. One way of keeping track of a nation's economic performance is by watching the ups and downs of so-called indicators. Some of these constitute an early-warning system, the leading indicators, so called because they turn up or down months ahead of a general upward or downward swing of the economy at large. New orders of durable goods, change in inventories, new business formation, plant and equipment orders, and composite stock prices are among such leading indicators.

Unfortunately, these indicators do not always move in the same direction. At any given time, some will indicate that the economy is expansionary, others will indicate the contrary, and still others will indicate no change in economic performance. A considerable amount of experience and personal judgment is required to make a meaningful interpretation of these data. This is where economists can normally be expected to disagree. The actual application of the policy tools, once a depression has been identified, is less controversial. But the recognition that a depression is developing or already existing in a mild form is, and always will be, highly controversial. Thus we have a third lag, namely the period of time that must necessarily elapse between the initial downturn of a business cycle and recognition of that fact by the relevant monetary or fiscal authorities.

Quantification of Policies

Economic theory is full of so-called multipliers. There are the money multiplier and the Keynesian multiplier, for example. As we will see in Part 4, the money multiplier refers to the ability of each added reserve dollar to add several dollars to the existing stock of money. But how many? The answer is, no one knows. The upper limit of the money multiplier is usually well defined, but it is probably never reached.

The Keynesian multiplier gives recognition to the fact that each dollar that is invested at conditions of under-capacity production will give rise to an increase in total output worth several dollars. Again, while no economist today seriously questions the existence of this multiplier, no one has been able to quantify it with precision. More will be said on the Keynesian multiplier in Chapter 13.

In discussing monetary and fiscal policies, we assumed that the responsible authorities knew by how much AD had to be raised to stimulate the economy to return to the full-employment level. There it was pointed out, however, that we used the 20/20 hindsight approach. We posed the following question: Suppose we know by how much AD has to be raised, and by how much the monetary and fiscal policy under discussion will under appropriate conditions raise the AD, how do these policies work? The truth is, we do not know how much money, for example, needs to be injected to raise the AD a given amount, nor by how much a given increase in AD will raise total output. Our 20/20 hindsight approach was merely a convenient expository device that allowed us to center our attention on the mechanics of monetary and fiscal policy actions.

Of course, the government is not totally without precedent in its anti-depression policies. The type of policy action and the required order of magnitude are by and large known; what is not known is the exact quantity of antidote needed to reach full employment. In fact, we have pointed out previously that the term full employment is itself less than well defined. Like the *homo oeconomicus* or the principle of profit maximization, the term full employment is nothing but a sweeping generalization. It is a not-very-precise but highly convenient concept without which a meaningful discussion of macroeconomic theory is impossible.

The advent of computers has contributed a great deal toward the quantification of policy actions. The main impact of these machines has been to facilitate the handling of a great number of variables. Still, it is doubtful that computers can give precise answers to patently imprecise questions. It is doubtful that computers can quantify the psychology of a people, and nothing less is involved: The marginal propensity to consume, expectations, patriotism, the love and the hate of people all affect their economic behavior. As long as they do, economics will remain an inexact science.

This is not to say that computers are not useful in economics. Of course they are: Anything we can handle computers can handle better, and some things we cannot handle they can. But some of the things we cannot do they cannot do either, only they do not always know it. The danger lies not in the use of computers per se but in the supreme confidence with which we are handed machine-calculated results that may or may not be correct.

Problems

1. Analytically explain anti-recession monetary policies. Use a geometric presentation to clarify your reasoning.

Note: You are *not* asked to elaborate the mechanics of money expansion. Instead, you are asked to explain what happens when (no matter how) the supply of money is increased.

2. Analytically explain anti-inflation monetary policies. Use a geometric presentation to clarify your reasoning.

3. In mid-1971, when unemployment was running at near 6% of the labor force, and the price level was rising at about 6% per year, the executive branch of our government, in a slowly evolving dispute with the Federal Reserve System, was reported to be in favor of an easy-money policy.

    As a citizen committed to neither side of the dispute, analyze the effects of such an easy-money policy.

Hint: If you can, verbalize the entire process, but it would help if you used the following geometric procedure.

a. Assume a pure recession due to insufficient aggregate demand. Graphically show, and discuss, the effect of the proposed policy upon the final GNP. I am talking about the four-panel figure (commodity market, money market, *IS–LM, AD–AS*).

b. Having gone through the mechanics for a pure recession, redraw just the *AD–AS* graph (one figure) reflecting the stipulated reflation. Superimpose the result of the proposed policy on that graph, and lay bare the real problem of the economic situation. Show the results of the proposed policy and discuss its feasibility, advantages, shortcomings.

4. It is sometimes proposed that monetary and fiscal policies ought to be used in combination: fiscal policies to prevent major fluctuations in GNP, and monetary policies for "fine-tuning." Comment on the feasibility, advantages, shortcomings of such an approach.

Suggested Readings

M. Friedman, "A Monetary and Fiscal Framework for Economic Stability," *The American Economic Review*, 38 (June 1948), 245–264.

M. Friedman, *A Program for Monetary Stability* (New York: Fordham University Press, 1960).

G. Horwich, "A Framework for Monetary Policy," in K. Brunner, ed., *Targets and Indicators of Monetary Policy* (San Francisco: Chandler Publishing Co., 1969), pp. 124–164.

D. E. W. Laidler, *The Demand for Money: Theories and Evidence* (Scranton, Pennsylvania: International Textbook Company, 1970).

B. P. Pesek and T. R. Saving, *The Foundations of Money and Banking* (New York: The Macmillan Company, 1968), Chapter 24.

J. Tobin, "Monetary Semantics," in K. Brunner, ed., *Targets and Indicators of Monetary Policy* (San Francisco: Chandler Publishing Co., 1969), pp. 165–174.

12 Current Macroeconomic Issues

It was pointed out in the preceding chapter that there are some things that our model fails to capture, notably lags and the quantification of multipliers. But this is only part of the reason why we cannot always hold the economy on an even keel. In addition to this lack of knowledge in the application of corrective policies, there is one area where knowledge is present but the corrective tool missing, where the government is powerless to remedy the situation even though the reasons for the disturbance are well understood. We are referring to the concept of cost-push inflation. Some inflation of this kind coupled with a mild recession can very well result in that very inconvenient and hotly disputed phenomenon, an inflationary recession, where unemployment plagues the nation while prices continue to rise.

Demand-Pull, Cost-Push Inflation

By way of introduction let us look first at the so-called demand-pull inflation. Suppose that the people in this country consume so many gallons of milk each day at a given average retail price of $1.00 per gallon. Suppose, now, that the demand for milk suddenly rises; that is, at the price of $1.00 per gallon, people wish to consume more milk. The increase in demand may have a variety of causes: more people, higher incomes, distribution of free milk to the poor, etc. In a free market, the demand pressures will make their way to the produc-

157

tive origin. Faced by insufficient supplies, the grocers will place larger orders with the dairy wholesalers who, in turn, will place larger orders with the dairy farmers. In order to obtain the increase in the quantity of milk that is demanded, through their grocers, by the consuming public, the dairy wholesalers will bid up the price. In the short run, the farmers will obtain a rent, a larger-than-normal profit if you wish, on the production of milk. But in the long run, as they step up their production of milk either by running more cows on the given pasture land or by using less-desirable pasture land for dairy purposes, their costs will rise and the rent will ultimately disappear. Nevertheless, it was the increase in the demand for milk that caused the price of milk to rise.

The wholesalers, having bid up the price of milk in order to satisfy the increase in demand for it, will pass on the incremental cost to the grocers. The grocers, who had nothing to do with the pricing process at the dairy, will view this as an increase in cost pure and simple, to be passed on to consumers. Chances are, the grocer does not know that the cost increase was caused by the increase in demand by his customers. Nor would this explanation sound very convincing to the irate housewife, but the fact is that this is one, though not the only, factor in a price increase. A geometric presentation of demand-pull inflation is given in Figure 12–1.

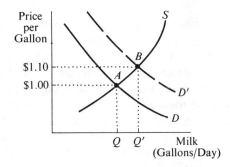

Figure 12–1   Demand-Pull Inflation

Given the familiar demand-and-supply apparatus of Figure 12–1, the initial equilibrium condition is defined by Point *A*. At a milk price of $1.00 per gallon, a given quantity *Q* is sold and consumed each day. As the demand for milk rises from *D* to the dashed *D'* curve, the equilibrium quantity of milk rises to *Q'* and the price rises to $1.10 per gallon, Point *B*. Thus, it is said that the increase in demand pulled up the price (and the quantity sold) of milk: demand-pull inflation.

On the macroeconomic scale, an increase in *AD* is inflationary, i.e., pulls up the price level, while a decrease in *AD* causes unemployment. The monetary and fiscal policies we have discussed all work through the *AD* curve. That is, governmental policies designed to minimize business cycle fluctuations aim at stimulating the *AD* in the case of a recession or at reducing *AD* in the opposite case of an inflation. But demand is only half of the demand and supply apparatus. What about shifts of the supply curve? Leftward shifts of the supply curve give rise to the so-called cost-push inflation.

Let us again begin on the microeconomic level. Suppose our dairy industry sells a given quantity, *Q*, of milk per day at a price of $1.00 per unit, Point *A*. Let the demand for milk remain the same while the supply of milk falls. This is indicated by the leftward shift of the supply curve from *S* to *S'* in Figure 12–2. The new equilibrium position is at Point *B*, where output has decreased and the price of milk has risen to $1.10 per gallon.

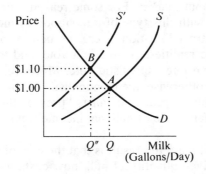

Figure 12–2   Cost-Push Inflation

The leftward shift of the supply curve may have one of two causes, each one hotly disputed by the relevant economic unit.

1. The retail industry may turn from a competitive to a monopolistic market structure. In a pure monopoly it is true that there is no supply curve. The profit-maximizing monopolist finds that output and price combination at which his profits are maximized or losses minimized. Having found that level of output, he will not vary it ever.

    But there is no such thing as a black-and-white economy. Our pure monopoly, which among other things abstracts from the realities of space and distance, is a fiction, a very useful one, to be sure, but a fiction nevertheless. Moreover, if there were such a thing as an overt monopoly preying on, of all things, milk-consuming widows and infants, antitrust litigation would be initiated at once.

But, then, neither is there such a thing as perfect competition, where economic profit is exactly zero, entry is totally unconstrained, and perfect knowledge is the order of the day. Between the two extremes, pure monopoly and perfect competition, we find our real-life firms and industries. A move away from competitive market structures will cause the industry's supply curve to shift to the left.

2. Suppose that our dairy retail industry is, by and large, overwhelmingly competitive. Let us assume, on the other hand, that the dairy farmers believe that they fail to get a fair share of the national income. Suppose further that they all combine into a huge cooperative and press for an increase in income, threatening to go on strike (spill the milk) unless their demands are met.

Our otherwise competitive dairy industry is now faced by a monopolistic input market. For some reason, our legal setup is not geared to deal with this type of a monopoly, which therefore is not subject to antitrust litigation. Here, as before, political issues obscure economic realities. A vote is a vote, and ten dairy votes are worth more than one capitalistic vote. Moreover, be it for reasons of solidarity or otherwise, the monopolistic factor market has always had greater public appeal. Capitalists "prey on their victims," workers ask for a "fair share of national income"; both do this by raising prices.

Be this as it may, the result is that the cost of milk production is increased. A given quantity of milk now costs more to produce or, what is the same thing, for a given price less milk will be produced. That is, the milk-supply curve in Figure 12–2 is shifted to the left. In this case, the increase in the price of milk is not the result of an increase in demand. Rather, the increase in the cost of producing milk takes the form of higher incomes to dairy farmers. This increase in cost is said to have pushed up the price: cost-push inflation.

In macroeconomic terms, Point *B* in Figure 12–2 is the result of cost-push inflation: The reduction of the aggregate supply causes total output to fall while the price level rises. Since monetary and fiscal policies can affect only the aggregate demand, the cost-push type of economic affliction has no known remedy. Ideally, of course, a perfectly perfect state of perfect competition, both in the commodity market and in the factor market, would not allow a leftward shift of the aggregate supply curve. Unfortunately, as we pointed out earlier, competition is less than perfect, and to the extent that it is, a leftward shift of the aggregate supply curve is a distinct possibility and, moreover, an economic reality.

In real life we encounter varied mixtures of demand-pull and cost-push forces. This we know. What we don't know is to what extent a given inflationary situation is caused by the one or the other force. Suppose we know that a recent price-level increase was primarily the result of demand-pull forces. A policy action designed to reduce the *AD* would be the correct remedy. In monetary policy, this would entail a reduction of the money supply. In fiscal policies, a reduction of government spending accompanied by either a reduction in borrowing or the accumulation of budgetary surpluses would reduce the *AD*. Similarly, imposing a corporate or income tax while holding government spending at the same level would cause a decline in *AD*. Since the assumed price-level increase was the result of demand-pull forces, any one of the preceding remedies would work.

Suppose, however, the price-level increase was a pure form of cost-push inflation, as indicated in Figure 12–3. Let Point *A* in this figure correspond to

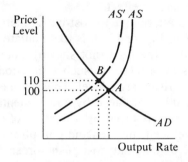

*Figure 12–3   Cost-Push and
Economic Policies*

the initial full-employment equilibrium. Suppose that the aggregate supply is shifted leftward from the solid *AS* curve to the dashed *AS'* curve. As a result, the price will rise and output will fall as indicated by Point *B*. Unemployment will prevail in the country. If the responsible authorities did not recognize the source of their troubles, they might be tempted to combat the "inflationary" price-level increase by reducing *AD*. The result would be a fall in the price level, but at the cost of greater unemployment. That is, a leftward shift of the *AD* curve (not shown) would fail to bring the hoped-for results.

The government, of course, knows all that: After all, the price level is not the only indicator it keeps tabs on; in particular, unemployment is itself a closely watched indicator. Suppose, then, the government wishes to take corrective action after our economy has reached the unemployment-inflation position of Point *B* in Figure 12–3. If the leftward shift of the *AS'* curve is due to monopolistic behavior in the commodity market, antitrust litigation will tend to shift the curve back to the right with the result that for a given level of output the cost to the buyer (the price level) is reduced.[1] This is, of course, a continuous process rather than a one-time policy objective, a process that is performed with more or less vigor, depending upon many, including political, factors. Many claims and counterclaims have been voiced regarding the theoretical relevance as well as the effectiveness of antitrust policies. On effectiveness, empirical evidence is scant and room is left for debate, but no room is left for debate regarding the theoretical relevance of antitrust policies. They will increase aggregate supply, or at least they will keep it from being reduced.

If the leftward shift of the dashed AS' curve in Figure 12–3 is the result of monopolistic behavior in the factor market, there is very little the government can do about it. Cartels in the labor market are not subject to antitrust laws.[2] Cooling-off periods and nonbinding arbitration are the only medicine at the disposal of the government. These are chiefly one-time tranquilizers, they wear off quickly and have no lasting effect.

Thus, the unpleasant alternative to cost-push inflation and unemployment, represented by Point B in Figure 12–3, is to stimulate aggregate demand. As the AD curve is shifted to the right (not shown), unemployment is reduced, but the price level rises even more. In such a situation, full employment will necessarily bring about a rising price level. This is the essence of the inflation-versus-full-employment dilemma faced by governmental authorities.

In real life, an economy is faced by a mixture of cost-push and demand-pull forces. As we have seen, the demand-pull portion can be handled with moderate ease. To the extent that cost-push forces assert themselves, the government is at best inefficient, at worst helpless, depending on the name of the culprit. Needless to say, the capitalist points his finger at labor, and labor

---

[1] To give one somewhat extreme example: After antitrust litigation in 1962, the cost of 100 capsules of the antibiotic tetracycline dropped from \$30.60 to \$4.25 (from testimony presented by R. W. McLaren, then Assistant Attorney General, Antitrust Division, Department of Justice, before the Joint Economic Committee, *The 1970 Midyear Review of the State of the Economy,* Part 1, p. 146).

[2] Nor are they very likely to be made subject to antitrust laws. This feeling is reflected by the following testimony by R. W. McLaren (M, see footnote 1) to the Joint Economic Committee, Senator Proxmire (P) questioning:

   M: Labor Relations are not under the antitrust laws, they are under their own set of labor-management relations.

   P: Yes.

   M: And I think that is appropriate.

   P: I agree.

   M: They shouldn't be under the antitrust laws. . . . Personally, I think there is something very wrong about the Congress having to step in and pass a special statute to settle a railroad labor dispute. I think there is something wrong about a handful of people being able to tie up the whole harbor of New York City, of a relatively small union tying up all trucking in Chicago. I think that in the interests of the public we need to study the situation further. I don't think it is right for labor, I don't think it is right for business, and I think it is very very wrong for the public.

   P: I think it is good to study it. . . . Frankly, I don't want to break up labor unions, and I don't think you do either.

   M: I don't.

The 1970 Midyear Review of the State of the Economy, Part 1, pp. 167 and 168.

accuses the capitalist. Chances are, both are partially correct. In any event, many economists have come to agree, and so have many noneconomists on a more intuitive basis, that full employment can only be had at the cost of inflation. As we now know, this is true to the extent that cost-push forces are active.

The Wage-Price Spiral

A one-time increase in the price level shown in Figure 12–3 is by no means the end of the story. Suppose our economy experiences a leftward shift of the *AS* curve, as shown by Point *B* in Figure 12–4. To facilitate the discussion, let us assume that this shift is induced by labor-related cost-push forces. If the

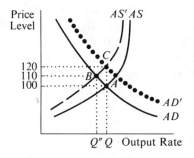

Figure 12–4   The Wage-Price Spiral

reader prefers, he may replace the word labor by capitalist in what follows; the sequence of events will be essentially the same.

Starting at the full-employment equilibrium position denoted by Point *A* in Figure 12–4, the leftward shift of the solid *AS* curve to *AS'* leads to the now-familiar disequilibrium position *B*, where unemployment exists, while the price level rises. Suppose now that the government decides to swallow the bitter pill and to reestablish full employment by increasing aggregate demand, i.e., to move the *AD* curve to the dotted *AD'* curve so that it intersects the *AS'* curve at the full-employment output *Q*. The result of such a move, as we have seen before, causes the price level to rise, say, from 110 at Point *B* to 120 at Point *C*. If this were a one-time phenomenon, there would be no ground for concern. But it is not a one-time remedy. At Point *C*, the gains in income that accrued to labor are diluted by the higher price level. Labor did not get what it wanted. The answer is, of course, to try again. What labor can do once, it can certainly do twice. Thus, the aggregate supply curve is shifted one more time (not shown), causing total output to fall again and the price level to rise further. If the government is committed to a policy of full employment, its response will be a further upward shift of the aggregate demand curve, raising the price level even more.

Rather than having one sector, labor or the capitalists, push the *AS* curve to the left, both may do this alternatively, thus playing a game of tug of war against the government. Suppose labor has succeeded in obtaining higher wages, thereby pushing the *AS* curve to the left, Point *B* in Figure 12–4. Suppose the capitalists wish to regain the loss this move has brought to them. The remedy is to raise prices over and above the labor-induced cost increase. This will shift the aggregate supply curve even further to the left. The price level is now under a double attack. The government, wanting to reestablish full employment, will raise it and so will labor, wanting to recoup the losses it incurred by the capitalist-induced price increase. This game can be played over many rounds. The primary loser is neither the capitalist nor organized labor. It is that sector of the economy that has to live on fixed incomes, normally the poorer sector in the economy, the one that can least afford to lose. However, that sector is not totally without recourse: It represents a substantial number of votes which, if sufficiently aroused, may be cast as one block. (But, again, we have slipped out of the area of pure economics.)

Empirical Evidence on Cost-Push Inflation

We have stressed the point throughout Part 3 that monetary and fiscal policies work solely through the *AD* side. These policies, then, are only effective in combating inflations or recessions that originate with the *AD* side. In fact, we were careful to develop an unemployment situation in Chapter 9 that resulted from a decline in consumer spending. That kind of a recession can be brought to an end by means of fiscal policies (Chapter 10) or monetary policies (Chapter 11) or a combination of these. But if cost-push forces assert themselves in an economy, monetary and fiscal policies are totally ineffective. Unemployment can be reduced in such cases, but only at the expense of a substantial price-level increase. In fact, as we pointed out earlier in the book, this new creature called the recession-inflation, or reflation, is thrust upon us as a result of newly developing cost-push forces in the economy.

Cost-push forces, as we have seen, are forces that assert themselves on a nation's *AS* side. For example—and you may wish to refer to the last section in Chapter 6 to review the details of cartel-induced shifts of the *AS* curve—a move towards monopolistic input markets (labor cartels) or monopolistic output markets (management cartels) raises the price of a given quantity of output.

In the first case, labor cartels, the incremental money receipts flow to labor in the form of wage increases; in the second case, management cartels, they flow to capitalists in the form of excess profits. In recent years, labor, and in par-
. ticular organized labor, has been exerting its power more forcefully and more skillfully than ever before. The undeniable fact is that wage settlements greatly surpassing productivity increases and unparalleled in pre-1965 settlements have been the major cause of shifts in the *AS* curve. The fact that the first substantial inflationary recession occured in 1970 is not a coincidence. Rather, the reflation is the inevitable consequence of greater-than-productivity wage settlements. This is not to say that labor is the sole culprit in creating the reflation. But labor has played a more dominant role in its creation than any other sector in the economy. This is a very serious charge, but the record is clear. Let us, by way of an example, review some of the more sensational wage settlements that were made during the first nine months of 1970.

1. In March 1970, the federal government was hit by its first major walkout in this century. The postal strike, which affected over 20% of all organized postal workers, was ultimately settled by a 14% wage increase.
2. A new wage settlement with the Teamsters Union called for an upward revision in wages of $1.85 per hour over 39 months, about triple the wage settlement of the preceding three-year contract. The new contract contained other benefits, in particular a cost-of-living escalator.
3. The Rubber Workers settled for an 82 cents an hour wage boost, to be spread over three years.
4. The Automobile Workers, after a lengthy strike at General Motors, settled for a 51 cents an hour wage increase in the first year. An unlimited escalator was part of the settlement.
5. The Railroad Workers obtained a 13.5% wage increase in late 1970.
6. The Air Line Employees Association obtained a 33% wage increase spread over three years.

The U.S. Department of Labor, in its Handbook of Labor Statistics, maintains a record of wage changes in major collective bargaining situations. Part of the data shown there is reproduced here as Table 12–1. To bring out the abrupt changes in wage settlements that occurred after 1965, these data have also been plotted in Figure 12–5.

As can be seen from Figure 12–5, median wage increases in the pre-1965 period have fluctuated roughly between 3 and 4%. Starting in 1966, wage settlements began to climb. The steepest increase has been in nonmanufacturing industries, where the median wage settlement in 1970 was 14.2%.

Table 12-1
General Wage Changes in Major Collective
Bargaining Situations

Median Increase, First-Year Changes in Contracts (%)

Year	All Industries	Manufacturing	Selected Nonmanu-facturing Industries
1959	3.9	3.7	4.0
1960	3.2	3.2	3.3
1961	2.9	2.5	3.6
1962	3.6	2.9	4.1
1963	3.4	3.0	3.5
1964	3.2	2.2	3.6
1965	3.9	4.1	3.7
1966	4.5	4.2	5.0
1966*	4.8	4.2	5.0
1967	5.7	6.4	5.0
1968	7.2	6.9	7.5
1969	8.0	7.0	10.0
1970	10.0	7.5	14.2

* In 1966, the data were expanded to include additional nonmanufacturing industries (construction, finance, insurance, real estate, service industries).
Source: *Handbook of Labor Statistics 1970*, U.S. Department of Labor.

As a matter of interest, this manifestation of increasing labor power over the last few years does not occur exclusively in the United States. Rather, it is a well-noted international trend. For example, in April 1971, striking Ford workers in Great Britain accepted a 32% wage increase, spread over a period of two years. Similarly, wildcat strikes, heretofore unknown in Western Germany, made their appearance there in 1970 and have since become part of that country's economic life.

How can we best deal with these new forces in the economy? Monetary and fiscal policies, as we have seen, are totally ineffective in solving the problem. The answer, in the United States, has been to provide a lot of fireworks with little illumination. During the 1970 reflation, for example, the executive branch wished to pursue a liberal credit and money policy, but the Federal Reserve System refused to go along, pointing out that this would set up inflationary pressures, which is the last thing anyone wants during a reflation. The Fed talked about productivity, thereby hinting at the problem, but leaving the solu-

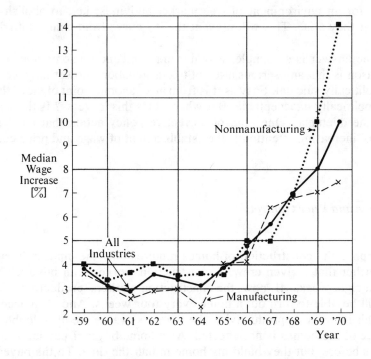

Figure 12–5   General Wage Changes,
Major Collective Bargaining Situations
Source: *Handbook of Labor Statistics 1970*, U.S. Department of Labor.

tion in the political arena.[3] The public generally was convinced that the problem lay with the government's deficit spending: It wanted less of it, to reduce inflationary pressures, but also more of it, to provide for full employment. In short, it was confused, a state of mind it shared with Congress.

Having looked at both the *AD* and *AS* side of our economy, we know that deficit spending (a fiscal policy) or an accelerated growth of the U.S. money stock are of limited effectiveness for the simple reason that they have no bearing on the *AS* curve. But if the problem has its roots on this nation's *AS* side, as it does with increasing severity, then corrective action is needed there. Economically speaking, the solution to the problem is disarmingly simple: to

[3] See, for example, Arthur F. Burns' testimony before the Joint Economic Committee, on February 19, 1971. The most easily accessible transcript of this statement is a reprint in the March 1971 issue of the *Federal Reserve Bulletin*, pp. 233–240. In his testimony, the Chairman of the Fed's Board of Governors pointed to the cost-push problem. Moreover, he quite candidly admitted the inability of monetary and fiscal policies to solve the "new problem."

provide for an environment of free market activities; i.e., to abolish cartels wherever they arise. This will prevent the *AS* curve from being shifted to the left.

If the answer is so simple, why doesn't someone do something about it? The reason is that any serious attempt to curtail labor's power may well prove to be politically suicidal. Easy as it is from an economic point of view, the solution is politically unacceptable. But where does this leave us? Is there no way out of the dilemma? One kind of corrective policy action that has been the center of increasing attention is the establishment of wage and price controls.[4]

Wage and Price Controls

Suppose the construction of homes requires only the input of labor. Suppose further that a given crew of construction workers can build a $30,000-home in eight weeks. If, now, the construction workers' productivity doubles, they will be able to turn out a home every four weeks. And if, in accordance with their increase in productivity, the workers' wages are also doubled, then the price of the homes is not affected. As a home buyer, I pay labor twice as much as before, but they build my home in half the time. To the buyer, then, the net effect is zero. This is the idea that lies behind the productivity concept of labor compensation. And the term wage control ordinarily refers to tying labor's wage increases to increases in productivity.

Price controls, on the other hand, are directed towards management. Their purpose is to prevent managers from developing monopolistic output markets. That is, price controls are intended to establish normal profit rates by preventing arbitrary upward adjustments of prices over and above costs (including normal profits).

Wage and price controls, then, are measures that are directed towards the *AS* side of an economy. Still, they find only lukewarm support among the majority of economists. The reason for this apparently contradictory phenomenon is that wage and price controls deal only with the symptoms of the problem, not its cause. But that in itself does not negate their effectiveness.

Some of the specific problems associated with such controls are:

Establishment of price controls requires freezing of *all* prices. If prices were frozen on selected goods only, with others free to rise, the industry producing fixed-price goods would soon be at a competitive disadvantage due to rising wages, thus causing output to contract and, perhaps, ultimately to disappear. But if all prices are frozen, the price mechanism is deprived of its most important function, that of allocating resources to the various outputs. The supply curve of each good would simply be its horizontal price line, and

---

[4]These have since been introduced in the U.S. economy.

changes in demand would not be reflected by price and quantity changes, as
in the case of a free interplay of supply and demand, but would simply bring
about changes in output at the fixed price. The allocation problems associated
with this approach are best discussed with the aid of a geometric presentation.

Suppose the normal supply and demand curves are as shown by the curves
labeled *S* and *D* in the two panels of Figure 12–6. By "normal" we mean here

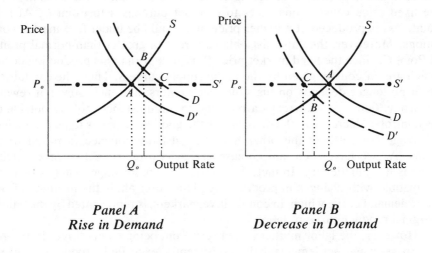

Panel A
Rise in Demand

Panel B
Decrease in Demand

Figure 12–6   Price Controls

what these curves would look like in the absence of price controls. If price
controls are established, the supply curves are shifted and assume the horizontal positions indicated by *S'*. These new pseudo-supply curves must, of
course, go through the initial equilibrium positions *A* if it is assumed that prices
are frozen at their given equilibrium levels.

If the demand for a good increases, panel *A* of Figure 12–6 shows the resulting sequence of events. In the absence of price controls, the new output
would be at Point *B:* In response to an increase in demand, both the output and
the price would rise. But with the price held at P_o, buyers will want to move to
Point *C*. At that output rate, however, production costs greatly exceed the
sales price. No manufacturer will be willing to supply that output. In fact,
at price P_o the most that will ever be supplied is Q_o below Point *A*. Thus an
increase in demand in the face of a fixed price will create a shortage of output.
Fewer goods will be produced than would be produced in a free market, causing fewer resources to be allocated to the production of these goods: This is
the concept of the misallocation of resources.

Moreover, at Point *A* the buyers are willing to pay considerably higher prices than the sellers are allowed to charge. The inevitable result would be the development of black markets to a greater or lesser extent, depending on the vigilance of the police and the severity of the courts. In fact, the creation of additional administrative and enforcement agencies to monitor the prices might in itself be viewed as a misallocation of resources, not to mention bribes and other costs of corruption that seem always to appear when large-scale government controls replace free-market forces.

Panel B in Figure 12–6 shows the sequence of events resulting from a decrease in demand. Instead of having output move to Point *B* with a fall in price, the fixed price causes consumers to contract purchases to Point *C*. At that point, less is produced at a higher price than would be under free-market conditions. Moreover, the capitalist obtains a rent (a greater-than-normal profit) at Point *C*, since the fixed market price P_0 is greater than his production costs, which are, of course, given by the initial supply curve *S*. Thus, the capitalist's profit no longer depends on his skill. Luck enters, and luck does not reward efficiency. Our capitalist reaps a rent due to circumstances totally outside of his control: a decrease in the demand for the good he happens to be producing.

Wage controls, on the other hand, are usually couched in productivity terms. As we have seen, an increase in wages proportional to productivity gains is not inflationary. In fact, free markets promote wage changes that are compatible with changes in productivity. This, after all, is the meaning of the labor-demand curve which, in competitive markets, is represented by the value-marginal-product curve of labor.

However, the labor market is a far cry from being competitive. In the recent past, wage settlements have consistently exceeded productivity gains and, therefore, these settlements have been inflationary. The resulting inflation is of the cost-push variety, not susceptible to manipulation by monetary or fiscal policy tools.

Actual measurements of productivity gains is a sticky subject. The investigating agency which would have to be created for this task (another misallocation of resources) would have to come up with productivity indices for thousands of different professions in various regions in the United States. This is a hopeless task. The alternative would be an across-the-board increase in wages tied to average increases in national productivity. Such a procedure, had it been instituted early enough, would have assured the survival and growth in compensation of the fireman on the diesel locomotive.

Let us illustrate by a specific example the resource-allocation problem that is inherent in price controls. Suppose Colombia, which is a major coffee producing and exporting country, is the sole supplier of coffee to the world market. In that market, it faces a definite demand structure, and the world price of coffee is determined by the interplay of demand and supply forces. But since, as a matter of fact, Colombia is highly specialized in the production of coffee, to the extent that over 90% of its exports are in coffee, that country's economy becomes very vulnerable to relatively small fluctuations in world coffee prices.

This may well give rise to a demand by Colombia that a world price stabilization board for coffee be set up. The function of such a board would be to purchase excess coffee rather than letting the coffee price deteriorate.

Suppose, now, that the people generally take a fancy to tea instead of coffee. This situation is depicted by panel B in Figure 12-6. The switch from coffee to tea is reflected by a leftward shift of the coffee-demand curve. In a free market system, the news of the change in consumption pattern is flashed to the producer: Less coffee is wanted, and as a result, less money will be paid for a given quantity of coffee. This would ordinarily cause the producer to cut back the production of coffee, Point B; but now our price stabilization board springs to life. In an attempt to prevent the price decline, it begins to buy up coffee. If, as a result of this activity, the coffee price is maintained at P_o, the consumers respond by buying even less than they would under free market conditions, Point C. The difference, namely quantity $(A-C)$, now goes into silos maintained by our board. Translated into noneconomic terms, this is the result of the price support policy: At the given price P_o, the consumers have put Colombia on notice that they will only buy the quantity given by Point C. Would Colombia please convert some of its coffee-producing land to the production of other goods? But no, the price stabilization board intercepts and perverts this message and, in effect, tells Colombia to merrily go on producing coffee, whether it is wanted or not. Colombia will happily comply, using some of its scarce resource, land, to produce coffee that nobody wants. Colombia, in this instance, is said to be misallocating its resources, which, we will remember, was caused by price controls.

Of course, the enforcement of domestic price controls does not necessitate the creation of price stabilization boards. The freezing of prices can be administered by a legislative process, coupled with an indispensible enforcement mechanism. Still, the application of such a system of price controls to an entire economy producing some 200,000 different goods and services gives rise to an enormous distortion of that economy's resource allocation. Initially, such a system may fairly well represent demand and supply patterns. But give the system a year or two, when significant shifts in demand have occurred, when people no longer want certain goods, when they want new goods that did not exist earlier, then the prices will be hopelessly out of tune and the nation's resources will be very seriously misallocated. Moreover, the introduction of price controls requires an administrative enforcement procedure which means, as it now does in various foreign countries, that government employees visit the various stores in the disguise of buyers, checking up on prices. Quite apart from the fact that the creation of this new bureaucracy in itself constitutes a misallocation of resources, this smacks of a police state, to say the least. It involves more government interference, when less is needed.

There has been a small but highly vocal group among economists who claim that prices are not really set by supply and demand forces, that the big bad corporations simply set their prices, and the public's preferences (demand) be damned. The public, by the way, has been lending increasing credence to this allegation. There exists a very simple one-word answer to this accusation, an answer involving a very, very big corporation, indeed. And that answer is: Edsel.

Let us summarize our argument to this point. Monetary and fiscal policies can only deal with demand-pull forces. To the extent that cost-push forces assert themselves with increasing severity in our economy, these policies are ineffective. To deal with cost-push forces, a return to free markets would be highly effective, but this solution is not politically feasible. Wage and price controls, on the other hand, introduce serious distortions in the economy. The following question now arises, a question that must ultimately be faced by this nation: given the fact that the abolition of cartels is politically unacceptable, would it not be better to institute a system of wage and price controls, rather than doing nothing? The science of economics does not have an answer to this question.

You may object and say that I have led you all the way into the heart of the problem, but now that you are there, I refuse to show you the way out. This is true, and I offer my apologies. The only thing I have to say in my defense is this: The alternative, for me to indicate a valid solution in the name of the science of economics, would be far worse than to confess my ignorance. There are economists who have offered "economic" solutions to inherently political problems, but the trouble is, these various solutions do not all agree and, in fact, contradict each other in part. It would be far more honest for economists who offer solutions to call them what they are, namely opinions. Generally—and this is what most economists will do—it is better for them to take up and analyze "solutions" that have been proposed by the political sector, to point out to that sector the economic effects of these solutions, and to leave the final decision to that sector. This is what I have done in discussing wage and price controls.

We mentioned earlier in the chapter that cost-push forces and demand-pull forces oftentimes assert themselves simultaneously in an economy. Having devoted a number of pages to the cost-push problem, we may well ask whether demand-pull forces have also been active in the late sixties and why. The answer to this question leads us to the problems of deficit spending and our national debt.

Our National Debt

When this nation came into being as an independent entity in 1789, it had an accumulated public debt of $77 million. Of this amount, something like $15 million were defaulted interest payments. In those days all debts, national, business, or personal, were viewed with suspicion: In the short run, having to go into debt was unfortunate; in the long run, i.e., to give the appearance of deliberately staying in debt, was downright immoral. Accordingly, this country's first Secretary-Treasurer, Alexander Hamilton, and his successors believed it to be their primary duty to eliminate the national debt. In this they succeeded some 45 years later. In 1835, for the first and only time, the United States found itself free of a national debt. In fact, the federal government was faced with budgetary surpluses which it set out to redistribute to the states. The idea of revenue sharing, as we can see, is not exactly a twentieth century invention.

The problem of how to dispose of budgetary surpluses soon solved itself. After 1835, the government, by and large, spent more than it received through taxation. The Mexican War increased our national debt by some $50 million. The point of no return, however, was the Civil War. Of its total cost of $3.5 billion, no less than $2.5 billion were raised by borrowing. The national debt at the end of the Civil War stood at $2.8 billion. Thus, it was the Civil War debt that brought about a change in the scale of measurement of our national debt. Before the war it was measured in millions of dollars; after the war that scale was too small, the national debt was measured in billions of dollars, and has been to this day.

By the end of World War I, our national debt stood at $25.4 billion. Significantly, the Great Depression "cost" almost exactly as much as World War I in deficit spending, causing the national debt to rise to $48.5 billion by 1940. After World War II, which cost an estimated $288 billion, most of which was debt-financed, our national debt stood at $280 billion (February 1946). The Korean War, the Vietnam War, and internal recessions all have contributed to continued deficit spending. Fiscal 1971, ending on June 30, 1971, saw the second largest peacetime deficit in U.S. history, a whopping $23.5 billion. The national debt by this time had risen to more than $410 billion.

Over the ten-year period from 1962 through 1971, the United States had incurred budgetary deficits nine times out of ten, raising the national debt during that period by some $80 billion. Certainly, in so doing, the government stimulated this nation's aggregate demand. It has often been said that wars are inflationary. As we pointed out earlier, that statement is ambiguous. But wars, historically, have always been financed, at least in part, by governmental deficit spending. And deficit spending, not a war in and of itself, does stimulate *AD*. Whether or not an increase in *AD* is inflationary depends on the nation's initial economic condition. For example, this country was still very much caught in the aftermath of the Great Depression when World War II broke out. Whatever one's personal view of that war may be, economically it did much to reactivate the U.S. economy.[5]

To come back to the question raised initially: Has the U.S. economy been subject to demand-pull forces during the sixties, and why? The answer should be clear by now: To the extent that this nation has engaged in heavy deficit

---

[5] If this statement sounds to you like an implicit justification of World War II on economic grounds, go back and read footnote 5 in Chapter 2. No war can ever be justified on economic grounds. If you can't see that, ask the family members of the men killed in action whether it was worth it. Again, the issue is subjective, not economic.

spending, demand-pull forces have played an active role in that decade. It was not exclusively labor, then, that contributed to the inflationary trend of the late sixties. Both demand-pull and cost-push forces were present, and on an unprecedented scale.[6] Still, the predominating influence was the cost-push phenomenon. After all, a simultaneous occurrence of inflation and recession *did* take place. If both the *AD* and the *AS* curves were shifted up, the very existence of a reflation can only mean that the *AS* curve was shifted up higher; i.e., that cost-push forces asserted themselves more vigorously.

Before we abandon this subject, a few words may be in order concerning the burden of the national debt. We are often reminded by public speakers and the press that the national debt represents a per capita burden of approximately $2000. While this is true, it is also misleading, since the statement implicitly conjures the image of our turning over to the government $2000 for every member in our family, probably by taxation. We would, if the government today felt about the national debt in the same way it did almost 200 years ago, that is, if the government were bent on extinguishing it. Suppose, however, the government has no intention to reduce or eliminate the national debt. In that case it is not the sum total of that debt, expressed as a stock variable, that interests us, but the annual cost to service that debt (a flow variable). That cost, called interest payments, amounted to some $20 billion in 1971, or $100 per annum, per capita.

What about the morality of maintaining, or even increasing, the national debt? The answer to that question may be provided in a course in moral philosophy or ethics or what-have-you: It is not an economic question.

Morality aside, the size of our national debt is an economic question. There are some very good arguments to the effect that we may have been too concerned with the issue. After all, there is hardly a major business, and hardly a family in the United States, for that matter, that does not operate on a long-run and intentional debt. Moreover, if you express the national debt as a percent of our GNP, it has been falling ever since World War II. If you take the more meaningful ratio of the interest on the national debt divided by the GNP (both are flow variables), it has remained at a constant 1.9%, more or less, since 1950. Finally, compared to the growth rate of the private debt, the federal debt seems to be standing still; from 1960 to 1970, the federal debt increased by about 32%, while the private debt more than doubled.

Still, servicing the national debt is a burden. To say that if it wishes the government can always eliminate the debt by printing money or by simple legislative annulment begs the question. And the argument that there is no burden, because as a nation we owe that debt to ourselves is formally correct but misses the point. It is true, of course, that the $100 per capita that the public is paying each year to service the national debt is not retained by the government. That money is paid out to the private and institutional holders of U.S.

---

[6] Excepting World War II, when deficit spending ran upward of $50 billion per year for three successive years.

government bonds and in that sense, the effect is distributional rather than consumptive. But then, taxes too are redistributed. And just as there is believed to be an upper limit to taxation above which taxes become oppressive and economic activity is stifled, there exists an upper limit in the annual cost of our national debt. After all, that cost is covered either by taxation, thereby adding to the present tax burden, or by further deficit spending, thereby adding to additional future annual interest charges.

Having argued that there exists an upper limit in our national debt, the question may well be asked: Where is that limit? To that question, I have for once a very simple four-word answer: *I do not know.* By and large, that is one of the many unresolved questions in economics.

This brings us to the end of Chapter 12. We have fairly covered the topic of short-run macroeconomic problems and policies. In dealing with our model, we have dealt implicitly with some very important economic concepts that deserve explicit discussion. Concepts like the Keynesian and other multipliers, the accelerator, the Phillips curve, and others form the topic of the final chapter in Part 3.

Problems

1. Using only the *AD-AS* figure, show geometrically and explain verbally the concept of cost-push inflation.
2. Using only the *AD-AS* figure, show geometrically and explain verbally the concept of demand-pull inflation.
3. Explain the wage-price spiral with the aid of a diagram. Be sure to identify the power groups responsible for the spiral.
4. "With unemployment currently running at about 6%, all we need to do is stimulate the economy by increasing the money supply." Take issue with this statement.
5. State the reasons for, intent of, and advantages and disadvantages of wage and price controls as a macroeconomic policy tool.
6. Explain the concept of the misallocation of resources that arises with controlled wages and prices.
7. Suppose some ten or so leading unions achieve wage settlements substantially in excess of productivity increases. Using the simple model, show geometrically how this affects the nation. Suppose the contracts also contain full price-index escalator clauses. Do you agree that this inevitably brings about inflationary pressures for several years to come? Justify your position.
8. During late 1970 and in early 1971, the executive branch devised the famous and ill-famed two-phase game plan. The objective was to reduce

the rate of inflation in Phase I, and subsequently, in Phase II, to stimulate the economy in an attempt to bring about full employment. The period was marked by the simultaneous occurrence of rapidly rising prices and disturbing unemployment rates. As it turned out, the subsequent imposition of different and more drastic methods (the wage and price freeze) was an implicit admission that the game plan had failed. Why the failure?

Suggested Readings

An excellent summary of the demand-pull vs. cost-push problem is given in:

F. Machlup, "Another View of Cost-Push and Demand-Pull Inflation," *Review of Economics and Statistics*, XLII (1960), 125–139.

Of the substantial literature on wage and price controls, the following articles are among the best and most easily accessible:

G. Ackley, "A Third Approach to the Analysis and Control of Inflation," in *The Relationship of Prices to Economic Stability*, Compendium of Papers, 85th Congress, 2nd Session (1958), pp. 619–636.

A. P. Lerner, "Inflationary Depression and the Regulation of Administered Prices," in *The Relationship of Prices to Economic Stability and Growth*, Compendium of Papers, 85th Congress, 2nd Session (1958), pp. 257–268.

P. Samuelson, "Wage-Price Guideposts and the Need for Informal Controls in a Mixed Economy," in *Full Employment, Guideposts, and Economic Stability: Rational Debate Seminars* (Washington, D.C.: American Enterprise Institute for Public Policy Research, 1967), pp. 46–66.

On the national debt and its management:

T. A. Beard, "Debt Management: Its Relationship to Monetary Policy, 1951–1962," *The National Banking Review*, II (September 1964), 61–76.

W. E. Laird, "The Changing Views on Debt Management," *The Quarterly Review of Economics and Business*, 3 (Autumn 1963), 7–17.

A. P. Lerner, "Functional Finance and the Federal Debt," *Social Research*, 10 (February 1943), 38–51.

Chamber of Commerce of the United States, *Debt: Public and Private* (Washington, D.C., 1956).

13 Important Macroeconomic Concepts

One of the problems faced by practicing economists is the immense competition in the field. There are some 200 million people living in the United States. It is a fair guess that 150 million are old enough to read and write. Thus, there are 150 million self-styled economists in this country. At a cocktail party no one ever talks about how to correctly perform an appendectomy. If you as a budding economist broached the subject while talking with your physician, chances are he would feel insulted, especially if your approach is prescriptive rather than inquisitive. Yet, *he* will have no qualms in telling *you* authoritatively what is wrong with the state of the economy. The embarrassing aspect of this is that he has all the answers, while you do not. It does you little good to know that his solutions are based on (economic) ignorance, you are left on the defensive. All he has to do is to point at the current state of affairs; that is your fault. Then he gives his solution, and since no one is ever going to give it a try, you cannot easily prove him wrong. That is, empirically you cannot, and theoretically you cannot either, because he would not understand you.

Some of the primary conversation topics at cocktail parties are the Keynesian multiplier, the Phillips curve, and other macroeconomic concepts. We have used all of these in our model without referring to them by name. Let us now deal with them explicitly, not to provide you with ammunition at parties, but because these terms describe certain macroeconomic concepts that are of the utmost importance.

The Keynesian Multiplier

Suppose a given industrial area in the United States is particularly hard hit by a recession. That is, the total output in the area has declined and a state of unemployment prevails. Suppose, now, that for some unexplained reason a giant electronics firm invests in a multi-million dollar plant in that area. We will assume that the construction operations are of such a scale that they give rise to 1000 newly created jobs, either directly on the construction site or indirectly through local suppliers. Thus, the initial impact of the new investment is to provide jobs for 1000 people. If that were the end of the story, there would be no such thing as a Keynesian multiplier, the total investment would simply be transformed into wages and profits, and that would be the end.

However, a thousand people do not find or lose employment in a community without marked repercussions. In the case at hand, our newly employed people are going to spend most of their incomes, and as they do the community's consumption demand rises. For example, several hundred cars will be operated daily in taking the new labor force to and from their respective work places, causing gasoline and car sales to go up and giving rise to additional employment in the retail trade area. The same holds true for almost any consumer good. Our newly employed labor force is going to spend money on every durable and nondurable consumer good as well as on services, and as they increase their consumption spending, each and every economic activity in the community is affected. But the circle is not closed yet by simply taking into consideration the additional work force that was hired in the retail trade or in the service industry to accommodate the increased consumption spending of the primary additional work force, i.e., the original one thousand workers. The secondary work force, the people who found employment as a result of the spending streams emanating from the primary force—those people, too, will spend most of their incomes, thereby further increasing the community's spending level or economic activity. In fact, the more these people spend out of their incomes (the greater the community's marginal propensity to consume, to use economic jargon) the greater will be the impact of the newly employed people upon our community's spending level. Thus the secondary work force, by adding its spending stream to that of the community as a whole, will induce the employment of a tertiary work force. That force, too, will spend most of its income, etc., etc. If everyone were to spend each and every dime he made, there would be no end to the economic expansion resulting from the initial investment in the electronics plant. But people do not spend their entire incomes, and as a result, after so many rounds of additional spending, the impact wears out. A new level of economic activity is finally reached, one that is greatly in excess of the initial investment stream pouring into our community. Thus, the effect of that investment has been to provide an additional spending stream which is a multiple of the investment itself: the investment multiplier. This is the most talked about of the Keynesian multipliers.[1]

Another Keynesian multiplier, for example, described the increase in total spending that is brought about by a unit increase in government spending. Replace the electronics plant with the construction of a large dam for irrigation or power-generation, and you can complete the effects by analogy with the plant. There is one important difference between the two examples, however, and it might be time well-spent to dwell on it.

In the case of the electronics plant, completion of the construction phase gives rise to further employment when the plant goes on production. If we assume that the same number of workers will be employed in the plant as was used in its construction, then the total spending stream of the primary work force is not affected and the multiplier remains in effect, even though different people are now employed.

In the case of our dam, on the other hand, particularly if it is an irrigation dam, the number of people remaining employed in its operation is negligible. This means that termination of the construction job results in heavy lay-offs, and the Keynesian multiplier now asserts itself in reverse, with repercussions felt in all phases of our community's economic activity. A one-shot investment

---

[1] In equation form, the Keynesian investment multiplier is usually explained as follows. Let there be a GNP, consisting of consumption spending C, investment spending I, and government expenditures G. Then

$$GNP = C + I + G, \text{ and} \tag{a}$$
$$\Delta GNP = \Delta C + \Delta I + \Delta G. \tag{b}$$

Furthermore, let us assume that the marginal propensity to consume (MPC) out of this nation's GNP is 65% or 0.65. That is, a \$100 rise in GNP is consistent with a \$65 rise in consumption spending. Then, from equation (b),

$$\Delta GNP = MPC \times \Delta GNP + \Delta I + \Delta G, \tag{c}$$

and

$$\Delta GNP = \frac{1}{1 - MPC} [\Delta I + \Delta G]. \tag{d}$$

Given our assumed $MPC = .65$, equation (d) reduces to

$$\Delta GNP = 2.9[\Delta I + \Delta G].$$

Assuming no change in government expenditures, the usual conclusion is that one additional dollar invested thus gives rise to a \$2.9 increase in the GNP: the Keynesian investment multiplier.

project, in other words, even if it extends over several years, will not, in and of itself, and permanently, reverse our community's economic stagnation.

Figure 10-3 on page 140 comes close to providing a geometric description of the investment multiplier. If you wish to adapt that figure to the case at hand, simply assume that the increase in total spending was the result of an increase in investment spending pure and simple, i.e., assume away the reduction in consumption spending in the first panel of that figure. The increase in investment spending, then, raises total spending from Point D to a point on the TS' curve vertically above D. This, as we have seen, is a position of excess demand; In the aggregate, people wish to spend more, and as a result production is stimulated. This gives rise to further consumption spending, since the people who now find employment in order to produce and sell the required additional output add their spending streams to that of the economy. In short, the economy now moves *along* the dashed TS' curve to its new equilibrium position that is designated by Point A in Figure 10-3. The corresponding moves in the money market, the IS-LM graph and the AD-AS graph have been explained earlier and need not be repeated here.

The Accelerator

In the preceding section covering the multiplier we were concerned with the effect of additional investment or government spending upon the level of consumption spending and on the GNP as a whole. The question may well be asked if this effect also works in reverse, i.e., if consumption spending, in and of itself, affects investment. The answer is that it does, particularly in the long run. This phenomenon is called the accelerator.

Consider, for example, the bicycle fad that swept the country in the early seventies. America discovered the speed bike and everybody, well practically everybody, had to have one. The result was a sudden and substantial increase in the demand for bikes. Economic theory tells us that such an increase in the demand for bicycles has a dual effect: Both the price and the sales of bikes will rise. If the increase in the sales volume of bicycles is substantial, new capital investment may be required in the bicycle industry to facilitate the new output. It so happens that a significant portion of the bicycles was imported from abroad. This does not detract from the need for additional investment, some of which took place in the United States and the rest abroad. In our model we are dealing with a closed economy. Thus, if all newly produced bikes are assumed to be U.S. made, all new investment takes place in this country.

Our model implicitly contains the accelerator principle. To see this, suppose that our bike industry is producing at or near full capacity, i.e., in long-run equilibrium, when the new bicycle craze sweeps the country. The resulting increase in demand for bicycles, given a temporarily fixed output rate, will only raise prices. This gives our bicycle manufacturers a greater-than-normal rate of return. But investment spending, in our model in Chapter 7, was shown to be positively related to the rate of return. Our bicycle manufacturers, faced by an unexpected surge in the profit margin on each of the bikes they sell, will want more of the same via an increase in output. Since they are already producing at capacity, such an increase in output requires additional capital outlays to increase their productive capacity. Thus, a round of investment spending is induced in the bike manufacturing industry as a result of an increase in the demand for bicycles, and this is the concept underlying the accelerator principle.

What holds true for one industry holds true for all. A surge in aggregate consumer spending, especially if the nation is producing at or near full capacity, will tend to induce additional investment spending.

Automatic Stabilizers

In describing the Keynesian multiplier in reverse, we used the example of an irrigation dam; as we mentioned at the time, when the construction of the dam is terminated and 1000 workers are laid off, such a reduction in the work force has multiple repercussions in practically all the economic activities of the community in which the mass lay-off takes place. There exist, however, institutional and behavioral phenomena that tend to dampen the impact of the blow. These are called automatic stabilizers. The term automatic refers to the fact that the reactions to the mass lay-offs are spontaneous, i.e., without intervention from outside the system. Let us list the more important automatic stabilizers.

1. *Unemployment Compensation*   When our 1000 construction workers are laid off, their incomes do not really go to zero, as we implied in our preceding discussion. Our workers are entitled to and will receive unemployment compensation which will allow them to maintain a certain, even though reduced, level of consumption spending. Thus, the impact of the lay-offs on the total spending level is dampened. Other welfare programs such as the issuance of food stamps or financial aid to depressed areas also tend to reduce the disruptive effect of greatly reduced incomes.

2. *Induced Deficit Spending*   The government sector in our economy does not ordinarily adjust downward its expenditures in response to short-run reductions in tax receipts. When a substantial number of laborers is laid off, the government sector does experience such a reduction in tax receipts, and for two reasons: First, the laborers themselves, being out of work and deriving no income, are no longer paying personal income taxes; and second, the general decline in economic activity in the retail and service industries, as well as in

the manufacturing area, will cause corporate profits to decline, thereby reducing the government's receipts from corporate profit taxes.

The decline in tax receipts in the face of a given level of government spending gives rise to deficit spending. This tends to stimulate the economy's aggregate demand (see Chapter 10). Since the decline in economic activity was the original cause of the resulting deficit spending, the latter cannot also be the cause of a return to full employment. That is, the induced level of deficit spending cannot possibly provide the economy with a sufficient stimulation in aggregate demand to offset the effect of our initial mass lay-offs. But to the extent that deficit spending does develop in reaction to these lay-offs, the deflationary effect is dampened.

3. Dissaving   In addition to the various welfare programs that spring into action on the occasion of mass lay-offs, people have one more source of funds available to them, namely their savings. Typically, people faced by unemployment seem to be unwilling to make instant downward adjustments in their living standards. This is especially true when they believe that this condition is temporary. That is, people do not ordinarily move into smaller homes or sell one of their cars as soon as they are laid off. They will, for a while, as long as they can do so comfortably, make up for their loss in income by dipping into savings, by dissaving as the economists call this process. To the extent that they do so, the reduction in total spending resulting from the lay-offs is dampened.

The automatic stabilizers listed in the preceding section work in both directions. That is, a policy that is designed to stimulate economic activity must take into consideration that the hoped-for stimulus will also be subject to the dampening effect of the automatic stabilizers. For example, unemployed people will not add the full amount of their normal spending streams to the nation's total spending level when they find employment. Rather, the net effect will be their spending streams less any unemployment compensation or dissaving that they were subject to in their unemployment days. Similarly, to the extent that these people now produce tax receipts to the government, directly by income taxes and indirectly by corporate taxes, the government's level of deficit spending is reduced. Such a reduction in deficit spending, as we have seen, will destimulate aggregate demand and thus dampen the effect of our expansionary policy.

The Phillips Curve

In Chapter 12 we discussed the inflation-versus-full-employment dilemma faced by governmental authorities. A. W. Phillips, in 1958, developed a curve, subsequently named after him, which neatly summarizes this dilemma.[2]

The original Phillips curve correlates changes in wage rates with con-current levels of unemployment. This curve has subsequently been refined, so that many economists today use a modified Phillips curve which correlates changes in the price level with unemployment. As might have been expected, this curve is negatively sloped so that a reduction in unemployment is shown to be consistent with a rising price level, and vice versa. While the Phillips curve is in essence the result of an empirical study, there is theoretical content to it, as we will see in Figure 13–1.

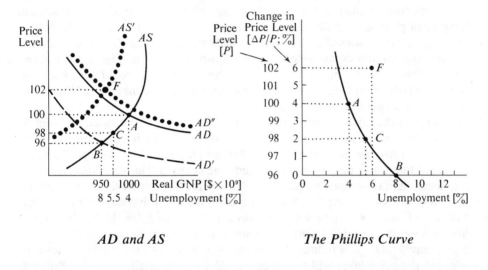

AD and AS   The Phillips Curve

Figure 13–1

Let there be an *AD-AS* system as shown on the left panel of Figure 13–1. The "full-employment" equilibrium condition, designated by Point *A*, is characterized by a price level of 100 and an unemployment rate of 4%. On the Phillips curve on the right panel of Figure 13–1, this corresponds to Point *A*.

Now let us assume that the *AD* declines to *AD'* and let us plot the result of this decline in terms of the price level and the rate of unemployment. To make our discussion meaningful, we will assume the price level to be com-pletely flexible downward. This, of course, is not the case we pursued in most

[2]A. W. Phillips, "The Relation between Unemployment and the Rate of Change of Money Wage Rates in the United Kingdom, 1861–1957," *Economica*, XXV (November 1958) 283–300.

of our policy discussions, where the price level was assumed to be rigid downward. We have discussed the merits of the fixed versus the flexible price level in Chapter 9. In particular, we pointed out there that the truth lies between the two extremes, i.e., that the price level is flexible downward, but that the price-level flexibility is less than complete. A theoretical interpretation of the Phillips curve must take this flexibility into consideration. In the discussion that follows, we will assume completely flexible prices, not because complete flexibility is essential to the argument, but because it makes the discussion considerably easier, without distorting its theoretical validity.

A decline from *AD,* then, to *AD'* in Figure 13-1 causes both the price level and the real GNP to decline, Point *B*. The reduction in real GNP gives rise to an increased rate of unemployment. In fact, Point *B* is characterized by a 4% reduction in the price level and an unemployment rate of 8%. These data have been plotted onto the right-hand panel of Figure 13-1, where the resulting point is also labeled *B*. Finally, an intermediate Point *C* is found on the *AD-AS* system and crossplotted on the right-hand panel of Figure 13-1. Connecting Points *A, B,* and *C,* and several other points that could have been derived similarly, results in the so-called Phillips curve. The meaning of this curve can now be explained as follows.

Suppose the government is in a genuine recession, as indicated by Point *B*. Any of the previously discussed monetary or fiscal policies that will stimulate *AD* will return the economy to the "full employment" position at Point *A,* provided that the fiscal or monetary medicine is applied in the correct amount. An insufficient dose may move the *AD'* curve partially upward to intersect the *AS* curve at Point *C*. At that point, the price level will have risen by 2%, and the rate of unemployment will have been reduced to 5.5%. If that is still too high a level of unemployment, a further stimulation of the aggregate demand curve, say to *AD,* will reduce the unemployment rate to the minimum level of 4%, but the price level will be raised by 4% over its original starting Point *B*. The Phillips curve on the right-hand side of Figure 13-1 summarizes the trade-off between falling unemployment and increasing price levels.

Now let us introduce a new element into our discussion: Let the *AS* curve be shifted upward by the combined effect of managerial and labor cartels as shown by the dotted *AS'* curve; at the same time, let the government engage in sufficient deficit spending so that the aggregate demand curve is partially stimulated; this is shown by the dotted *AD''* curve. The final point of intersection, Point *F,* is fairly indicative of the year 1971, when the unemployment rate and the price-level rise both stood at about 6%. In terms of our Phillips curve, what does this mean? It means, as the right-hand panel shows, that Point *F* is located clearly to the right of our Phillips curve. Empirically, the extreme location of Point *F* may be the result of one of two events: Either we are confronted by a random deviation or, and this is what the theoretical interpretation on the left-hand side suggests, the Phillips curve has been shifted to the right as a result of newly emerging cost-push forces. Whether or not this diagnosis is correct only time will tell.

This discussion brings up the weakness of the Phillips curve. It shows only the results of certain underlying forces, and consequently it deals with the symptoms rather than the causes of economic disturbances. For any newly plotted point in the system that fails to fall onto the Phillips curve itself, one can never tell in advance whether or not this is indicative of a shift in the curve. In other words, the curve fails to separate out cost-push and demand-pull forces, while the *AD-AS* system does not. Still, the Phillips curve has the advantage of spelling out very clearly the *AD*-related inevitability of the price level versus unemployment trade-off that exists in any economy.

Keynesian versus Non-Keynesian — Post-, Pre-, Anti-, Pro-, Neo-Keynesian?

Certainly, John Maynard Keynes was by far the most influential twentieth century economist in the Western world. In his epoch-making book entitled *The General Theory of Employment, Interest, and Money,* published in December 1935, Keynes presented the world with a new approach to economic theory, an approach that to this day remains the foundation of much current economic thinking. A brilliant mathematician in his own right, Keynes stated his General Theory mostly in words, with only occasional uses of formal mathematical presentations. In fact, in speaking of the purely mathematical approach, Keynes has this to say:[3]

I do not myself attach much value to manipulations of this kind; and I would repeat the warning, which I have given above, that they involve just as much tacit assumption as to what variables are taken as independent (partial differentials being ignored throughout) as does ordinary discourse, whilst I doubt if they can carry us further than ordinary discourse can.

And elsewhere in the same chapter, Keynes extolls the virtues of ordinary discourse vis-à-vis "symbolic pseudo-mathematical methods of formalising a system of economic analysis." In ordinary discourse, so writes Keynes, "we can keep 'at the back of our heads' the necessary reserves and qualifica-

---

[3]J. M. Keynes (1935), *The General Theory of Employment, Interest, and Money* (New York: Harcourt Brace Jovanovich, First Harbinger Edition, 1965), p. 305.

tions and the adjustments which we will have to make later on. . . ."[4] And so, in refusing to formalize his theory in mathematical terms and by keeping at the back of his head certain qualifications that are either introduced much later in the text, or perhaps not at all, Keynes left himself open to all kinds of interpretations. A truly massive literature evolved around the common theme of what Keynes said or really meant to say. Furthermore, where Keynes refused to formalize his theory, many of his successors did not, and indeed, the model that is developed in Chapters 6–8 in this book contains a great deal of formalized Keynesian doctrine.

Some of the early attempts at interpreting the General Theory, be it in formalized or verbal terms, have come to be regarded as *the* interpretations, and much writing has subsequently centered not on Keynes' original work itself, but on interpretations of this work. J. R. Hicks' article "Mr. Keynes and The 'Classics'; A Suggested Interpretation" may serve as an example to support this contention.[5] This article has become the basis of much discussion concerning the validity of the theory it attempts to interpret, even though the interpretation in and of itself is less than exhaustive. Hicks, in his celebrated article, develops the *IS-LM* analysis. And having defined the intersection of the *IS* and *LM* curves as equilibrium positions, he stops there. In reference to our Figure 10–1, p. 135, this takes us through the third panel; i.e., it ignores an economy's aggregate supply. And sure enough, Keynes, not Hicks, on the basis of the cited article by Hicks, has been accused of neglecting the *AS* side. Moreover, and for a reason that is a little hard to see, Keynes has also been accused of dealing in real terms only, i.e., of leaving aside monetary considerations.

Both accusations are unjust. First, Keynes was a monetarist in his own right, having previously published a well-received scholarly book on money.[6] A great deal of the discussion in his *General Theory,* it is true, takes place in real, rather than monetary, terms. But that, in and of itself, does not negate the effects of money. Even Hicks' interpretation of Keynes very explicitly contains the *LM* curve, and rightly so. After all, Keynes did have what we would today call a money market in his system, as his celebrated passage on the liquidity preference confirms.

What Hicks failed to realize in his model, and this neglect has subsequently been frozen into a great many post-Keynesian models, is the fact that the intersection of the *IS* and *LM* curves is *one* point on an economy's *AD* curve. It is not the final equilibrium position in the economy, since it ignores the *AS* conditions in that economy.

What did Keynes have to say on the subject? Did he fail to consider aggregate supply, as many of his successors did, or was his theory broad enough to encompass *AS?* As we might have expected, Keynes himself was aware of the

---

[4] J. M. Keynes (1935), p. 297.

[5] J. R. Hicks, "Mr. Keynes and the 'Classics'; A Suggested Interpretation," *Econometrica,* V (1937), 147–159.

[6] J. M. Keynes, *A Treatise on Money* (New York: Harcourt Brace Jovanovich, 1930).

aggregate supply in an economy. He might have given it a bit more emphasis, it is true, but the idea is clearly present. Here is what he has to say on the subject, in the jargon of his time:[7]

> When a further increase in the quantity of effective demand produces no further increase in output and entirely spends itself on an increase in the cost-unit fully proportionate to the increase in effective demand, we have reached a condition which might be appropriately designated as one of true inflation.

This somewhat obscure description of an economy's production-possibility frontier implicitly rests on the concept of an *AS* curve which Keynes prefers to hold at the back of his head, to use his own term.

In view of the discrepancy between Keynes' own theory and the commonly accepted Keynesian models, one wonders if Keynes himself was a Keynesian. The question is deliberately absurd, but the alternative assumption is not, namely that much of the currently accepted Keynesian doctrine may not do justice to the original General Theory, that a generation of economists has become strapped into an economic doctrine which only partly reflects the master's thinking. Maybe it has.

This brings us to the end of Chapter 13. There remains one loose end we need to pick up in order to round out our understanding of this nation's economy. You will remember that we prefaced our monetary policy discussion by the simple statement that the Federal Reserve System in this country is authorized to change the money supply. Having said this, we preferred not to confuse the issue by introducing the mechanics of money at that point. As it turns out, this is really a somewhat complicated topic that will be taken up in the following, and last, part of this book.

Problems

1. Suppose the level of investment spending is drastically reduced in some community. Verbalize the effects and develop the Keynesian multiplier in reverse.

---

[7] J. M. Keynes (1935), p. 303.

2. Suppose some underdeveloped country has a marginal propensity to consume out of its GNP of 100: The entire income is spent on consumer goods with no funds left over for investment. In that case, the Keynesian multiplier is infinity. Why? The implication of an infinitely large multiplier is that a one-dollar investment in each underdeveloped country will increase their GNPs without bound. Thus, our foreign aid should have been limited to $1.00 per country and their problems should be solved by now. They are not. Why? Which vital concept is left out of the Keynesian multiplier?
3. Develop a two-sector geometric S & D model using cars on one graph and capital goods on the other. Show how an increase in the demand for cars affects the level of investment in capital goods.
4. Suppose you are told that there is no substance to the assertion that union-induced cost-push forces can raise the price level because, if they did, the Phillips curve would be positively sloped. Take issue with the argument.

Suggested Readings

On the Keynesian multiplier:

G. C. Chow, "Multiplier, Accelerator, and Liquidity Preference in the Determination of National Income in the United States," *The Review of Economics and Statistics,* 49 (February 1967), 1–15.
P. A. Samuelson, "Interactions between the Multiplier Analysis and the Principle of Acceleration," *The Review of Economics and Statistics,* 21 (May 1939), 75–78.
W. L. Smith, "A Graphical Exposition of the Complete Keynesian System," *Journal of Political Economy,* 23 (October 1956), 115–125.

On the accelerator, in addition to the preceding papers by Chow and Samuelson, see:

A. D. Knox, "The Acceleration Principle and the Theory of Investment: A Survey," *Economica,* New Series, 19 (August 1952), 269–297.

On the concept of automatic stabilization:

G. Ackley, *Macroeconomic Theory* (New York: The Macmillan Company, 1961), pp. 299–305.

P. Eilbott, "The Effectiveness of Automatic Stabilizers," *The American Economic Review,* LVI (June 1966), 450–465.

D. J. Smyth, "Built-in Flexibility of Taxation and Automatic Stabilization," *Journal of Political Economy,* LXXIV (1966), 396–400.

On the Phillips Curve:

A. W. Phillips, "The Relation Between Unemployment and the Rate of Change of Money Wage Rates in the United Kingdom, 1861–1957," *Economica,* XXV (November 1958), 283–300.

A. W. Phillips, "Employment, Inflation, and Growth," *Economica,* New Series, 29 (February 1962), 1–16.

On the Keynesian theory:

A. H. Hansen, *A Guide to Keynes* (New York: McGraw-Hill Book Company, Inc., 1953).

J. R. Hicks, "Mr. Keynes and the 'Classics'; A Suggested Interpretation," *Econometrica,* 5 (April 1937), 147–159.

J. M. Keynes (1936), *The General Theory of Employment, Interest, and Money* (New York: Harcourt Brace Jovanovich, 1965).

Part Four
Money and Credit

14 Money

Let us quickly summarize what we have achieved so far. In macroeconomic theory we are primarily concerned with the welfare of a people, individually and collectively. The methods of measuring a people's welfare are less than perfect: Ideally, a person's happiness or well-being depends on his consumption of material goods and services and on his possession of intangible goods; that is, the food and the shelter and other physical amenities of life make up only a part of a person's welfare. In addition there are intangibles, among them the so-called costless rights, which are part and parcel of an individual's consumption goods. In this and many other countries, these costless rights are constitutionally guaranteed: freedom of speech and worship, for example.

Note, however, that some "rights" are not costless and do not fall into the category of intangibles, as people often claim they do. The "right" to adequate health standards is not an absolute right. It can only be achieved by increasing the number of medical personnel and equipment, i.e., by reducing labor and capital used for other purposes. There exists a trade-off between medical standards and the availability of other consumption goods. The cost to society of an increase in health care or, for that matter, in the purity of its environment is the resulting reduction of other consumption. The cost to society of the people's freedom of speech is zero.

If we attempted to include intangible goods as a measure of a people's welfare, we would immediately be in trouble. Intangible goods are patently non-quantifiable. How many skirts or pairs of shoes is the right to worship worth to us? Some people have valued that right more highly than any material good, even life itself. But not all of us are martyrs.

From necessity rather than from virtue, we omit intangible consumption goods in macroeconomic theory. This implies that all people benefit to the same degree from, e.g., the freedom to worship or, for that matter, from the freedom from pursuit for not worshipping. We only consider material consumption goods, including services, when we talk about the people's welfare or living standards. Rather than expressing these goods in real terms, we measure them in value terms—in dollars. This corresponds to popular usage: In speaking of a man's welfare or standard of living we are inclined to say that he has a monthly income of $1000; we do not say that per month he enjoys 2000 square feet of housing, two cars, one refrigerator, one TV set, a lawn mower, ten steaks, etc., etc.

In macroeconomic theory, we are even less precise than that. We add up in dollars the total consumption of all people. If we include government services and the consumption of future goods in total consumption, the resulting measure is called gross national product or GNP. The definition and description of this measure was the topic of Part 1 of this book.

Part 2 dealt with the development of a macroeconomic model. Since this model was to be used to observe and explain short-run fluctuations in GNP, several simplifying assumptions could be used in constructing it. In particular, it was assumed that the state of the art remained the same, i.e., that technological progress is not a very important factor in the short run. Similarly, in deriving the aggregate supply curve, a nation's resource base, its capital stock, and the skill of its labor force were considered constant. The aggregate demand curve was derived by dividing the economy into three sectors: households, government, and business. Each sector's desired level of spending was determined separately. The sum of these three spending curves gave us the total spending curve and, ultimately, the *AD* curve.

In its final version, our macroeconomic model takes the form of the well-known supply and demand apparatus. Needless to say, our model turned out to be a bit more complicated than the usual microeconomic supply and demand analysis. There are several sectors; there is, in addition to the price level, an entirely new variable, namely the rate of interest; there is a greater interdependence of variables; and there are more variables in the first place.

Our model having been developed, Part 3 of the book was devoted to its application to the U.S. economy—in particular, to the problem of inflations and recessions and to ways by which these business cycle fluctuations may be stabilized. Monetary and fiscal policies were described analytically, and their advantages and shortcomings considered.

In dealing with monetary policies, we have stipulated that the money supply in this country can be increased or reduced by a semi-autonomous agency called the Federal Reserve System. For the sake of continuity in the development and application of our model, we did not stop to show precisely how this is done; in fact, the mechanics of money need not be understood in using our model. It suffices to know that the stock of money can be changed by policy action, and everything else follows. But in practical terms, this is not enough. Monetary policy, because of its almost daily effect on economic life, is more widely discussed in financial papers, such as *The Wall Street Journal* and *Barron's,* than fiscal policy. Government bonds are sold or bought by the Federal Reserve System almost every working day. There is talk of reserve balances and excess reserves, of prices and yields of a bewildering array of credit instruments; there are very short-term overnight loans, oftentimes involving no more than two pairs of book entries at widely different locations; there are short-term bonds and long-term bonds; there are repurchase agreements and repurchase agreements in reverse. All of these things are somehow affected by changes in the money supply, primarily through a common variable, the rate of interest.

In spite of an occasional appearance to this effect, the emphasis of this book is not on macroeconomic *theory.* The purpose of this book is to implant an awareness of macroeconomic forces in the reader's mind. It is hoped that having read this book, you will be able to follow the public debate concerning our welfare; that you will recognize the alternative policy actions that can be used to this end; that there are limitations in our economy that no person or policy action can overcome. And it is hoped, also, that you will attempt to stay abreast of at least the major macroeconomic issues that will be confronting you and the nation in the future. To be informed requires, of course, that available information must be made intelligible. This is the function of Part 4, to provide the reader with a set of terminological tools with which to connect the macroeconomic model of Parts 1–3 with the information as it is found in the press and in statements as they are released by various commercial and governmental economic units. If a modern analogy may be used: Parts 1–3 are in the nature of a (macroeconomic) computer program; Part 4 deals with the input data and the translation of these data into acceptable machine language. The mechanics of money, the U.S. banking institution, and the credit market form the specific topics of Part 4.

The Mechanics of Money

Imagine the following scene: It is past midnight; the president of your friendly neighborhood bank busies himself behind a money printing press in the basement of the bank building; a hushed cough from outside the building, originating from the bank's vice president and the president's accomplice, assures the man on the inside that all is quiet. Quickly and efficiently he begins to make money, money, money. Fiction or fact? It is both. Your neighborhood banker, as well as every banker in this country, is a creator of money. So much money, in fact, that they outproduce the government at the rate of three to one.

That part of our nightly story is fact. The printing press, the ungodly hour, the veil of secrecy and the hint of a criminal conspiracy are fiction. Our banks create money quite legitimately and under strict supervision by the government. How they do it we will see later. Let us first turn to a discussion of the role of money in our economy.

That money is a medium of exchange is, perhaps, a trite statement. As we have seen earlier, the use of money facilitates the exchange of goods and eliminates the need for a double coincidence of wants that is required in all barter deals: if I wish to exchange a pair of newly made boots for two shirts, I must find someone, in the absence of money, who wishes to trade two shirts for a pair of boots. By the time I find that man, I might have built a second pair of boots.

The three prevalent types of money used in this country and their creators are, in order of their importance:

1. Checking accounts, also called demand deposits, created by commercial banks.
2. Federal Reserve Notes made by the Federal Reserve System, an independent regulatory body.
3. Coin made by the Treasury.

The latter two kinds of money, Federal Reserve Notes and Treasury coins are money to the extent that they are held by or circulated in the public. Currency held in bank vaults is not money. Rather, it is part of the important raw material, called bank reserves, that is needed for the production of checking-account money. Thus, if I hold $100 in Federal Reserve Notes and $5 in Treasury coin in my pocket, while my checking account contains $500, I may be said to have money holdings worth $605.

There are, then, three institutions in this country engaged in the business of making money, each making its own kind. The result is not confusion but assurance of an orderly flow of money through the economy. Of the $215 billion of money that were in existence in January 1971, the banks had made $165 billion. The Federal Reserve System was circulating approximately $44 billion. The Treasury had the smallest output of money, a skimpy six billion dollars of fractional coin.

How do banks create money? Suppose you open a bank and receive 100 deposits over $100 each by trusting clients. That is, you are holding $10,000 in currency in your bank vault. Suppose further that, as time goes by, you observe that your currency holdings remain more or less the same. The withdrawals of cash by some clients are offset by additional payments into their checking accounts by other clients. You are in effect holding $10,000 in your vault that is not much use to anyone. If only you could put this sum to work for yourself. . . .

But you can. Suppose a borrower approaches you who wishes to take up a loan of $8000 to buy an equity on a home. Having convinced yourself of the credit worthiness of your client and of the security of the loan (by a first lien and adequate insurance) you make him that loan out of the $10,000 that you have idle in your bank. In making the loan you either give the borrower $8000 in Federal Reserve Notes or you open a checking account for him and credit that account with $8000, i.e., you give him $8000 in privately produced checking-account money. Almost invariably, the loan is actually made by the checking-account procedure, but the effect on the money supply is the same. We will trace through the subsequent steps by pretending that all loans are made by handing over Federal Reserve Notes to the borrowers. This simplifies matters considerably. Whether you, as the banker, made the loan by handing over $8000 in Federal Reserve Notes or by crediting the borrower's checking account, the important point is that you have just created $8000. Somehow there are $8000 available to the economy that were not there before.

Your initial one hundred depositors continue to add to and deduct from their balances against which you now hold not the original $10,000, but a fractional reserve of $2000. This, however, is sufficient to let any one depositor withdraw all his deposits at once. Only a general run on the bank would reveal that you are insolvent. But why should anyone start a run on the bank, if he knows his account is insured up to $20,000 by the FDIC, the Federal Deposit Insurance Corporation?

If it is so easy for a banker to create money, why does he ever stop cranking the handle? There is, first of all, the very practical consideration of holding sufficient working balances in his vault. No matter how hard he tries, he cannot stretch a dime to finance his entire operation. In that respect, the banker's problem is similar to that of every one of us. We, too, would like to reduce our cash holdings to a minimum, since they produce no income. We, too, must hold more than a dime to finance this intricate operation called life.

But there is another, more compelling reason for the banker to hold his money balances at a certain level. The Federal Reserve System is authorized by Congress to tell the banker how much of his total balances he must hold in reserve. These reserve balances must be in the form of vault cash, the case we have discussed so far, or of deposits made by the banks with the relevant Federal Reserve Bank. The great majority of reserve balances are of the deposit variety. By setting the reserve requirements, the Federal Reserve System in effect controls the brakes of the money machine, while the banker is allowed to crank the handle.

Consider again the case of our newly opened bank. Suppose the Federal Reserve System sets the minimum reserve requirements at 20%. This means that you as the banker are holding reserve balances just sufficient to meet the requirements set forth by the Fed. That is, you are holding $2000 in vault cash on ten thousand dollars' worth of checking accounts, since you made a loan over $8000.

Our borrower now buys his equity and pays $8000 in cash to the former homeowner who in turn deposits the money in his bank. Again strictly for simplicity, we will assume that the homeowner's bank is not the same as the borrower's bank. Since there is money to be made in loaning out money, the homeowner's bank will promptly loan out as much of the newly acquired $8000 that the Fed allows, namely $6400. That sum will find its way into a third bank, which will in turn loan out $5120, etc., etc. The sequence of loans and the concomitant creation of money that is facilitated by the initial deposit of $10,000 is illustrated in Table 14–1.

Table 14–1
The Creation of Money

		New Money	Remaining Reserves
Bank #1	.8 × 10,000 =	$ 8,000	$ 2,000
Bank #2	.8 × 8,000 =	6,400	1,600
Bank #3	.8 × 6,400 =	5,120	1,280
Bank #4	.8 × 5,120 =	4,096	1,024
.	.	.	.
.	.	.	.
.	.	.	.
	Total	$50,000	$10,000

Try to let this concept sink in for a minute. People have deposited $10,000 of Federal Reserve money, and the banks subsequently converted that sum into $50,000 of private money called checking accounts. There has been a net money addition of $40,000, since the $10,000 of vault cash held by the commercial banks are not money. This follows from the definition of money which consists of demand deposits and currency held by the *nonbank* public.

You think that is just book-entry money? But it bought an equity of $8000 for a borrower in bank #1. The $6400-loan in bank #2 may have been used to open a small business; the $5120 loaned out by bank #3 may have been used for a new car, etc., etc. The point is, the newly created money has been accepted in the market for the purchase of goods or services. Moreover, the new money has been created through a series of loan transactions: As the money stock was increased, the amount of loans outstanding was also increased. This is why we speak of a money and credit expansion as a result of an "easy-money policy." This institutional link between money and credit was referred to earlier.

The depositors in our first bank, and all other banks for that matter, have not been consulted by the banker when he awarded this $8000 loan. In fact, most depositors think that they still have $100 each on their accounts, and *all* depositors behave as though they still have it. And indeed, individually they do.

There is one flaw in the above procedure. We stipulated that the money came originally from the public. If, when we opened our bank, the one hundred new clients made their new deposits by reducing their under-the-mattress cash holdings, we have correctly described what is called the money multiplier. If, on the other hand, the money came from deposits held with other banks, then the creation of new money by the receiving bank would be accompanied by an equivalent destruction of money in the other banks. To put it in other words, in the case of a transfer of deposits from one bank to another, the banking system as a whole has gained nothing. As a result, there will be no net creation of money.

Let us summarize the chain of events that led to the creation of money. People reduced their currency holdings and deposited $10,000 in a bank. The net effect of this operation on the money supply, up to this point, is zero. That is, the people have simply decided to exchange $10,000 in Federal Reserve money for $10,000 in commercial bank money, i.e., they have swapped Federal Reserve Notes for checking accounts. But currency held by commercial banks, commonly called vault cash, no longer is money. Currency, as we will remember from our definition of money, is money only to the extent that it is held by the nonbank public.

The newly deposited $10,000 held in currency by the commercial banks are called reserve balances. Given a 20% reserve requirement, these reserve balances are capable of supporting a money stock five times their own value. The money stock is expanded through a series of loan transactions in the banking system. The important point to note is that no such money expansion can occur unless the commercial banks have unused reserves.

This is where the Fed exerts its control over the money supply in this country. It can affect the reserve position of the U.S. banking system. For example, the Federal Reserve System can increase commercial bank reserves by direct infusion. One way of doing this is by the so-called open market operations: The Fed buys government bonds from the public; the money that goes to the public in payment for these bonds will eventually find its way into commercial banks; once there, it ceases to be money, but it represents a net addition to reserve balances, subject to the money multiplier. For this reason, the Federal Reserve System is said to have supplied "high powered" money to commercial banks. Alternatively, by selling bonds to the public, the Federal Reserve System can reduce the banking system's reserves and thus force a multiple contraction of the money supply.

Open market operations are not the only method of direct reserve infusion. Another way for the Federal Reserve System to increase the money stock is to function as a banker's bank by making loans to commercial banks. Such a loan also involves a shift of money from the Federal Reserve System to commercial banks, subject to the money multiplier.

Finally, the Federal Reserve System can change the money supply in this country without affecting the volume of reserves held by commercial banks. It can do this by simply changing the money-supporting capacity of existing reserves, i.e., by changing the reserve requirements. For example, a change in reserve requirements from 20% to 10% will raise the money multiplier from five to ten, thus doubling the money-supporting capacity of currently held bank reserves.

These three monetary policies, then, are open to the Federal Reserve System:

1. Open Market Operations.
2. Loans to Commercial Banks.
3. Changes in Reserve Requirements.

Each of these policies works through the Federal Reserve System's ability to manipulate either the volume or the expansionary power of reserve balances held by commercial banks. Having taken an overview of these monetary policies, let us provide a few practical details. In particular, let us begin by describing the institutional setup of the Federal Reserve System or Central Bank in the United States.

The Federal Reserve System

The Federal Reserve System was created in 1913 through the Federal Reserve Act. The original intent of the law was to provide an elastic money supply. The inelasticity of the currency prior to 1913 had given rise to recurring money crises, especially during the harvesting seasons when our then largely agricultural nation was subject to unusually great credit demands. The Federal Reserve System was given the power to meet these seasonal demands for money and credit. This was to be accomplished through the reserve balances of commercial banks.

Soon after the creation of the Federal Reserve System it became apparent that the System's influence extended much farther than the addition to or subtraction from the nation's money stock in response to seasonal needs. Full employment, price-level stability, and economic growth came to be affected by changes in the supply of money, and these broader concepts have subsequently evolved into the primary objectives of monetary policies. A relatively recent addition has been the balance-of-payment objective.

The Structure of the Fed

To facilitate the functioning of the Federal Reserve System, a decentralized institutional arrangement was provided. The territory of the United States was divided into twelve Federal Reserve Districts, each one headed up by a Federal Reserve Bank. All but two Reserve Banks have branch offices. Figure 14–1 shows the boundaries of the Federal Reserve districts.

Central coordination is provided by the Board of Governors in Washington, D.C. Thus, the Federal Reserve System is a national system that is well attuned to local and regional economic conditions. Each Reserve Bank transacts business with the member banks in its territory, and through these commercial banks it keeps in constant touch with the local business community.

Each of the twelve Federal Reserve Banks is incorporated. However, the Federal Reserve Banks differ from commercial banks, and from other business enterprises for that matter, in that they are not operated for profit. Their function is strictly a public service. The shares of Federal Reserve Banks are held by member banks, but these shares are nonvoting.

The public nature of Federal Reserve Banks is best illustrated by the provision for selecting each bank's nine directors: Three of these directors are representatives of member banks and are usually bankers themselves; they are elected by the member banks. One of these directors is elected by and represents large banks, one represents medium-sized banks, and one small banks. Another three of the nine directors, while elected by member banks, must not be bankers. Rather, they are representatives of the business community. The remaining three directors, designated by the Board of Governors in Washington, must not be connected with the commercial banking industry in any way. One of these centrally designated directors is nominated chairman of the Reserve Bank's board of directors.

Thus, the fact that six of the nine directors, the majority, are nonbankers ensures that the Federal Reserve System, at least on a local or regional level, cannot be used as a tool to further the interest of the banking industry at the expense of the public. There are other checks built into the system. For example, the conduct of affairs of each Federal Reserve Bank is subject to supervision by the Board of Governors.

The corporate structure of the Federal Reserve Banks is evident in its officer-director relationship. As in any corporation, the board of directors appoints the officers who are given the responsibility of conducting the daily operations of the Reserve Banks. Again, the public nature of these banks is revealed by certain additional checks built into the structure: Reserve Bank officers are appointed for five-year terms, but the appointment of Reserve Bank presidents and vice presidents is subject to ratification by the Board of Governors.

Central guidance throughout the Federal Reserve System comes from the Board of Governors, which has seven members. Each member is appointed by the President of the United States, subject to ratification by the Senate.

Figure 14-1   The Federal Reserve System

Legend:

——Boundaries of Federal Reserve Districts ——Boundaries of Federal Reserve Branch Territories

★ Board of Governors of the Federal Reserve System

◉ Federal Reserve Bank Cities   • Federal Reserve Branch Cities

Reproduced from The Federal Reserve Bulletin, March 1971.

Tenure of the full-time governorship is fourteen years and the terms are staggered so that one expires every two years. This removes the Board of Governors from direct political pressure. During his four-year tenure, the President of the United States can appoint only two Governors. If a President succeeds himself in office, he can at most appoint four Governors, a bare majority of the Board. Regional representation on the Board is assured by the rule that no two Board members may come from the same Federal Reserve district.

The Board of Governors retains budgetary control over the Federal Reserve System, and it passes on the salaries of all officers and employees of the Reserve Banks. Furthermore, the Board of Governors provides for an annual audit of all Federal Reserve Banks and their branches.

Control over one of the three most important instruments of monetary policy, changes in reserve requirements, rests exclusively with the Board of Governors. The other two policies, open market operations and the discount rate, are under the effective, if not exclusive, control of the Board.

Open market operations are controlled by the Federal Open Market Committee. Of its twelve members, the seven governors form an absolute majority. The other five members are presidents of Federal Reserve Banks who are appointed to the Open Market Committee on rotation, except for the president of the Federal Reserve Bank of New York, who is a permanent member.

All presidents of the Federal Reserve Banks are invited to, and attend, the Open Market Committee meetings which are held once a month. In these meetings they participate in policy discussions. The right to vote, however, is reserved to the current twelve official members. The presence of all presidents at these meetings serves a twofold purpose. It keeps nonmember presidents apprised of current policy problems and enables them to better understand and to more meaningfully comply with policy instructions emanating from the Open Market Committee. On the other hand, it allows the twelve policy-setting committee members to draw on the experience and regional observations of the entire Federal Reserve System.

In addition to changes in reserve requirements and open market operations, another major monetary policy is the change in discount rates. Requests for such a change normally originate with the Federal Reserve Banks, but they are subject to approval by the Board of Governors; thus, the Board retains ultimate control over discount rates. It should be noted that different Reserve Banks may, at times, have slightly different discount rates. This is especially true during periods of changing rates, when different Reserve Banks act with different speeds in following or setting the trends in credit markets.

We have briefly described the twelve Federal Reserve Banks, the Board of Governors, and the Open Market Committee. These three institutions constitute the main administrative and policy-setting units of the Federal Reserve System. In addition, there are numerous advisory committees providing channels of communication and coordination. Among these, the Federal Advisory Council deserves special mention: This Council, made up of one representative banker from each Federal Reserve District, provides a channel of communication between the Board of Governors and the banking and business community. The Federal Advisory Council meets quarterly in Washington, D.C.

Without its member banks, the Federal Reserve System would be about as important as a university without students. Not all commercial banks in the United States—in fact, not even half of them—are members of the Federal Reserve System, but almost all large banks are. As a result, the approximately 42% of all commercial banks belonging to the Federal Reserve System produce more than 80% of the demand deposits held in this country.

There are two types of commercial banks in the United States. Those that are chartered by the Comptroller of the Currency, a federal government official, are called national banks, whose membership in the Federal Reserve System is compulsory. In addition, there are state chartered banks, called state banks, whose membership in the Federal Reserve System is voluntary. Table 14–2 shows the composition of the commercial banking system and the money holdings by types of banks. FDIC insurance is mandatory for all member banks of the Federal Reserve System. Nonmember banks may join the Federal Deposit Insurance Corporation and, as Table 14–2 shows, they overwhelmingly elect to do so.

Table 14–2
The U.S. Banking System

	U.S. Banks (Dec. 31, 1970)		Demand Deposits (June 30, 1970)	
	Number	*Percent*	*Billion $*	*Percent*
Fed Member Banks				
National	4621	33.8	113.3	58.7
State	1147	8.4	42.6	22.1
Nonmember Banks				
FDIC Insured	7735	56.5	35.8	18.6
Noninsured	185	1.3	1.2	0.6
Total	13,688	100.0	192.9	100.0

Source: Federal Reserve Bulletin, February 1971.

Each Federal Reserve Bank is financed through the purchase of nonvoting shares by its member banks. The member banks are required to provide funds equal to 3% of their capital and surplus; another 3% is subject to call. When banks become members of the Federal Reserve System, they assumc ccrtain obligations. They must maintain minimum reserve balances as set by the Federal Reserve System. These reserve balances are to be held either in the form of deposits without interest at the relevant Federal Reserve Bank, or in the form of vault cash. Furthermore, all checks presented by the Reserve Bank—and to member banks that means practically all checks— must be remitted at par. In addition, member banks are subject to various federal laws and regulations, as well as to supervision and an annual examination by the Federal Reserve System.

These obligations are in part offset by certain privileges. Member banks may borrow from Federal Reserve Banks, at the discount window, to cover temporary reserve deficiencies. It is important to note, however, that such discounting is a privilege, not a right: The availability of loans through the discount window is at the discretion of the Federal Reserve Bank. Other member-bank privileges are the use of Federal Reserve facilities to collect checks, to serve as an interbank clearing house, and to transfer funds by the Federal Reserve wire system. Furthermore, member banks are provided currency upon request; they also receive a 6% dividend on their paid-in capital. Since member banks elect six of the nine Federal Reserve Bank directors, they participate to some degree in the administrative and policy-setting process of the Federal Reserve System.

Federal Reserve Policies

In discussing monetary policies, we stated that the Federal Reserve System can increase or reduce the supply of money, and by three methods or policies; but we concentrated our discussion upon the effects, rather than the mechanics, of these policies. Let us now take up some of the details of money mechanics. In particular, this section will show how, precisely, the money supply is changed by means of open market operations, changes in reserve requirements, and through the discount window.

Open Market Operations   Our previous discussion showed that a given quantity of commercial bank reserve balances is capable of supporting so much privately produced money, called demand deposits. Thus, any change in the quantity or the supporting capacity of reserve balances affects the total supply of demand deposits. And since demand deposits constitute approximately 75% of the total money supply, such a change directly and noticeably affects the supply of money. All Federal Reserve System policies, the so-called monetary policies, work through the reserve balances of commercial banks.

The most frequently used monetary policy is open market operations, whereby reserve balances of commercial banks are changed through the purchase or sale of government securities by the Federal Reserve System. Let us trace through the sequence of events of, say, a purchase of government securities.

Suppose our economy is in a recession caused by insufficient *AD,* and an expansionary monetary policy is deemed desirable. In that case, the Federal Reserve System will buy up government securities. Even though typical Federal Reserve transactions run into millions of dollars, we will assume in this and subsequent policy discussions that the amount purchased or sold is $100.

In order to pay for the government bond, the Federal Reserve System writes out a check, drawn on itself and payable to the selling dealer. The dealer deposits this check in his bank and the bank remits it to its Federal Reserve Bank for deposit and credit on its reserve balances. The effect is the same as when people draw down their under-the-mattress cash holdings and open up demand deposits in banks: The banking system as a whole experiences an increase in reserve balances. In the case at hand, the purchase of $100 of government securities gives rise to an increase in reserve balances by $100. If we assume a reserve requirement of 20%, the resulting increase in demand deposits may reach a high of $500. Again, the creation of this privately produced money takes place through many successive rounds of loan transactions, causing the supply of credit to increase. The Federal Reserve System is said to follow an expansionary monetary, or easy-money, policy when it increases the money supply.

A reduction in the money supply, a tight monetary policy, is one way to check inflationary demand-pull forces. In open market operations, the procedure is the exact reverse of the preceding sequence. The Federal Reserve System sells government securities, bought by dealers specializing in this market, who transact orders for their own accounts as well as for banks or corporations wishing to hold a riskless but nonsterile asset of high liquidity. The dealer remits payment by a check, drawn on a demand deposit at his bank. Suppose again that the transaction involves the sum of $100. Since the member banks' reserve balances are also routinely used as working balances in the Federal Reserve System's clearing house operations, this check over $100 will be treated like any other claim upon the issuing bank's deposits: it will be debited to, i.e., deducted from, its reserve balances. But the transaction differs from ordinary money transfers in that no corresponding amount is credited to some other bank's reserve balances. Thus, the banking system as a whole loses $100 in reserves.

If a $100 increase in reserve balances gives rise to a money expansion of $500, a $100 decrease in reserves has the opposite effect: The money stock held in the economy is reduced by $500. Thus, a round of loan and demand deposit contractions is set in motion, until the reduction in bank reserves is balanced by the required multiple reduction in demand deposits.

In practice, all sales and purchases of government securities are effected through some twenty dealers. Headquarters of most dealers are in New York City, but a network of branch offices covers the entire nation. The Federal Reserve System sells and buys government bonds through the Federal Reserve

Bank of New York. Five or six Federal Reserve traders sit on the outside of a U-shaped trading desk, facing a large quotation board where the latest bid and offer prices of various government securities are posted. Each Federal Reserve trader is connected by private wire to each of the government security dealers.

The decision to buy or sell securities on any given day depends on many factors. So-called defensive operations involve the sale or purchase of government securities by the Federal Reserve System, in an attempt to offset destabilizing forces in the market and thus to ensure the continuation of an existing policy. Oftentimes, the purchase or sale of government securities is at the initiative of the Federal Reserve System to comply with current monetary policy directives.

Proximity to the market enables the New York Federal Reserve Bank to continuously collect and analyze market indicators such as reserve positions of commercial banks, amount of currency in circulation, Treasury operations, opening bids of government securities, gold and foreign operations, and others. Moreover, personal contact is maintained by the Manager of Open Market Operations, who has a daily meeting, on a rotating basis, with two of the government securities dealers.

Even though, at the close of Open Market Committee meetings, policy directives are issued to the Open Market Operations Manager, the latter remains in daily contact with some members of the Committee through a three-way telephone hookup. A member of the Board of Governors and one of the presidents currently serving on the Open Market Committee participate in these meetings, the purpose of which is to discuss existing policy directives in the light of the latest available market conditions. Any decision to buy, sell, or do nothing on that day is usually taken at the close of this eleven o'clock telephone meeting. Moreover, if an unusual situation arises, the entire Open Market Committee may meet over the telephone.

Actual sales and purchases are made on a strictly competitive basis in an over-the-counter type of market. Suppose the decision has been made to sell government securities: Each of the five or six traders at the trading desk is instructed to contact two or three government security dealers by telephone and to invite them to submit bids on the impending sale. A dealer may bid on all or on part of the securities that are up for sale.

The normal "go around" to all dealers takes no more than five minutes. This nearly simultaneous notification prevents any one dealer from deriving a competitive advantage in the fast-moving market. Offers to buy are tabulated as they are phoned in by the dealers. If the offers to buy exceed the number of securities to be sold, as is usually the case, the highest discount offerings will be accepted, and the dealers notified. The entire operation, notification of dealers, preparation of bids by dealers, acceptance, tabulation, and selection by the Federal Reserve trading desk takes less than twenty minutes. Amounts of $100 million and more are often involved.

One variant of these outright sales and purchases is the repurchase agreement. This is a frequently used and discussed tool and, for that reason, deserves mention. Suppose the Federal Reserve System wishes to temporarily inject funds into the economy, say to provide liquid funds over the Labor-Day weekend. Instead of buying government securities outright and then selling them outright after the holiday season, the Federal Reserve System may prefer to buy the securities with the understanding that they are to be repurchased by the selling dealer after a specified interval, usually a few days and never more than fifteen days. Since this is well known at the time of the initial purchase by the Federal Reserve System, the repurchase by dealers, as well as the initial sale, is less unsettling in the market. That is, the announced repurchase transaction does not give rise to speculation about a new monetary policy decision.

The Discount Window   In spite of the establishment of minimum reserve requirements by the Federal Reserve System, it may at times occur that a member bank finds itself faced by temporary reserve deficiencies. Suppose, for example, a bank has $1000 of demand deposits, and the reserve requirement is 20%. Suppose further that our bank has loaned out $800 and holds $200 in reserve. Thus, our bank does not violate its reserve requirements. Now let one of the bank's clients withdraw $100 from his demand deposit, say for payment of a bill to a store that maintains its accounts at a different bank. Again, through the Federal Reserve System's routine clearing house operations, using the various reserve balances as operating funds, this check will be debited to our bank's reserve balances and credited to the recipient bank's accounts. Our bank suddenly finds itself holding $900 in demand deposits, which are offset by loans over $800 and reserve balances of only $100. Thus, through the initiative of someone else, namely its client, the bank incurs a reserve deficiency. One way for our bank to overcome this reserve deficiency would be to call loans covering $80 and to transfer this amount to its reserve balances. This would give our bank a total reserve of $180, which is equal to the required 20% of its remaining demand deposit holdings of $900.

Suppose that no loans are maturing or callable, what can our bank do to cover its reserve deficiency? Several alternatives are available to a bank. It can restrict its lending, call in correspondent balances it keeps in other banks, sell government securities from its portfolio, borrow from another member bank via the federal funds market, or it can borrow the required reserve from its Federal Reserve Bank, provided it is a member bank. This latter procedure is normally referred to as discounting. It usually takes the form of a promissory note, made out by the bank and secured by eligible papers such as government securities, that are accepted as collateral by the Federal Reserve Bank. As the name implies, such a loan is obtained via the discounting procedure: The bank receives less than the nominal value of the loan and pays the full nominal value back to the Federal Reserve Bank. The difference between the nominal and discount prices can be converted into the so-called discount rate. This is the interest rate that the Federal Reserve Bank charges its member bank for the loan. As was pointed out before, access to loans from the Federal Reserve

System through the discount window is a privilege, not a right. The System may at its discretion refuse to make such a loan. Furthermore, since the System has discretionary power to set the discount rate, it may discourage such loans by making their costs higher than those of other alternatives that are open to banks in need of reserve funds.

The preceding discussion gives the impression that member banks must maintain sufficient reserves daily. This is not exactly true: Depending upon the type of member bank, reserve requirements must be met, on the average, over a one- or two-week period. A member bank incurring a temporary reserve deficiency on a given day may make up for it by carrying an offsetting excess reserve some other day of the relevant period.

An individual member bank is likely to view the discount window simply as a tool to offset temporary reserve deficiencies. In fact, most banks are somewhat reluctant to make use of the discount window, and some banks never do. Still, in the aggregate, some discount window loans are always outstanding. To the extent that they exist, they represent added reserve balances giving rise to additional demand deposits, or at least forestalling a forced contraction of such deposits. The total money supply is, therefore, affected by these loans, by the money multiplier. For this reason, discount operations are effective tools in the toolbox of monetary policies.

Changes in Reserve Requirements   Open market operations and borrowing by member banks affect the supply of money by changing the quantity of reserve balances held by member banks. Alternatively, the Federal Reserve System may change the money supply for a given quantity of reserve balances, by changing the money supporting capacity of these balances, i.e., by changing the reserve requirements.

Suppose, for example, a given bank holds demand deposits over $1000, loans in the amount of $800 and reserve balances in the amount of $200. If the reserve requirement is 20%, our bank has no excess reserves, nor does it have a reserve deficiency. Suppose the Federal Reserve System wishes to increase the money supply without changing the quantity of reserve balances. A reduction in reserve requirements will accomplish this. Let the reserve requirement be reduced from 20% to 15%. This will allow our bank, on the basis of its existing reserve balances of $200, to expand demand deposits from $200/.20 = $1000 to $200/.15 = $1333. A similar expansion will be made possible for all member banks, so that the banking system as a whole may produce more demand deposits.

In practice, there is no such thing as *the* reserve requirement. Different types of banks and different types of deposits are subject to different reserve requirements. For example, the Federal Reserve System classifies member banks into reserve city banks and country banks. Reserve city banks are located in the major financial centers of the United States. They have more direct access to the money and credit markets. These banks tend to be large in size and as a result have the sophistication and almost instant liquidity that the smaller country banks cannot afford. Thus, reserve city banks tend to have a relatively small amount of unused reserves – or excess reserves, as they are called in financial circles.

If equal reserve requirements were levied on reserve city banks and on country banks, the latter would suffer a competitive disadvantage. Therefore, reserve city banks are subject to higher reserve requirements. Moreover, the statutory maximum and minimum values between which the Board of Governors may set reserve requirements for member banks recognizes the need for different requirements for the different types of banks. This is illustrated in Table 14–3.

Table 14–3
Reserve Requirements of Member Banks

| | Demand Deposits | | Time Deposits |
	Reserve City Banks	Country Banks	All Member Banks
In Effect in Mid-1971	17	12½	3
Legal Minimum	10	7	3
Legal Maximum	22	14	10

Source: Federal Reserve Bulletin.

As can be seen from Table 14–3, time deposits, or savings accounts, are also subject to reserve requirements. In fact, since time deposits are more stable than demand deposits, fewer reserves have to be held against them. This means that a dollar held as reserve balances will give rise to different quantities of money, depending upon the type of bank where it is held and also depending upon the kind of deposit it is going to support. In a reserve city bank one such dollar will support demand deposits of approximately $5.90; the equivalent figure for a country bank is $8.00. One reserve dollar will support time deposits in the amount of $33.33, but to the extent that it supports time deposits, it contributes nothing toward the creation of money, simply because time deposits are not money.[1]

---

[1] At least not in terms of our model. Just what is and is not money is by no means a clear-cut issue. Our definition, namely currency held by the nonbank public plus demand deposits, has been called the M_1 money stock. The M_2 money stock, by contrast, consists of the M_1 stock plus all time deposits. Thus, M_2 is larger than M_1, in fact almost exactly twice as large. For our model in Part 2, the results remain unaltered whether the M_1 or M_2 concept is used.

The difference in reserve requirements gives rise to changes in the supply of money due to interdeposit transfers. For example, if I transfer $100 from a checking account to a savings account in a reserve city bank, the net decrease in demand deposits implies an immediate reduction in the money supply by the same amount. However, the reduction in demand deposits by $100 also means that $17 of reserve balances are freed, while the new time deposit only needs $3 of reserve balances to support it. Thus, there has been a net gain in unused reserve balances in the amount of $14. If this amount went to support only demand deposits, the initial reduction in the money supply by $100 would be partially offset by newly created money (demand deposits) in the amount of $14/.17 = $82.50. The overall result, then, of converting $100 from demand deposits to time deposits would be a net money loss of $17.50. This change in the money supply is not, however, at the initiative of the Federal Reserve System. Rather, it is the public that brings about such a "monetary policy." If this move runs counter to current official policies, the Federal Reserve System may have to initiate offsetting or defensive monetary policies.

There are other incidental "monetary policies" against which the Federal Reserve System must be prepared to take countermeasures: The conversion of privately held currency into demand deposits (or time deposits) has already been mentioned; certain Treasury actions have a similar effect and, incredible as it appears, the weather, as we shall see later in this chapter, may also bring about a temporary change in the supply of money. These effects will be discussed in a later section of this chapter.

Within the statutory limits set forth in Table 14–3, the Board of Governors has sole authority to set the reserve requirements for different types of banks or accounts. Still, this monetary tool is not used as frequently as open market operations or discount loans. There are several reasons for this. First, a unilateral change, by a given percentage, of the reserve requirements on all deposits has a large and widespread impact. An increase as small as one half of one percentage point may cause the existing demand deposits to be contracted by as much as 5%. At the present time, this corresponds to a contraction by approximately seven to eight billion dollars. Second, the change in reserve requirements affects all member banks more or less to the same degree, regardless of their current reserve position. Thus, unlike the other two major monetary policies, this tool is very inflexible. By contrast, member bank borrowing from the Federal Reserve System is at the initiative of the individual banks and is likely to be used only by those banks that have temporary reserve deficiencies. Similarly, to the extent that banks are themselves holders of government securities, open market operations offer a limited degree of control to member banks insofar as their reserve balances are concerned. Finally, changes of reserve requirements become effective as of a certain preannounced date. Thus, the tool lacks the discretion of the other two policies, and as a result it is more unsettling in the money and credit markets. Frequent changes in reserve requirements unduly complicate investment and bank management decisions.

One additional regulatory tool under the jurisdiction of the Federal Reserve System deserves mention, even though it is not a monetary tool. Since 1934, the System has been authorized to curb the excessive use of credit for speculative purchases of securities. In particular, the Federal Reserve System sets margin requirements on the purchase of stocks or corporate bonds that are convertible into stocks. In April 1971, these stock margin requirements were set at 65 and 50 percent, for stocks and bonds respectively. At a 65% stock margin requirement, for example, the ultimate purchaser must fund 65% of the purchase price of the stock, i.e., the bank or the dealer can, at most, loan the purchaser 35% of that price. A high stock margin requirement will have the effect of restricting credit for stock transactions. A margin requirement of 100% was set once, for a period of about a year. That was in 1946, after World War II, when drastic measures were required to contain pent-up inflationary pressures.

Independent Factors Changing Bank Reserves   We have briefly mentioned the fact that the Federal Reserve System is at times forced to take defensive policy measures. This happens when, through forces outside the System, the money supply is changed in a direction that is incompatible with current official policies. Let us take a closer look at this problem. In particular, we will list and describe the major factors that can, and at times do, change the supply of money.

1. Changes in Currency Holdings   This process has been dealt with previously. In fact, we introduced the concept of the money multiplier and the creation of money from this angle. Thus, we will content ourselves with a brief review of this privately induced "monetary policy."

Suppose I take $10 out of my son's cookie jar and deposit this money in a checking account. My son has lost ten dollars's worth of currency, but he has gained the same amount in the form of privately produced money, called demand deposits. He is, therefore, no worse off. The bank, on the other hand, is better off: it has increased its liabilities, accounts payable if you wish, by $10. That is, the new checking account is a liability to the bank, payable upon request. On the asset side, the bank has received currency in the amount of $10. Let us suppose that this currency is placed in the vault, where it is counted as new bank reserves. This money will allow the banking industry as a whole to expand its demand deposits to $50, assuming a reserve requirement of 20%. Thus, between my son's cookie jar and the commercial banking industry, the money supply has been increased. Of note is that the Federal Reserve System had nothing to do with this creation of money.

If a sizable sector of the population begins to reduce its currency holdings and to increase demand deposit holdings, the resulting increase in the supply of money may be large enough to act as a destabilizing force. Suppose, for example, that the Federal Reserve System currently pursues a tight money policy. Wholesale conversions of currency into demand deposits may create enough money to completely negate this policy. This is one instance where the System may be compelled to undo the damage done by the public. For example, the Federal Reserve System may sell government securities through open market operations. This would have the effect of destroying the money that the public has unwittingly created.

Just as wholesale conversions of currency into demand deposits increase the money supply, so do conversions of demand deposits into currency reduce it. One way for the Federal Reserve System to offset the decrease in the supply of money would be through open market purchases of government securities. This is precisely what happens during the Christmas season and on major holidays. At those times people tend to carry more currency on hand. They obtain this currency by drawing down their checking accounts. During these recurring times of peak currency demand, the Federal Reserve System routinely provides the required funds by purchasing government securities, only to sell them again after the holiday season.

2. Changes in Treasury Deposits   Not all independent monetary effects are initiated by the public. The Treasury, in its routine operations, also influences the supply of money. To understand the reasons for this, let us take a brief look at the way the Treasury takes in and disburses its money.

All Treasury receipts are deposited in the so-called "tax and loan" accounts at commercial banks throughout the nation. All disbursements are made through Federal Reserve Banks, where the Treasury maintains small working balances for that purpose. As the working balances are depleted, the Treasury replenishes them from its tax and loan accounts.

The Treasury's money holdings at commercial banks are subject to reserve requirements just like demand deposits. As a result, when the Treasury transfers funds from its tax and loan accounts to the Federal Reserve Banks, the effect is the same as an increase in currency holdings by the public. For example, such a transfer in the amount of $100 reduces bank reserves by $100 and thus forces a contraction of demand deposits by $500, assuming again a 20% reserve requirement.

Large transfers of this nature will substantially reduce the money supply. Conversely, large disbursements by the Treasury from Federal Reserve accounts will increase the money supply. Either event takes place at the initiative of the Treasury. The destabilizing effects of such Treasury operations may be offset by defensive moves on the part of the Federal Reserve System.

The reason that the Treasury carries the bulk of its money holdings at commercial banks is precisely to minimize these destabilizing forces. Suppose the Treasury held all its money in Federal Reserve Banks. A huge decrease in the supply of money would then occur each April, for example, when personal income taxes are due. Similarly, when quarterly corporate taxes are paid, large amounts of money would be destroyed through a forced contraction of demand deposits. To the extent that the bulk of these payments remains on deposit with commercial banks, the effect of such tax payments on the supply of money is nil.[2]

3. Foreign and Other Deposits   Member banks and the Treasury are not the only clients of the Federal Reserve System. In addition, foreign central banks and international institutions maintain funds in Federal Reserve Banks. These funds are usually built up from balances these institutions hold with member banks.

Suppose a foreign central bank wishes to buy U.S. government securities and pays for them by drawing down its balances held at the Federal Reserve Bank. The securities dealer will deposit the check he receives from the central bank in his commercial bank, where that money gives rise to additional demand deposits, through the money multiplier.

The only difference between this case and the preceding case of a change in the money supply through Treasury operations is that the destabilizing force is now triggered by a foreign central bank. Again, offsetting monetary moves may be undertaken by the Federal Reserve System.

4. Changes in Gold Holdings   The Federal Reserve System acts as an agent for the Treasury in purchasing or selling gold. Since no gold is currently produced in this country and U.S. citizens are not allowed to own gold other than in the forms of jewelry and teeth, there is in effect no such thing as a domestic gold market. Foreign central banks are the primary customers of the Treasury; they may be either buyers or sellers of gold.

The basic reason for international gold transactions, as far as the U.S. Treasury is concerned, is the fact that our dollar is backed by a committment that it can always be exchanged for gold by foreign governments, at the rate of U.S. $35 per fine troy ounce of gold (approximately 31.1 mg).[3] Thus, if a foreign government accumulates U.S. dollars in the course of its international trade transactions or as a result of capital movements, it can always sell these dollars to the Treasury and receive gold in return. Suppose, for example, Country A exports more goods to the United States than it imports from it. For every dollar's worth of exports to the United States, Country A receives one U.S. dollar in payment. Similarly, since the U.S. dollar is commonly used as international currency, Country A pays out one dollar for every dollar's worth of imports from the U.S. If Country A has a positive trade balance with the U.S., i.e., it exports more than it imports, more U.S. dollars will be re-

---

[2] Actually, according to the Federal Reserve System, funds held by the Treasury in tax and loan accounts are not money. These funds are, however, subject to reserve requirements. Thus, our description, while somewhat simplified, is basically correct.

[3] This provision has been suspended by the new economic policy that was announced by President Nixon on August 15, 1971. The value of the U.S. dollar was reduced subsequently such that it takes $38 to buy one fine troy ounce of gold. However, the convertibility of foreign-held U.S. dollars into gold has not yet been restored.

ceived than disbursed and Country A is faced by a growing volume of U.S. dollar holdings.

Suppose Country A now wishes to convert these dollar holdings into gold. Again, for simplicity, let us stipulate that the amount involved is $100. Country A, then, makes out a check for $100, drawn on its account in a commercial U.S. bank, and payable to the Federal Reserve System as agent for the Treasury. Since the Federal Reserve System makes collection by deducting $100 from the commercial bank's reserve balances, our bank loses $100 in demand deposits on the liability side, and the same amount in reserve balances on the asset side. The loss of $100 of reserve balances forces a further contraction of demand deposits: The money supply is reduced.

An influx of gold into the United States has, of course, the opposite effect: Reserve balances are increased and with them the supply of money. Recent history shows that the United States has been mostly a net seller of gold. In some years, these sales have been substantial. The resulting decrease in reserve balances required offsetting monetary policies. The magnitude of recent net gold transactions is shown in Table 14–4.

Table 14–4
U.S. Net Monetary Gold Transactions
with Foreign Countries
(*Exclusive of IMF Transactions*)

Year	*Net Sales**	*Year*	*Net Sales**
1961	970	1966	608
1962	833	1967	1031
1963	392	1968	1118
1964	36	1969	−957
1965	1322	1970	631

* Millions of dollars.

Source: Federal Reserve Bulletin, March 1971.

As can be seen from Table 14–4, in nine years out of ten, the United States has experienced a net outflow of gold. In 1965, the net loss of gold to foreign countries was in the amount of $1322 million. Of this, France alone withdrew nearly $900 million. Gold transactions are the single most important exogenous cause of change in the money supply. In a way, the Federal Reserve System's hand is forced by the monetary decisions of foreign governments. But the balance of payments itself can be influenced through Federal Reserve System policies. An unfavorable balance of payments can be eliminated, or at least reduced, through tight money policies. The trouble is, this objective may be incompatible with that of full employment, which may at times require easy money policies, regardless of the balance of payments situation.

5. Federal Reserve Bank Float   Suppose member bank A receives a check for $100, payable to one of its customers and drawn on an out-of-town bank B. When this check arrives at the Federal Reserve Bank, the reserve balances of bank A will be credited with this amount no later than two days after receipt of this check by the Fed, whether collection has been made from bank B or not. In practice there are always some collections yet to be made when checks are credited to receiving banks' reserves. The total credit outstanding, called float, constitutes a net addition to reserve balances and gives rise to the money multiplier. Thus, an increase in float causes the money supply to be increased and vice versa.

The actual magnitude of the float is fairly stable in the long run. In 1970, for example, it ran between two and three billion dollars. But the float is subject to violent daily fluctuations, causing temporary imbalances in the money market. In particular, spells of bad weather, especially blizzards, hurricanes, etc., tend to delay air traffic and thus retard the collection on out-of-town checks. Since the Federal Reserve Banks credit these checks to the receiving bank's reserves in accordance with a given schedule, regardless of the prevailing weather conditions, the amount of float increases sharply during such bad weather spells.

For monetary policy, because changes in float are of a temporary nature, they are, perhaps, less destabilizing than the other independent factors discussed under points one to four. The interesting fact that the weather can (temporarily) affect the money supply did, however, deserve mention. Chances are, the Federal Reserve System encounters fewer problems in predicting the weather than it does in outguessing the actions of the private sector, the Treasury, and foreign governments.

A Final Note on the Federal Reserve System

In our discussion of monetary policies and of independent factors affecting the money supply, we made several simplifying assumptions. For example, we assumed that a one-dollar increase in reserve balances would give rise to $5 of privately produced money, provided the reserve requirement is 20%. In practice, we do not know the exact money multiplier, and for several reasons.

1. As bank reserves are increased, the public may wish to hold a portion of the resulting increase in the money supply in the form of cur-

rency. To the extent that this happens, each additional reserve dollar gives rise to only one dollar of money.

2. To the extent that some of the newly created reserves will support time deposits, the increase in the supply of money is zero.

3. We have mentioned the fact that different types of banks are subject to different reserve requirements. Since the money multiplier usually involves a number of transactions at various banks, probably of both types, the money multiplier is actually a weighted average with the weights unknown.

4. Banks usually keep excess reserves on hand: funds held with the Federal Reserve System or cash in vaults over and above those that are legally required. These excess reserves are in the nature of safety cushions; they help prevent banks from having reserve deficiencies. As the Federal Reserve System increases reserve balances through monetary policies, the desired deposit expansion may fail to take place if the banks simply add the newly created reserves to their excess reserves. Of course, commercial banks are profit-making institutions, and they have a powerful incentive to put these newly created reserves to work. Similarly, a reduction of reserve balances may be in part absorbed by a reduction of excess reserves.

The American Banking System

The financial sector of the U.S. economy produces approximately 10% of the national income, yet it employs less than 5% of the U.S. labor force. In total and per capita income produced, therefore, the financial sector is of vital importance.

The significance of the financial sector goes beyond the output statistics, however. The sector is the most important creator of liquid assets and, as a result, it affects each and every economic unit in this country. Within the financial sector, the banking industry occupies a unique position: It is the largest subsector in absolute terms and, more importantly, it is the only subsector that has the power to create and destroy money. As far as sheer size is concerned, the banking industry's share in the private financial sector is approximately 39%. In the order of decreasing relative importance, other industries normally included in the financial sector are: savings institutions (20%), insurance companies (16%), finance and investment companies (9%), and pension plans (8%). These and other members of the financial sector will be discussed in more detail in Chapter 15.

In the month of February 1971, there were 13,688 commercial banks in existence in the United States. Approximately 80% of these were unit banks, that is, they operate only one office and are not controlled by other banks or corporations. By far the majority of the other banks were branch banks which are operated and controlled by other banks. Banks are not free to open branches wherever and whenever they wish. The establishment of branch banks is subject to approval by state regulatory authorities. These authorities, in an attempt to prevent the concentration of economic power in a few hands, place severe restrictions on the number of new branches. In some states, notably California, New York, and Pennsylvania, branch banking is the prevalent form of banking. Other states either do not allow branch banking, Florida, Texas and Missouri, to name a few, or place very severe restrictions on it, like Wisconsin, Iowa, and Oklahoma. Since all banks, whether they are Federal Reserve member banks or not, are subject to their relevant state legislations, none are permitted to establish U.S. branches outside their home state. However, they may have foreign branches.

Chain banking and group banking form the remaining two forms of banking. Neither system is of any importance in the U.S. economy. Chain banking is characterized by interlocking directorates of various banks. Group banking refers to a holding company arrangement, whereby the holding company, not necessarily itself a bank, holds the controlling interest in other banks.

Commercial banks, as we have pointed out before, are profit-seeking enterprises. Their profits are almost exclusively derived from loans and investments. In fact, over 80% of the banking industry's assets are in the form of loans or investments. By far the largest part of its funds are derived from checking and savings accounts, which make up a little less than 80% of its liabilities. Less than 10% of the bank's funds are provided by equity capital. This is illustrated in Table 14–5 which presents an abbreviated balance sheet for all commercial banks as of February 24, 1971.

Table 14–5
All Commercial Bank Assets and Liabilities
February 24, 1971 (Billions of Dollars)

Asset (Uses of Funds)	Amount	Percent	Liability (Sources of Funds)	Amount	Percent
Cash	81.9	14.6	Demand Deposits	194.5	34.6
Loans	307.5	54.8	Time Deposits	240.6	43.0
Investments	150.0	26.8	Other Liabilities	82.7	14.7
Other Assets	21.4	3.8	Equity Capital	43.0	7.7
Total Assets	560.8	100.0	Total Liabilities	560.8	100.0

Source: Federal Reserve Bulletin, March 1971.

As indicated by the terms in parentheses in Table 14–5, the assets of a bank are usually called "uses of funds," the liabilities usually "sources of funds." A loan made by a bank to an individual, for example, may be viewed by the bank as an account receivable and thus as an asset. Alternatively, it may be viewed as a money-earning outlet of bank funds or a use of funds. Similarly, a demand or time deposit is in the nature of an account payable (to the deposit holder) and, therefore, a liability. The various liabilities of a bank constitute its sources of funds.

The cash assets of banks consist of reserve deposits held with Federal Reserve banks, vault currency, balances held with other banks, and an entry called "cash items in the process of collection." These are checks drawn on other banks that have not yet been collected. As was pointed out in connection with the Federal Reserve System, bank reserves held with the Federal Reserve banks serve the dual purpose of fulfilling deposit margin requirements and of providing operating funds for the System's clearing house function. Currency is needed to provide for the working cash in a bank's day-to-day operations. In particular, this vault cash enables the bank to convert its clients' deposits into currency upon demand. Balances held with other banks enable smaller banks to gain access to the services of their larger correspondent banks. For example, many small nonmember banks hold accounts with larger member banks. Through these member banks, they participate indirectly in the services provided by the Federal Reserve System, such as obtaining currency or check clearing. The smaller banks' deposits with their larger correspondent banks are then used as working balances for the clearing of checks between the two banks.

Loans are by far the banks' most important assets in their portfolios. More than 50% of all bank assets were in this form in 1971; about 42% of these are commercial, industrial, and agricultural loans, 25% are real estate loans, and 22% are consumer loans to individuals, for cars, other durable goods, and home improvements. Also included are personal loans. The remaining 11% of the banks' loan portfolios are made for the purpose of purchasing or carrying securities, or they are loans to other banks or nonbank financial institutions, etc.

In addition to loans, banks hold direct investments in securities. These are, of course, also in the nature of loans but they are normally more liquid and less risky. By far the most important securities held by commercial banks are U.S. government securities and tax exempt state and local bonds. U.S. government securities constitute approximately 41% of the investment portfolio of all commercial banks. If held to maturity, these securities are virtually risk free. Furthermore, there exists a well-developed secondary market for these securities, giving them a high degree of liquidity. U.S. government securities may also be used as collateral in discount loans from the Federal Reserve System. All of these characteristics make U.S. government securities a highly desirable investment good from the banks' point of view. Tax exempt state and local bonds make up approximately 49% of the investment portfolio of commercial banks. The predominance of these bonds over U.S. bonds is a recent development, dating back to about 1969. The remaining 10% are corporate bonds. Commercial banks are not permitted to invest in corporate stock.

As was pointed out before, demand deposits and time deposits constitute by far the largest source of funds for commercial banks. About 80% of these deposits are held by individuals, partnerships, and corporations. The rest are held by various governments, local, state, and federal, and by banks in the form of interbank deposits.

Problems

1. Explain briefly the mechanics of open-market operations and show how they can be used to
   a. increase the money supply,
   b. reduce the money supply.
2. Explain the mechanics of changes in reserve requirements and show how they can be used to
   a. increase the money supply,
   b. reduce the money supply.
3. Explain the mechanics of discount loans as a monetary policy tool.
4. Give at least two reasons why the expansion of reserve balances may not reach the theoretical maximum as indicated by the money multiplier.
5. What are the primary sources and uses of commercial banks?
6. List and discuss two incentives for a bank to join the Fed, i.e., two privileges that come to a bank by reason of its membership.
7. List and discuss two reasons why a bank may refrain from joining the Fed, i.e., two obligations that go with the membership.
8. Discuss some of the checks and balances that have been built into the structure of the Fed.
9. The U.S. Treasury is in a position where it, too, can affect monetary policies. Would you agree? Discuss the issue.
10. Suppose the Banque de France (the French Central Bank) buys U.S. securities by drawing on its U.S. commercial bank accounts. How will this affect the U.S. money supply? Explain.

Suggested Readings

On the mechanics of money, perhaps the three most important sources are:

The Federal Reserve System, *The Federal Reserve System, Purposes and Functions* (Washington, D.C., 1963). This 300-page book may be obtained without charge individually or in quantities for classroom use from: Division of Administrative Services, Board of Governors of the Federal Reserve System, Washington, D.C. 20551. It is an excellent manual that should be owned and read by every student of either macroeconomics or money and banking courses.

For current monetary issues and problems, the following monthly magazine is an important primary source:

Federal Reserve System, *Federal Reserve Bulletin* (Washington, D.C.).

Finally, there are the *Annual Reports,* issued by the Board of Governors of the Federal Reserve System (Washington, D.C.).

15 Credit

One important sector in the U.S. economy is the credit market. In fact, total credit outstanding as of January 1, 1970, was approximately $2700 billion. This is thirteen times the total money stock of $205 billion at that time, or almost three times the size of the corresponding GNP. How can it be that credit exceeds the money supply, and what is the purpose of credit in the first place?

As we have seen in Chapter 14, money is a productive commodity, produced chiefly by commercial banks under the supervision of the Federal Reserve System. To maintain its purchasing power, it must always be scarce. Credit makes the use of scarce money more efficient. For example, if I save $100 by putting a $100 bill under my mattress, that money is not available to anyone else. On the other hand, if I lend the money to a bank, via a savings account, it will eventually be loaned out by the bank. The under-the-mattress case is an example of a highly inefficient use of money. As long as I keep it in its hiding place, it will contribute nothing towards the production or merchandising of any good. Lending the money to a bank, however, may only be the initial link of a multiple chain of credit transactions.

This ability of credit to give rise to further credit is the reason for the huge amount of credit outstanding relative to the money stock. Suppose a rural grocery store sells its goods to some customers on credit; that is, the customers are permitted to put their purchases on a running bill which they pay at the end of the month out of their paychecks. This, for example, may be done by a small grocer in order to remain competitive with a nearby cash-only supermarket. Suppose further, our grocer can offer to sell on credit, because his wholesaler permits him to hold his inventories on credit. In fact, the wholesaler himself may operate on the basis of a credit arrangement with a food manufacturer. However, let us assume that our manufacturer must pay cash for his labor and food inputs. Thus there is a gap: On the manufacturing level, all inputs demand payment; on the sales side, credit is demanded. One way out of the dilemma is a bank loan to the manufacturer. This is another form of credit. Thus the original bank credit to the manufacturer facilitates three rounds of derivative credits: to the wholesaler, to the grocer, and to the consumer. Needless to say, the chain of credit events can be lengthened at will.

Until after World War II, credit was the neglected stepchild of economists—not so much because its importance was underestimated, as because the collection of credit data seemed hopeless. There exist a great number of

Table 15–1
Flow of Funds Matrix
Credit Outstanding as of January 1, 1970
(Billions of Dollars)

Source: Computer Printout, from the Flow of Funds Section, Board of Governors, Federal Reserve System.

		Private Domestic Nonfinancial Sectors								
		Households		Business		State & Local Governments		Total		U.S. Government
		(1)		(2)		(3)		(4)		(5)
		A	L	A	L	A	L	A	L	A	L
1	Time and Savings Accts.										
2	At Commercial Banks	155.4	–	17.0	–	11.6	–	184.1	–	0.3	–
3	At Savings Instit.	215.5	–	–	–	–	–	215.5	–	–	–
4	Life Insurance Reserves	124.7	–	–	–	–	–	124.7	–	–	7.3
5	Pension Fund Reserves	210.8	–	–	–	–	–	210.8	–	–	25.2
6	Interbank Claims	–	–	–	–	–	–	–	–	–	–
7	Credit Market Instr.										
8	U.S. Govt. Secur.	105.0	–	13.0	–	22.9	–	140.9	–	0.1	287.0
9	S. & L. Govt. Secur.	41.1	–	6.3	–	2.2	132.2	49.7	132.2	–	–
10	Corp. & Fgn. Bonds	25.4	–	–	147.6	10.3	–	35.7	147.6	–	–
11	Home Mortgages	12.6	260.4	–	2.5	2.5	–	15.1	262.8	6.1	1.6
12	Other Mortgages	27.1	18.9	–	139.0	–	–	27.1	157.9	3.0	–
13	Consumer Credit	–	122.5	28.5	–	–	–	28.5	122.5	–	–
14	Bank Loans N.E.C.	–	19.6	–	113.7	–	–	–	133.3	–	–
15	Other Loans	–	18.2	23.2	42.6	–	4.4	23.2	65.2	44.5	–
16	Security Credit										
17	To Brokers & Dealers	2.6	–	–	–	–	–	2.6	–	–	–
18	To Others	–	12.0	–	–	–	–	–	12.0	–	–
19	Taxes Payable	–	–	–	21.2	2.3	–	2.3	21.2	20.9	–
20	Trade Credit	–	4.5	198.2	126.0	–	5.7	198.2	136.2	7.3	4.8
21	Miscellaneous	23.7	4.7	88.0	80.8	–	–	111.7	85.4	4.1	0.6
22	Total	943.9	460.8	374.2	673.4	51.8	142.3	1370.1	1276.3	86.3	324.1

credit-lending and credit-seeking economic units. In fact most businesses, financial institutions, governmental units, and individuals simultaneously make and seek numerous kinds of credit. Starting in 1947, the Federal Reserve System, with the help of its sizable research staff, developed a credit matrix that shows the various uses of credit or assets (A) and sources of credit or liabilities (L) in the U.S. economy. Such a chart, as of January 1, 1970, is shown in Table 15-1.

Time and space do not permit discussion of each figure in Table 15-1. However, let us take a look at the totals along row number 22. This row shows that the private domestic nonfinancial sectors were net creditors in early 1970 by approximately \$94 billion (1370.1 − 1276.3). Within this category, households were net creditors in the amount of \$483 billion. This fact gives a hollow ring to the assertion that the American public lives ahead of itself. On the asset side, the bulk of household credit (approximately 75%) was held in the form of time and savings accounts, life insurance reserves, and pension fund reserves. On the liability side, mortgages on family housing (56%) and consumer credit (27%) constituted the bulk of credit obtained.

Financial Sectors													
Total		Federally Sponsored Credit Agencies		Monetary Authority		Commercial Banks		Private Nonbank Finance		Rest of the World		Total	
(6)		(7)		(8)		(9)		(10)		(11)		(12)	
A	L	A	L	A	L	A	L	A	L	A	L	A	L
0.1	192.8	–	–	–	–	–	192.8	0.1	–	8.4	–	192.9	192.8
0.8	216.3	–	–	–	–	–	–	0.8	216.3	–	–	216.3	216.3
–	117.4	–	–	–	–	–	–	–	117.4	–	–	124.7	124.7
–	185.5	–	–	–	–	–	–	–	185.5	–	–	210.8	210.8
33.7	33.7	–	–	3.6	29.4	30.0	4.2	–	–	–	–	33.7	33.7
165.2	30.6	2.3	30.6	57.2	–	64.3	–	41.4	–	11.4	–	317.6	317.6
82.5	–	–	–	–	–	60.2	–	22.3	–	–	–	132.2	132.2
146.4	22.7	–	–	–	–	1.5	2.3	144.9	20.3	1.2	13.0	183.3	183.3
245.6	2.5	11.0	–	–	–	41.1	–	193.5	2.5	–	–	266.8	266.9
127.8	–	6.8	–	–	–	29.2	–	91.9	–	–	–	159.7	157.9
94.0	–	–	–	–	–	48.2	–	45.8	–	–	–	122.5	122.5
152.9	13.1	15.3	–	–	–	152.9	–	–	13.1	–	6.5	152.9	152.9
57.6	34.1	–	–	0.1	–	6.4	4.2	35.8	29.8	3.7	29.7	129.0	129.0
7.4	10.4	–	–	–	–	6.5	–	0.9	10.4	0.4	–	10.4	10.4
12.3	–	–	–	–	–	4.1	–	8.2	–	–	0.3	12.3	12.3
–	2.0	–	–	–	0.2	–	0.8	–	1.1	–	–	23.2	23.2
3.8	–	–	–	–	–	–	–	3.8	–	3.7	5.6	212.9	146.5
36.6	121.4	0.5	1.1	–	1.5	12.3	50.5	23.7	64.8	30.7	70.8	183.0	278.3
1166.5	982.4	35.9	31.7	60.9	31.1	456.7	254.8	612.9	661.2	59.5	125.9	2682.4	2711.2

The business sector was a net borrower in early 1970, in the amount of $299 billion. Corporate bonds, mortgages, bank loans, and trade credit are the major liability accounts in this sector. State and local governments were also net borrowers. Their total borrowings of $91 billion were primarily in the form of bonds.

The largest single net borrower in the U.S. economy was the federal government, to the tune of $238 billion. Most of the U.S. government's borrowings are obtained by the sale of government securities.

The largest single net creditor in the financial sector was the commercial banking sector, whose net supply of credit, as of January 1, 1970, was $202 billion. The nonbank financial sector, consisting of life insurance companies, savings and loan associations, pension funds, mutual savings banks, and other institutions, was actually a net borrower, by some $48 billion. This is not surprising, since these institutions can only loan out funds that they manage to borrow. That is, they cannot create money and then loan it out, as can commercial banks. The discrepancy in the amount of $29 billion in the last column of Table 15–1 is due to statistical inaccuracies. This error of approximately 1% is not inordinate.

Needless to say, as the nation's GNP increases with time, so does the amount of credit outstanding. That is, the magnitudes of the various sectors' assets and liabilities change with time. But the relative credit and debit positions do not change. The household sector, to give an example, will always be a net creditor and the business sector a net debtor, etc. This is why, in our model, we have assumed that credit originates with households and that the primary credit seeker is the business sector. The government, it will be remembered, was also a demander of credit, but its credit demand originated outside the system.

Financial Intermediaries

Up to this point we have discussed the various sectors in terms of their net credit or net debit positions. This is not necessarily a valid criterion for the importance of the sectors. In particular, it tends to grossly underrate the nonbank financial sector which is listed in column 10 of Table 15–1. This sector, when measured in absolute terms, i.e., in total credit obtained and provided, is second only to the household sector.

The main function of the nonbank financial sector is to collect funds that are not currently spent in the market by some economic units, primarily individuals, and to make them available to other economic units. Individuals, through home mortgages, and corporations, through bonds, are the major fund seekers in the nonbank financial sector. This sector, in other words, provides an important market place for suppliers and demanders of credit.

The major nonbank financial intermediaries, in the order of decreasing total assets, are: life insurance companies, savings and loan associations, private pension funds, mutual savings banks, finance companies, and other financial institutions. The asset holdings of these intermediaries during the period of 1945–1969 are listed in Table 1 of Appendix C. Also shown there, for purposes of comparison, are the total assets of commercial banks and the annual growth rates of the various financial institutions. One interesting point that deserves emphasis is that all of the listed nonbank financial institutions had a growth rate larger, and in most cases substantially larger, than the commercial bank sector. Overall, the nonbank financial institutions exhibited an annual growth rate of 8% in the post-World War II period, compared to the commercial banking industry's 4.8%. This points up the growing relative importance of the nonbank financial sector in the U.S. economy. A brief discussion of each one of the major nonbank financial institutions is given in Appendix C.

Instruments of the Credit Market

The credit market, as we have seen, is impressive both in sheer size of credit outstanding and in the number and variety of institutions participating in that market. Moreover, there exists a bewildering number of credit instruments. To discuss all of these in detail would take us far beyond the scope of this book. However, every student of the U.S. economy should have some knowledge of the major credit instruments and of their characteristics.

Broadly speaking, credit instruments can be categorized into those with a repurchase clause and those without one. A repurchase clause is a promise on the part of the borrower, or issuer of the credit instrument, to repurchase it at a specified price. Such a repurchase may be on demand by the lender or bond holder. An example is a Series E Treasury bond; the borrower is the Treasury, which stands ready to repurchase the bond any time the lender, say a manufacturing corporation, wishes to convert that bond into cash. Call loans made by banks are another example of a credit instrument with a repurchase clause. In this case, it is the borrowing corporation or individual who is obligated to repay a loan at any time the lending bank desires.

Most credit instruments with repurchase clauses, however, have provisions that the loan may be called by the lender only after a specified number of days. For example, commercial banks have the right to delay payment to holders of savings accounts by thirty days. In practice this right is always waived by the banks, but it does nevertheless exist and might be used should the need arise. Accounts in mutual savings banks and shares in savings and loan associations are other examples of credit instruments with provisional repurchase clauses.

As a group, credit instruments with repurchase clauses comprise only about 20% of all the instruments in the market. The purpose of having the price of the instrument specified is to protect the lender against losses due to an increase in the rate of interest. This will be discussed shortly.

Credit instruments without a repurchase clause make up the overwhelming majority, namely 80%, of all credit instruments. Corporate and many types of government bonds, mortgages, and noncallable bank loans are examples of these. Since these credit instruments are fixed in their rate of interest, they yield a given income to maturity. Generally the borrower may not pay off his loan at face value before the maturity date. The exception is the callable corporate bond. Certain types of loans and mortgages make provision for early repayment, subject to a penalty.

The rate of interest is the price paid for credit. That is, the lender gives up the use of his funds for a specified time, and for this he expects to be compensated. A credit instrument without a repurchase clause is subject to price changes if the rate of interest changes. In particular, an increase in the rate of interest will reduce the current price of the instrument and vice versa. Moreover, long-term credit instruments are more sensitive to price changes than short-term instruments. The reason for this relation between the rate of interest and the price of a credit instrument may best be given by an example.

Suppose a $1000 bond has been issued, yielding 7% and having a maturity of twenty years. That is, the bond provides to its holder a yearly income of $70. Moreover, the borrower is obligated to repurchase the bond for the face amount at the end of twenty years. As long as the relevant market rate of interest remains 7%, the present value of the bond is exactly $1000. Why?

Suppose, however, that the rate of interest rises to 10% as soon as the bond is purchased by some lender. If that lender wishes to sell the bond, he could only get approximately $744 for it, because the prospective buyer would value the bond at the new 10%-rate which has now become the relevant opportunity cost. That is, in comparing the income stream of $70 per year and the final sale price of the bond, the prospective buyer will use a discount of 10%. For example, the present value, at 10%, of a twenty-year annuity in the amount of $70 is $70 × 8.51 or $596. Similarly, the present value of $1000, paid twenty years from now and discounted at 10%, is $148. The sum of these two figures, namely $744, represents the present value of the $1000-bond after the relevant rate of interest has risen from 7% to 10%. The present value factors have been taken from Tables 1 and 3 in Appendix A.

The upshot of this calculation is as follows: If our lender wishes to sell his bond after the rate of interest rose from 7% to 10%, he could at best get $744. Since he paid $1000 for it, our lender would incur a loss of $256 by selling. Chances are, our lender will not sell now. He may have reason to believe that the rate of interest will return to the initial level of 7%. If and when that happens, the bond's present value rises again to $1000. The lender, in a case like this, is said to be locked in on his bond.

We have stipulated that the price of a long-term bond is more sensitive to changes in the rate of interest than that of a shorter-term bond. Let us see why this is so. Suppose again a lender has just purchased a $1000-bond yielding a rate of interest of 7%; but this time, let the maturity date of our bond be ten years as compared with twenty years in the previous case.

If, right after the purchase of the newly issued bond, the rate of interest

Table 15–2
Bond Prices versus Interest Rates

| Rate of Interest | Maturity, Years | | | |
	20	10	5	1
3%	$1597	$1341	$1098	$1039
5	1252	1154	1049	1019
7*	1000	1000	1000	1000
10	744	815	923	973
15	497	598	818	931

* Initial Rate of Interest.

rises to 10%, by how much will the price of the bond fall? Again, using the new rate of interest as the relevant opportunity cost, a prospective buyer will calculate the present value of a ten-year annuity in the amount of $70 at $70 × 6.14 or $430. Similarly, the present value of the sales price of the bond will be $1000 × .385 or $385. Thus, the present value, or current price, of the bond is $815, and our initial buyer has lost $185.

Similar calculations have been made for bonds with maturity dates five years and one year in the future. As can be seen from Table 15–2, the respective bond prices are $923 and $973. Thus, for a given increase in the rate of interest, the longest-term bond has experienced the greatest price decrease. It is easy to see by extrapolation that a 90-day bond would have been subject to an even smaller price fluctuation. This is what is meant by the statement that long-term bond prices are more sensitive to changes in the rate of interest.

Table 15–2 also shows that a decrease in the rate of interest causes the price of a bond to rise. This, by the way, is one of the reasons the Federal Reserve System does not publish its policy decisions on open-market operations until well after their implementation. Suppose the Federal Reserve System decides upon an easy money policy; if the impending open-market purchase of government securities were known in advance, the public, anticipating a fall in the rate of interest and thus a rise in bond prices, would make a run on bond holdings, producing a destabilized and near-chaotic bond market.

Different Rates of Interest

In the development and application of our model, we have always referred to *the* rate of interest. This, of course, is an abstraction, as is the concept of *the* wage rate of labor. In practice, various credit instruments are subject to different rates of interest at a given point in time. Moreover, the interest rate of a specific type of credit instrument may change over time. Let us take a closer look at the difference in interest rates on different credit instruments.

As we have seen, interest payments are the compensation to a lender for temporarily relinquishing his funds. Suppose a lender has $1000 to loan out, and he is approached by two potential borrowers. Let borrower A be a respectable business man with a going business and an excellent credit rating. Let borrower B be an honest business man who, nevertheless, has been known to have been in financial difficulties. If both A and B offer our lender an interest rate of 5%, and if that is the highest offer he can get, which of the two business men will get the loan? The answer is, of course, that A gets it, because he is less likely to default on the loan.

Suppose, however, B offers 6%. Chances are, A will still get the loan. What if B raises his offer to 7% or 8%? There will be a level where the loan will be awarded to B. If that level is, for example, 8%, then the difference between A's 5% and B's 8% accounts for the greater risk associated with having B as a borrower. That is, B's rate of interest consists of the pure interest rate of 5% and an added risk factor of 3%.

Differences in risk associated with different credit instruments cause the rate of interest to vary. Long-term bonds, as we have seen, are more sensitive to interest fluctuations than are short-term bonds. Thus, long-term bonds are subject to greater risks and, accordingly, they generally yield higher interest rates.

There are other risks a lender must consider before he commits his funds to a borrower. An increase in the price level, for example, will transfer some of his wealth to the borrower who pays back his indebtedness with cheaper dollars. Therefore, if such a price-level increase is expected, the interest rate will reflect this risk; i.e., it will rise. Furthermore, the managerial ability of the corporate borrower must be considered, as well as the type of product he sells. For example, sudden changes in demand for fashions make the clothing industry relatively more risky than, say, a utility company that is assured of steadily increasing sales. No one creditor or financial intermediary can possibly evaluate the credit worthiness of all his potential borrowers. Luckily, he need not do this. Specialized firms exist whose sole purpose is to keep tabs on the credit ratings of other economic units. Moody's Investor Service, Inc., and the Standard and Poor's Corporation are the two major bond rating firms in this country. Both firms rate corporate bonds, but Moody also rates state and local government bonds. The two bond-rating firms use a different but comparable triple letter designation to express the risk worthiness of the bond under consideration. The letter ratings of both firms are shown in Table 15–3; the triple-A rating designates the highest-quality bond.

U.S. government securities are virtually risk-free. Unlike a corporation, the government can always raise taxes to meet its obligation. Such a convenient method of debt servicing is not available to a corporation. For this reason, U.S. government securities are subject to lower interest rates than corporate

Table 15-3
Interest Rates and Risk
Default-Free Bonds
April 15, 1971

Bond Ratings			Interest Rates (%)			
Moody		Standard and Poor	U.S. Govt.	State Govt.	Munici- pals	Corpo- rations
Not rated			5.74			
Aaa	↑	AAA		4.00	5.20	6.91
Aa	Invest-	AA		4.10	5.30	7.06
A	ment ↓	A			5.50	7.52
Baa	—	BBB			5.80	8.19
Ba	↑	BB		Interest rates are not listed,		
B	Specu-	B		since these issues are		
Caa	lative	CCC		considered too speculative		
Ca	↓	CC		for investment purposes.		
C	—	C				

Source: Moody's Bond Survey; April 19, 1971; p. 642.

bonds. This is borne out by Table 15-3, where the U.S. government bonds shown are long-term bonds. As a point of interest, the lower interest rates associated with state and local government bonds are the result of the tax-exempt status of these bonds.

For given types of bonds such as municipal bonds or corporate bonds, the interest rate is inversely related to the credit worthiness of the issuer. For example, on April 15, 1971, an investor had to be accorded a yield of 6.91% on a triple-A rated corporate bond, as can be seen in Table 15-3. A triple-B rated bond, on the other hand, sold for a yield of 8.19%. The spread of 1.28% (8.19 − 6.91) is substantial and, from a not so highly rated corporation's point of view, may be prohibitive. Consider, for example, the case of a firm whose credit rating has been lowered by just one notch, say, from AA to A. If that firm had floated a $50 million-bond issue over a period of five years, the interest cost to the firm would have been $17.65 million before the change in rating as compared to $18.80 million after the change. Thus, the cost increase in floating the loan would have been $1.15 million, a handsome amount of money that is solely attributable to the risk differential under consideration.

Needless to say, the fact that changes in risk ratings are immediately translated by the bond market into money terms gives a great deal of power to the individuals responsible for these ratings. It also subjects these individuals to great pressures and, in the case of downgradings, abuse. To quote one New York City Finance Administrator's reaction to the 1965-downgrading of New York City's municipal bonds from A to Baa: "The whole municipal bond rating system, now carried out largely by these two private agencies, is a horse-and-buggy system in a jet age."[1] Our irate administrator's feelings notwithstanding, both Moody and Standard and Poor are highly respected in financial circles for their impartiality and integrity. Moreover, to many investors they are the only easily accessible source of information on a great number of issues.

In spite of the great diversity in credit instruments, they all have one thing in common: They are close substitutes of each other. Even though different types of credit instruments are subject to different interest rates in the credit market — again primarily due to differences in risk — the interest rates on all instruments tend to rise or fall together. Tight money policies, for example, will raise the market rates of interest on all credit instruments. Easy money policies will reduce them. This interdependence of interest rates is illustrated in Figure 15-1.

The reason for this collective behavior of seemingly independent credit instruments is easy to see. The differences in interest rates of different instruments are held within more or less well-defined limits by arbitrage operations. Interest arbitrage is usually done by professional traders and institutional investors. They have the required sophistication to engage in this type of transaction and they deal in sufficient quantities to affect the interest rates. This arbitrage function of traders and investors, oftentimes viewed with suspicion by outsiders, especially noncapitalist outsiders, is nevertheless very important to the smooth operation of the credit market. Without it, monetary policies would be very difficult if not impossible to implement.

Suppose the Federal Reserve System buys a million dollars' worth of a given type of government securities. This would put a million dollars of high-powered money into the banking system, causing the interest rate in the money market to fall. But what about the credit market? In the first instance, the interest rate on the type of securities bought by the Fed would fall. But that was not what the Fed had on its mind when it bought them. It wanted the interest rate in the credit market to fall generally, not just on one specific instrument. In the absence of arbitrage operations by large-volume buyers, adjustments in interest rates of other types of credit would slowly and unevenly pervade the economy through the normal operations of commercial banks. These banks sell most of the newly produced money on credit. Thus, depending on the types of loans or investments they make, additional credit is eventually spread throughout the market. Direct arbitrage bypasses this slow adjustment process by banks. It works quickly and efficiently.

Let us demonstrate the effect of arbitrage operations with an example. Suppose the annual rate of interest on a given day is 5.5% on both 90-day Treasury bills and 90-day certificates of deposit. Rather than discussing the

---

[1] "The Men Who Make Treasurers Tremble," *Forbes*, Sept. 1, 1970, p. 19.

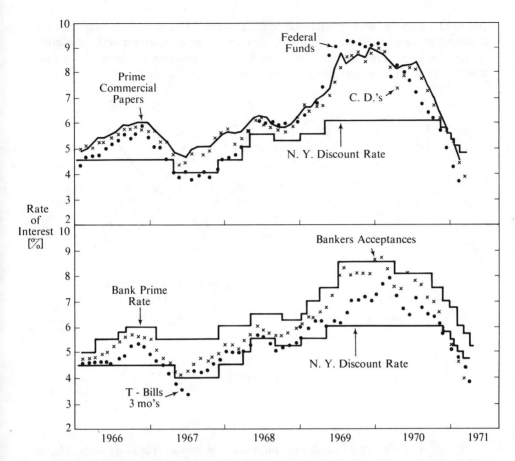

Figure 15–1   Short-Term Interest Rates

Source: Federal Reserve Bulletins, The Federal Reserve System.

credit market in terms of credit and the rate of interest, it is often more convenient to speak in terms of the credit instrument and its price. In the case at hand we may say that the government, through the sale of Treasury bills, is taking a loan from the public and that the yield or cost of this loan, depending on your point of view, is 5.5% per annum. Alternatively, we may say that the Treasury is selling short-term T-bills at a discount price of $986.62.[2] Similarly,

---

[2] This assumes that the bills are of a thousand-dollar denomination. The conversion formula reads as follows:

$$r = \frac{FV - DP}{DP} \times \frac{365}{90},$$

the C.D.s may be said to yield an annual interest rate of 5.5% or to sell at a discount price of $986.62, assuming, of course, a one-thousand dollar denomination for both credit instruments. The initial equilibrium position of our two credit instruments is illustrated by the solid lines in Figure 15–2.

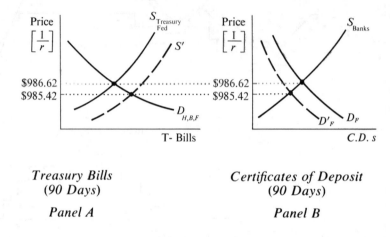

Treasury Bills
(90 Days)

Certificates of Deposit
(90 Days)

Panel A

Panel B

*Figure 15–2   Arbitrage on Credit
Instruments*

Panel A of Figure 15–2 shows the market in 90-day Treasury bills. These bills are supplied by the Treasury or by the Federal Reserve System and are purchased primarily by households, banks, and financial intermediaries, as indicated by the relevant subscripts (See Table 15–1 on page 220). The abscissa of panel A, labeled T-bills, simply measures the number of bills outstanding. The ordinate, labeled price, shows the discount price at which these bills trade in the market. To remind the reader that this discount price is inversely related to the rate of interest, the term $1/r$ is also shown on the ordinate. This is commonly done in economic literature, although, as we have seen, the price of our bill is not simply the direct inverse of the rate of interest.

where r = rate of interest,
         FV = face value of credit instrument,
         DP = discount price of credit instrument.
This is not the formula generally used in financial circles, and for two reasons: The Treasury's "year" contains 360 days, and the rate of interest is based not on the discount price actually paid by the investor, but on the face value of the bill. However, to the investor who wishes to compare the rate of return of a Treasury bill with other financial assets, the above formula is the relevant one to use.

Panel B of Figure 15–2 is in all respects equivalent to panel A, except that it represents the market of certificates of deposits, a credit instrument sold exclusively by large commercial banks and purchased predominantly by financial intermediaries. While C.D.s come in varying maturities, we will assume that they are all of the 90-day type. This makes them directly comparable with the 90-day Treasury bills of panel A.

The supply and demand curves of both instruments intersect at a discount price of $986.62. As we have seen, this corresponds to a rate of interest of 5.5%, which we assume to be our initial equilibrium position. Suppose the Treasury now begins to sell T-bills. This causes a rightward shift of the supply curve of these bills, as indicated by the dashed line S' in panel A of Figure 15–2. At equilibrium, there will be more bills in the market and the discount price will be lower (the rate of interest higher). But Treasury bills and certificates of deposit are very good substitutes of each other. They follow the same pattern that tea and coffee do in introductory microeconomic textbooks. As the price of tea falls, less of the relatively more expensive coffee will be demanded. Translation: As the price of T-bills falls, fewer of the now relatively more expensive C.D.s will be demanded. In panel B of Figure 15–2, the demand curve for C.D.s will be shifted to the left. This is indicated by the dashed D' curve. The result is that fewer C.D.s will be in the market and their price will fall. Equilibrium between the T-bill and C.D. markets is reestablished when the prices of the two instruments, and therefore the interest rates, coincide.

Actually, in real life the process is a bit more complicated. C.D.s are gotten rid of by simply not repurchasing them when they mature, and some of them always do. Instead, the financial intermediaries purchase the cheaper Treasury bills; that is, the demand for Treasury bills increases at the expense of C.D.s. But this and other fine points are of lesser importance. The one significant fact is that the prices, and therefore the rates of interest, of these two instruments are interdependent. Similarly, the prices and interest rates of all credit instruments are interdependent, even though they differ in risk factors associated with them. In fact, as a general rule, the interest rate on C.D.s runs somewhat higher than on equivalent Treasury bills. That is, commercial banks must compensate lenders at a little higher rate in order to attract their funds, since bank-issued credit instruments are not quite as risk-free as those of the federal government.

Types of Credit Instruments

As we have pointed out before, there exists a bewildering variety of credit instruments. New instruments, such as the now-popular C.D.s, are created in response to developing needs in the market; other instruments fade away when no longer needed. Some credit transactions do not even require marketable instruments, they are simply book entries that are reversed when the loans are paid off. Interbank borrowings of excess reserves, the so-called federal funds, are traded in this manner. These and other types of credit instruments are listed and discussed in Appendix D.

This terminates our discussion of the institutional aspects of money and credit. We have by now fairly covered most of the short-term aspects of macroeconomics, for both theory and policy. This is no claim to having provided exhaustive coverage of the subject. In fact, as we have pointed out throughout the text, we have purposefully refrained from pursuing each and every theoretical fine point to its logical conclusion, nor have we really taken issue with many of the raging controversies and divided opinions of which economics has its share. Lack of exhaustive rigor was the price we paid, but, hopefully, a fair understanding of the current economic issues facing this nation was the reward we obtained. There is, however, one area that requires discussion in this book, namely the long-term aspects of macroeconomics. This is the topic we will turn to in the sixteenth and final chapter.

Problems

1. The price of long-term bonds responds more, less, equally to given changes in the rate of interest, as compared with the price of short-term bonds. Circle the correct assertion and explain your answer.
2. Suppose you have just purchased a newly issued $1000 government bond having a maturity of ten years. The price you paid corresponds to an interest rate of 10%.

    Suppose the relevant interest rate declines the next morning to 5%. What is your bond worth now, in view of the new interest rate? Use your present-value tables.
3. Suppose you have just purchased a newly issued $1000 government bond having a maturity of ten years. The price you paid corresponds to an interest rate of 10%.

    Suppose the relevant interest rate rises the next morning to 15%. What is your bond worth now, in view of the new interest rate? Use your present-value tables.
4. You are the president of XYZ Corporation, and you want to float a corporate bond issue in the amount of $10 million over a period of ten years. This is your first time to consider such a step. Therefore, you do not now have a bond rating. Of course you assume that yours is a triple-A firm.

    Suppose Moody's Investor Service, Inc., rates you as A only. Using

Table 15–3, calculate the additional cost to your firm resulting from the difference in ratings.

5. With the aid of a geometric presentation and a minimum of words, explain why the interest rate of C.D.s falls when the Fed buys T-bills from the public.

Suggested Readings

T. R. Beard, "Debt Management: Its Relationship to Monetary Policy, 1951–1962," *National Banking Review,* II (1964), 61–76.

Chamber of Commerce of the United States, *Debt: Public and Private* (Revised Edition; Washington, D.C., 1966).

Federal Reserve System, *Flow of Funds Accounts, 1945–1968* (Washington, D.C., 1970).

Note: Supplements for the years after 1968 are provided on request.

L. T. Kendall, *The Savings and Loan Business* (Englewood Cliffs, N.J.: Prentice-Hall, Inc., 1962).

D. Patinkin, *Money, Interest, and Prices,* 2nd ed. (New York: Harper & Row, Publishers), Part II.

16 Long-term Macroeconomic Problems

The monetary and fiscal policy tools we have discussed have one thing in common: They are all used as short-term tools, designed and implemented for the purpose of correcting currently existing conditions. The nation has to be in the grips of, or at least be headed for, a recession or a reflation before any policy action is taken. That action, when it does come, is specifically aimed at currently pressing economic problems. Very little consideration is given the effect of a particular policy three, five, or ten years hence. These remarks also hold true for anti-inflationary policies.

The fact that there is an almost complete lack of long-term economic policies may come as a surprise. The argument supporting such a state of affairs is that a succession of short-term periods with optimum GNP levels will necessarily bring about a long-term optimal level in the GNP. To put this idea into the conceptually more meaningful terms of national wealth, a nation that pursues a policy of continuously maximizing its wealth in the short run will as a result maximize its wealth in the long run — or so goes the argument. This is a somewhat superficial point of view.

Consider, for example, two countries that are similar in all respects. In particular, let the two countries have equal GNPs of $100 billion at a given point in time and let both countries go through an extended subsequent period of full employment, for, say, ten years. We will assume that the state of full employment is being achieved by a judicious application of monetary and fiscal policies. That is, both countries attain their professed goals of short-term wealth maximization. In accordance with the previously stated argument, then, both countries are also maximizing their wealth in the long run. But are they?

Suppose country A chooses to take its national income only in the form of consumer goods and government services. That is, our country only replaces the capital equipment as it wears out; there is no net addition to the capital stock of country A. If for simplicity we assume away population growth and technological progress, i.e., the replacement of worn-out machines by more productive designs, country A will exhibit a zero growth rate. A given population, working with a given capital stock under conditions of full employment, will produce the same total output year after year. And since it sets aside a fixed amount each year to replace its worn-out capital equipment, its national wealth, measured in national income, will remain the same year after year.

Let us contrast this case with country B, which opts to invest more than what is needed to hold its capital stock constant. For the sake of the argument, let us assume that its net addition to capital stock is 10% of its national income. A country's current national income, as we have seen in Chapter 2, is not affected by its output mix. But its future national income is. In the case at hand, country B achieves an ever-growing stock of capital equipment. Its given labor force, since the population is assumed to be constant, uses more and more capital intensive processes, causing the total output and the national income to rise over the years. In fact, if we assume an annual growth rate in GNP of 5%, which is not incompatible with a net investment rate of 10% (the corresponding U.S. figures have been roughly 3.6% and 7–8%), then country B will have a GNP of $163 billion at the end of the indicated ten-year period. Country A, we remember, has been stagnating at $100 billion. Assuming a reasonable depreciation/GNP rate of 8%, country A will have a national income of $92 billion, compared to country B's $150 billion. The upshot of our discussion is this: Both countries maximized their national incomes in the short run; both had the option to expand their capital stock, but only country B did this. After ten years, country B was wealthier than country A. Since the national wealth of our two countries followed different long-term growth patterns, they cannot both have maximized their long-term national wealth. But both did maximize their wealth in the short run via monetary or fiscal policies. Thus, for one of the two countries at least, a given policy of short-term wealth maximization is not compatible with long-term wealth maximization. In other words, optimization in the short run is not in and of itself a guarantee for long-term optimization. In fact, the concept of a long-term optimum is somewhat nebulous. Is country B maximizing its wealth in the long run? Should it increase or reduce its net investment rate, thereby achieving a higher or lower long-run growth rate? And which growth rate is an optimum?

Since it is our national wealth today, not five years from now, that is of greater concern to us, it should come as no surprise that short-term macroeconomic models have received more attention in the past than long-term models or growth models. These growth models are ordinarily less involved; they normally make use of a net investment concept and some sort of a capital-output ratio. In fact, the preceding discussion concerning country B's growth rate is essentially an application of the Harrod-Domar model, named after two economists who developed this model independently after World War II.[1]

We have pointed out that the United States does not have a long-term macroeconomic policy. The fact that monetary and fiscal policies are pursued with short-term objectives in mind leads to sometimes curious phenomena. For example, monetary policies affect this nation's money supply. But since these policies are used to offset short-term disturbances, the national growth of the money stock is somewhat incidental in nature. This is illustrated in Figure 16-1, which shows the annual growth rates of the U.S. nominal money supply over the period 1955 to 1970.

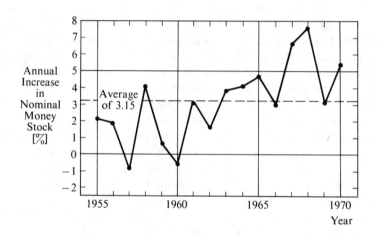

Figure 16-1   Annual Increase in
Nominal Money Stock
Source: Federal Reserve Bulletins, Federal Reserve System.

---

[1]Let
$$GNP = \text{total output or GNP,}$$
$$K = \text{a nation's capital stock,}$$
$$k = \Delta K/GNP = \text{net investment rate,}$$
$$\beta = \Delta K/\Delta GNP = \text{capital-output ratio, i.e., the amount of capital required to produce one additional dollar's worth of output.}$$

From: $k = \Delta K/GNP \;\Rightarrow\; GNP = \Delta K/k$
$\beta = \Delta K/\Delta GNP \Rightarrow \Delta GNP = \Delta K/\beta$ $\quad \dfrac{\Delta GNP}{GNP} = \dfrac{k}{\beta}$

The preceding discussion is based on a net investment rate of 10% and a capital-output ratio of 2. Thus, country *B*'s growth rate is:

$$\frac{\Delta GNP}{GNP} = \frac{k}{\beta} = \frac{.10}{2} = .05 \text{ or } 5\%.$$

As can be seen in that figure, the long-term monetary growth in the United States has been 3.15% per year. But year-to-year, the growth rate has fluctuated widely, from a maximum of 7.8% in 1968 to an actual contraction in the money supply of 0.9% in 1957. This erratic growth rate in our nation's money stock has not gone unnoticed. Many economists feel that a variable as important as the nation's money stock should be increased steadily over time.[2]

A similar problem exists in the implementation of fiscal policies. Suppose, for example, that in an attempt to stimulate aggregate demand the government embarks upon a policy of deficit spending. The very act of deficit spending increases the government's participation in the economy. Whether that is good or bad is beside the point. What matters here is that the level of government involvement is incidental in the sense that it varies with the vagaries of business cycle fluctuations. Over the past ten or so years, government spending has been on the order of 20% of our GNP. On the basis of the 1970 GNP of approximately one trillion dollars, a deficit of $10 billion will increase the involvement of the federal government in this nation's GNP by 1%. Thus, during fiscal 1971, which was marked by a deficit in the amount of $23.5 billion, the federal government's additional involvement has been on the order of 2.4% in terms of the GNP.

This discussion opens up the question of the desired level of government involvement. On the one extreme we have the centralized form of government, USSR-style, where the entire output formally originates with the government; that is, the entire stock of productive resources is owned by the government which, therefore, is the only producer in existence. On the other extreme are we, where the productive equipment is owned by the private sector. For the nation as a whole, which is the better system, and by which criterion are we to make our social choice?

For the nation, too, there exists an opportunity cost. There has been some discussion, for example, concerning the desirability of nationalizing the U.S. railroads. To the nation as a whole, the opportunity cost of having the government run the railroads is to have them run by private enterprise. The cost of running a railroad system in the first place is the production of goods and services that could be produced in lieu of running the railroad or, in other words, the output that is given up, the sacrifice that is incurred, as a result of having the railroads. If the sacrifice is greater with a government-run railroad than with one that is run by the private sector, then this nation's total output, and its wealth, are diminished by having the government operate the railroad system.

This argument holds true for every economic activity. If the government can perform a given task more efficiently, then the nation's wealth is increased by having the government assume that task. Otherwise not. For example, it is generally conceded that the federal government can more efficiently provide for

---

[2] M. Friedman (1960); *A Program For Monetary Stability;* Fordham University Press, New York.

this nation's national defense. The function of providing for this nation's primary and secondary education, to give another example, is assigned to local government in this country.

There are, of course, almost insurmountable problems in determining whether or not, in any given case, the government could operate more efficiently. The controversy that surrounded the defederalization of the Post Office is a good example of this. But *conceptually* there is no room left for ambiguities. The nation's wealth will be increased if the more efficient of the two sectors, public or private, performs the various functions.

But suppose you wish to take issue with the decision criterion of maximizing the national wealth. Suppose you tell me that material goods and services are not the only items on an individual's or a national welfare portfolio. Suppose you insist that such a portfolio includes intangibles such as religious freedom and personal bliss or misery derived from noneconomic and nonmaterial goods that are patently nonquantifiable. In short, suppose you raise the questions we originally posed in Chapter 1, before we became engrossed in the details of macroeconomic theory.

The answer we gave there still holds, namely that you are asking too much. That the exact quantification of human well-being requires nothing less than to fathom the human soul. And that this task had better be left to philosophers and religious leaders.

Maybe national wealth, the living standard of the people, is not the ultimate criterion. Certainly, it is not a perfect one. Whether you accept it or reject it is up to you. But if you choose to reject it, be sure to replace it with something that works. Analyze, do not emote. The problems facing a nation are rather involved, as you have seen in this book. There may be better solutions – who would seriously dispute that? But one thing is certain: There are no easy solutions. That, in and of itself, is a worthwhile discovery which, in my opinion, does much to justify your one-semester preoccupation with macroeconomic theory.

Appendices

Appendix A
Present Value Tables

Table 1
Present Value of One Future Dollar

Year	3%	4%	5%	6%	7%	8%	10%	12%	15%	20%	Year
1	.971	.962	.952	.943	.935	.926	.909	.893	.870	.833	1
2	.943	.925	.907	.890	.873	.857	.826	.797	.756	.694	2
3	.915	.890	.864	.839	.816	.794	.751	.711	.658	.578	3
4	.889	.855	.823	.792	.763	.735	.683	.636	.572	.482	4
5	.863	.823	.784	.747	.713	.681	.620	.567	.497	.402	5
6	.838	.790	.746	.705	.666	.630	.564	.507	.432	.335	6
7	.813	.760	.711	.665	.623	.583	.513	.452	.376	.279	7
8	.789	.731	.677	.627	.582	.540	.466	.404	.326	.233	8
9	.766	.703	.645	.591	.544	.500	.424	.360	.284	.194	9
10	.744	.676	.614	.558	.508	.463	.385	.322	.247	.162	10
11	.722	.650	.585	.526	.475	.429	.350	.287	.215	.134	11
12	.701	.625	.557	.497	.444	.397	.318	.257	.187	.112	12
13	.681	.601	.530	.468	.415	.368	.289	.229	.162	.0935	13
14	.661	.577	.505	.442	.388	.340	.263	.204	.141	.0779	14
15	.642	.555	.481	.417	.362	.315	.239	.183	.122	.0649	15
16	.623	.534	.458	.393	.339	.292	.217	.163	.107	.0541	16
17	.605	.513	.436	.371	.317	.270	.197	.146	.093	.0451	17
18	.587	.494	.416	.350	.296	.250	.179	.130	.0808	.0376	18
19	.570	.475	.396	.330	.277	.232	.163	.116	.0703	.0313	19
20	.554	.456	.377	.311	.258	.215	.148	.104	.0611	.0261	20
25	.478	.375	.295	.232	.184	.146	.0923	.0588	.0304	.0105	25
30	.412	.308	.231	.174	.131	.0994	.0573	.0334	.0151	.00421	30
40	.307	.208	.142	.0972	.067	.0460	.0221	.0107	.00373	.000680	40
50	.228	.141	.087	.0543	.034	.0213	.00852	.00346	.000922	.000109	50

Source: Alchian & Allen, *Exchange and Production: Theory in Use* (Belmont, California: Wadsworth Publishing Company, Inc., 1969).

Example: Suppose you are informed that you will receive $5000 exactly three years from now. If you take this note to a banker in order to get a loan *today* on the $5000 to be received in three years, he will give you less than $5000. How much less? That depends on the rate of interest he charges you. At 5%, he will loan you $.864 today for every $1.00 three years from today. Thus, for the total sum of $5000, he will loan you $5000 × .864 = $4320.

Table 2
Future Value of One Present Dollar

Year	3%	4%	5%	6%	7%	8%	10%	12%	15%	20%	Year
1	1.03	1.04	1.05	1.06	1.07	1.08	1.10	1.12	1.15	1.20	1
2	1.06	1.08	1.10	1.12	1.14	1.17	1.21	1.25	1.32	1.44	2
3	1.09	1.12	1.16	1.19	1.23	1.26	1.33	1.40	1.52	1.73	3
4	1.13	1.17	1.22	1.26	1.31	1.36	1.46	1.57	1.74	2.07	4
5	1.16	1.22	1.28	1.34	1.40	1.47	1.61	1.76	2.01	2.49	5
6	1.19	1.27	1.34	1.41	1.50	1.59	1.77	1.97	2.31	2.99	6
7	1.23	1.32	1.41	1.50	1.61	1.71	1.94	2.21	2.66	3.58	7
8	1.27	1.37	1.48	1.59	1.72	1.85	2.14	2.48	3.05	4.30	8
9	1.30	1.42	1.55	1.68	1.84	2.00	2.35	2.77	3.52	5.16	9
10	1.34	1.48	1.63	1.79	1.97	2.16	2.59	3.11	4.05	6.19	10
11	1.38	1.54	1.71	1.89	2.10	2.33	2.85	3.48	4.66	7.43	11
12	1.43	1.60	1.80	2.01	2.25	2.52	3.13	3.90	5.30	8.92	12
13	1.47	1.67	1.89	2.13	2.41	2.72	3.45	4.36	6.10	10.7	13
14	1.51	1.73	1.98	2.26	2.58	2.94	3.79	4.89	7.00	12.8	14
15	1.56	1.80	2.08	2.39	2.76	3.17	4.17	5.47	8.13	15.4	15
16	1.60	1.87	2.18	2.54	2.95	3.43	4.59	6.13	9.40	18.5	16
17	1.65	1.95	2.29	2.69	3.16	3.70	5.05	6.87	10.6	22.2	17
18	1.70	2.03	2.41	2.85	3.38	4.00	5.55	7.70	12.5	26.6	18
19	1.75	2.11	2.53	3.02	3.62	4.32	6.11	8.61	14.0	31.9	19
20	1.81	2.19	2.65	3.20	3.87	4.66	6.72	9.65	16.1	38.3	20
25	2.09	2.67	3.39	4.29	5.43	6.85	10.8	17.0	32.9	95.4	25
30	2.43	3.24	4.32	5.74	7.61	10.0	17.4	30.0	66.2	237	30
40	3.26	4.80	7.04	10.3	15.0	21.7	45.3	93.1	267.0	1470	40
50	4.38	7.11	11.5	18.4	29.5	46.9	117	289	1080	9100	50

Source: Alchian & Allen, *Exchange and Production: Theory in Use* (Belmont, California: Wadsworth Publishing Company, Inc., 1969).

Example: Suppose you put $500 into a savings account at 5%, compounded annually. How much will this amount grow to in ten years? For every one dollar invested at 5%, the value ten years from now is $1.63. Hence, the sum of $500 will grow to $500 × 1.63 = $815 at the end of ten years.

Table 3
Present Value of an Annuity of One Dollar

Year	3%	4%	5%	6%	7%	8%	10%	12%	15%	20%	Year
1	0.971	0.960	0.952	0.943	0.935	0.926	0.909	0.890	0.870	0.833	1
2	1.91	1.89	1.86	1.83	1.81	1.78	1.73	1.69	1.63	1.53	2
3	2.83	2.78	2.72	2.67	2.62	2.58	2.48	2.40	2.28	2.11	3
4	3.72	3.63	3.55	3.46	3.39	3.31	3.16	3.04	2.86	2.69	4
5	4.58	4.45	4.33	4.21	4.10	3.99	3.79	3.60	3.35	2.99	5
6	5.42	5.24	5.08	4.91	4.77	4.62	4.35	4.11	3.78	3.33	6
7	6.23	6.00	5.79	5.58	5.39	5.21	4.86	4.56	4.16	3.60	7
8	7.02	6.73	6.46	6.20	5.97	5.75	5.33	4.97	4.49	3.84	8
9	7.79	7.44	7.11	6.80	6.52	6.25	5.75	5.33	4.78	4.03	9
10	8.53	8.11	7.72	7.36	7.02	6.71	6.14	5.65	5.02	4.19	10
11	9.25	8.76	8.31	7.88	7.50	7.14	6.49	5.94	5.23	4.33	11
12	9.95	9.39	8.86	8.38	7.94	7.54	6.81	6.19	5.41	4.44	12
13	10.6	9.99	9.39	8.85	8.36	7.90	7.10	6.42	5.65	4.53	13
14	11.3	10.6	9.90	9.29	8.75	8.24	7.36	6.63	5.76	4.61	14
15	11.9	11.1	10.4	9.71	9.11	8.56	7.60	6.81	5.87	4.68	15
16	12.6	11.6	10.8	10.1	9.45	8.85	7.82	6.97	5.96	4.73	16
17	13.2	12.2	11.3	10.4	9.76	9.12	8.02	7.12	6.03	4.77	17
18	13.8	12.7	11.7	10.8	10.1	9.37	8.20	7.25	6.10	4.81	18
19	14.3	13.1	12.1	11.1	10.3	9.60	8.36	7.37	6.17	4.84	19
20	14.9	13.6	12.5	11.4	10.6	9.82	8.51	7.47	6.23	4.87	20
25	17.4	15.6	14.1	12.8	11.7	10.7	9.08	7.84	6.46	4.95	25
30	19.6	17.3	15.4	13.8	12.4	11.3	9.43	8.06	6.57	4.98	30
40	23.1	19.8	17.2	15.0	13.3	11.9	9.78	8.24	6.64	5.00	40
50	25.7	21.5	18.3	15.8	13.8	12.2	9.91	8.25	6.66	5.00	50

Source: Alchian & Allen, Exchange and Production: Theory in Use (Belmont, California: Wadsworth Publishing Company, Inc., 1969).

Example: Suppose you are informed that you will receive $2000 annually, at the end of each year, for a period of five years. If you take this note to a banker in order to get a loan *today* on the $10,000 you will receive in the course of the next five years, he will give you less than $10,000. How much less? That depends on the rate of interest. If he charges you 6%, he will loan you $4.21 in return for your promise to pay him $1.00 at the end of each year over a period of five years. Thus, your five-year annuity of $2000 will produce a loan of $2000 × 4.21 = $8420.

Table 4
Required Annuity Payments to Extinguish
a One-Dollar Debt

Year	3%	4%	5%	6%	7%	8%	10%	12%	15%	20%	Year
1	1.03	1.04	1.05	1.06	1.07	1.08	1.10	1.12	1.15	1.20	1
2	.524	.529	.538	.546	.552	.562	.578	.592	.613	.654	2
3	.353	.360	.368	.375	.381	.388	.403	.417	.439	.474	3
4	.269	.275	.282	.289	.295	.302	.316	.329	.350	.386	4
5	.218	.225	.231	.238	.244	.251	.267	.278	.299	.334	5
6	.185	.191	.197	.204	.210	.216	.230	.243	.265	.300	6
7	.161	.167	.173	.179	.186	.192	.206	.219	.240	.278	7
8	.142	.149	.155	.161	.168	.174	.188	.201	.223	.260	8
9	.128	.134	.141	.147	.153	.160	.174	.188	.209	.248	9
10	.117	.123	.130	.136	.142	.149	.163	.177	.199	.239	10
11	.108	.114	.120	.127	.133	.140	.154	.168	.191	.231	11
12	.101	.106	.113	.119	.126	.133	.147	.162	.185	.225	12
13	.0943	.100	.107	.113	.120	.127	.141	.156	.177	.221	13
14	.0885	.0943	.101	.108	.114	.121	.136	.151	.174	.217	14
15	.0840	.0901	.0982	.103	.110	.117	.132	.147	.170	.214	15
16	.0794	.0862	.0926	.0990	.106	.113	.128	.143	.168	.211	16
17	.0758	.0819	.0885	.0961	.102	.110	.125	.140	.166	.210	17
18	.0725	.0787	.0855	.0925	.0990	.107	.122	.138	.164	.208	18
19	.0699	.0763	.0826	.0901	.0971	.104	.120	.136	.162	.207	19
20	.0671	.0735	.0800	.0877	.0943	.102	.118	.134	.161	.205	20
25	.0575	.0641	.0709	.0781	.0855	.0935	.110	.128	.155	.202	25
30	.0510	.0578	.0649	.0724	.0806	.0885	.106	.124	.152	.201	30
40	.0433	.0505	.0581	.0666	.0752	.0840	.102	.121	.151	.200	40
50	.0389	.0465	.0546	.0632	.0725	.0820	.101	.120	.150	.200	50

Source: Alchian & Allen, *Exchange and Production: Theory in Use* (Belmont, California: Wadsworth Publishing Company, Inc., 1969).

Example: Suppose you owe your bank $3000, and your loan contract calls for annual repayments, at the end of each year, and over a period of five years. If the relevant rate of interest is 6%, then, for every one dollar thus owed, you have to pay $.238 each year. Thus, for your debt in the amount of $3000, your annual payments will be $.238 × 3000 = $714.

Appendix B
Partial Differentials

Starting in Chapter 7 and throughout the remainder of the text, the effect of given independent variables upon a dependent variable is shown in shorthand form. For example, the consumption function is given as follows:

$$C = c \left\{ (y - t), CG, \left(D + \frac{M}{P} \right), r, E \right\} \tag{7-3}$$

The effect of the aggregate income y on consumption spending is symbolically shown as follows:

$$\frac{\Delta C}{\Delta y} > 0.$$

The Δ signs actually take the place of partials (∂), and the fraction $\Delta C / \Delta y$ is really the partial derivative of C with respect to y. The meaning of the inequality is this:

Holding all other variables constant, an increase in income will increase consumption spending. Conversely, a decrease in income will decrease consumption spending.

Suppose, for example, y goes up by \$10 billion, i.e., $\Delta y = + \$10$ billion. Since $\Delta C/\Delta y > 0$, and $\Delta y > 0$, it follows that $\Delta C > 0$. ΔC may be $+ \$6$ billion or $+ \$4$ billion or (on empirical grounds) any positive number greater than zero and less than \$10 billion. ΔC cannot be zero; this would change our above inequality into $\Delta C/\Delta y = 0$. And ΔC cannot be negative; this would change our inequality into $\Delta C/\Delta y < 0$.

Similarly, the effect of the interest rate on consumption spending is shown symbolically as follows:

$$\frac{\Delta C}{\Delta r} < 0.$$

The meaning of the preceding inequality is this:

Holding all other variables constant, an increase in the rate of interest will reduce consumption spending. Conversely, a decrease in the rate of interest will increase consumption spending.

Appendix C
Financial
Intermediaries

As we have seen in Chapter 15, the nonbank financial sector, when measured in absolute terms, i.e., in total credit obtained and provided, is second only to the household sector. The major nonbank financial intermediaries, in order of decreasing total assets, are: life insurance companies, savings and loan associations, private pension funds, mutual savings banks, and others. The asset holdings of these intermediaries are listed in Table 1. Also shown, for comparison, are the total assets of commercial banks and the annual growth rates of the various financial institutions. We have already commented on the difference in growth rates between the commercial banks and the nonbank financial sector as a whole. Let us, therefore, turn to a brief description of the nonbank financial institutions that are listed in Table 1.

1. Life Insurance Companies

Life insurance is big business. By the end of 1967, three life insurance companies had resources exceeding $10 billion, seven had over $5 billion, and 28 had over $1 billion. Prudential, the nation's largest life insurance company ($25 billion) was the second largest corporation at that time, followed by yet another life insurance company (Metropolitan, $24.6 billion) for third place. Taken together, the life insurance companies were underwriting over a trillion dollars' worth of life insurance in 1967.

Practically all of the life insurance companies' funds come from one source: policy reserves that have been accumulated through policy holders' contributions. However, not all of these contributions go into policy reserves. Some people do die, and to the extent that they do, benefit payments are made to their beneficiaries. In the case of term insurance, the amount of premiums going into policy reserves is minimal. Apart from a normal rate of return, which in economic theory is a cost, payments to beneficiaries equal contributions by holders of term insurance policies. That is, funds received by life insurance companies for term insurance are payments for services rendered, namely readiness to compensate the beneficiaries on prearranged terms.

To the extent that many life insurance policies contain a built-in savings plan, the companies are financial intermediaries. They collect the savings of policy holders into their policy reserves out of which funds are channeled into various types of income-earning assets. Due to the public nature of life insurance companies, their primary investment criteria are safety of principal and stability of income. Accordingly, they favor fixed-income obligations, in particular domestic corporate bonds and mortgages, which made up over 76% of their assets at the end of 1969. The importance of life insurance companies in the corporate bond market can be judged from the fact that they hold approximately 55% of all outstanding corporate bonds. Only about 5% of the assets of life insurance companies are placed with corporate stocks. Since these are titles to real property rather than loans, life insurance companies are not "pure" financial intermediaries.

Life insurance companies are heavily regulated, primarily by state insurance boards. This is true even though the sale of insurance across state lines has been defined by the U.S. Supreme Court as interstate commerce, subject to congressional jurisdiction.

2. Savings and Loan Associations

Savings and loan associations may be chartered by federal law or by state law. Those that are chartered by state law oftentimes go under different names such as savings associations, homestead associations, building and loan associations, and others. Since their inception in 1831, savings and loan associations have shown substantial year-after-year growth. In particular, their average annual growth rate after World War II was 13%, placing them narrowly behind the number one financial intermediary in terms of asset holdings, namely life insurance companies. Moreover, extrapolation of their growth rates indicates that savings and loan associations may soon exceed life insurance companies in total asset holdings. Thus, savings and loan associations are big business. The largest individual association has assets close to $3 billion.

The impact of savings and loan associations in the credit market is exclusively in the area of residential home mortgages. The associations obtain

Table 1
Year-End Asset Holdings of Financial
Institutions 1945–1969, Billions of Dollars

End of Year	Commercial Banks	Life Insurance Companies	Savings and Loan Associations	Private Pension Funds	Mutual Savings Banks	Finance Companies	State, Local Gov't Retirem. Funds	Other Insur. Co.s	Open-end Investm. Co.s	Other Financial Institutions
1945	143.8	43.9	8.7	2.8	17.0	4.3	2.7	6.9	1.3	7.8
1946	133.3	47.5	10.2	3.2	18.7	4.9	2.9	7.7	1.3	6.1
1947	136.8	50.9	11.7	3.8	19.7	5.5	3.3	8.8	1.4	5.4
1948	137.8	54.5	13.0	4.4	20.5	6.7	3.7	9.9	1.5	6.0
1949	139.9	58.4	14.6	5.0	21.5	7.7	4.3	11.3	3.1	6.7
1950	147.8	62.6	16.9	6.7	22.4	9.3	5.0	12.6	3.3	7.4
1951	156.8	66.7	19.2	7.8	23.5	9.8	5.7	13.8	3.5	7.4
1952	166.1	71.4	22.7	9.6	25.3	10.8	6.7	15.4	3.9	8.4
1953	170.5	76.6	26.7	11.6	27.2	12.6	8.0	16.8	4.1	9.2
1954	179.7	82.1	31.6	13.8	29.4	13.0	9.5	19.2	6.1	10.8
1955	185.1	87.9	37.7	18.3	31.3	17.1	10.7	21.0	7.1	12.4
1956	191.3	93.2	42.9	21.0	33.4	17.8	12.1	21.8	9.0	12.2

Year										
1957	197.0	98.3	48.1	23.4	35.2	18.9	13.8	21.1	8.7	13.1
1958	211.7	104.3	55.1	29.2	37.8	18.2	15.3	24.8	13.2	14.5
1959	217.0	110.1	63.5	34.1	38.9	21.1	17.3	27.1	15.8	14.5
1960	226.0	115.9	71.5	38.2	40.6	24.1	19.6	28.2	17.0	16.0
1961	243.2	122.8	82.1	46.3	42.8	25.1	22.0	31.6	22.9	17.9
1962	264.4	129.2	93.6	47.3	46.1	27.6	24.5	32.6	21.3	19.5
1963	283.5	136.9	107.6	55.4	49.7	31.7	26.9	35.3	25.2	21.1
1964	307.0	144.9	119.4	63.9	54.2	35.6	29.7	38.1	27.2	23.1
1965	337.6	154.1	129.6	72.6	58.2	41.0	33.1	39.8	35.2	23.9
1966	356.6	161.8	133.9	73.8	61.0	43.6	37.1	40.0	34.8	25.7
1967	396.5	173.1	143.5	86.5	66.4	44.5	41.6	45.6	44.7	30.2
1968	439.7	182.6	152.8	98.3	71.2	49.9	46.0	48.4	52.7	35.8
1969	456.8	189.9	162.2	96.5	74.2	58.3	51.0	49.7	48.3	35.2
Percent of Total	—	24.8	21.2	12.6	9.7	7.6	6.7	6.5	6.3	4.6
Annual Growth (%)	4.8	6.3	13.0	15.9	6.3	13.7	12.9	8.6	16.7	6.3

Source: Flow of Funds Accounts 1945–1968, Board of Governors of Federal Reserve System, and 1969 supplementary computer output.

their funds by borrowing from the public; i.e., they sell savings and loan shares. In fact, approximately 90% of these funds come from savings accounts of individuals and trust funds. Thus the savings and loan associations are an important means of channeling the public's savings into the home mortgage market. In that market, the savings and loan associations hold approximately 44% of all outstanding residential mortgages. This is more than the combined market share of commercial banks, insurance companies, and mutual savings banks. Most of the loans made by savings and loan associations, in fact, some 90% of them, are of the conventional type; that is, these loans are not guaranteed by the Federal Housing Administration or the Veterans' Administration. About half the loans are made for existing homes, the remainder go for new homes or home improvements, mortgage refinancing, etc.

All federal savings and loan associations are subject to supervision and periodic examination by the Federal Home Loan Bank Board. This board also has jurisdiction over state associations that are insured by the Federal Savings and Loan Insurance Corporation, an insurance corporation that was patterned after the banking industry's FDIC. The purpose of this board is to insure the savings of depositors (share holders) up to $15,000 and thus to make savings and loan associations more attractive to the saver. Since 96% of the savings and loan associations deposits are insured (compared to a 99.4% FDIC coverage), the Federal Home Loan Bank Board effectively controls this number-two giant in the private nonbank credit market.

3. Private Pension Funds

Covered under this heading are the so-called noninsured pension funds. These funds are normally administered by trustees, usually banks. Their asset holdings are thus completely separated from those of the parent company. Regular pension funds provide given benefits to participants, in return for given contributions. Profitsharing plans do not guarantee given retirement benefits. Their company contributions vary depending upon the profits of the preceding year, causing benefits to be indeterminate in advance.

Interestingly enough, employer contributions are substantially higher than employee contributions. In 1967, the former made up 56% of that year's total receipts, compared to 7% of employee contributions. The remaining 37% came primarily from investment income. The phenomenal growth of private pension plans at the rate of 15.9% per annum over the 24-year span since World War II (Table 1) is in part attributable to the tax-exempt status of these funds. That is, company contributions to pension funds are fully tax deductible and capital gains tax liabilities by participants are deferred until withdrawal.

Private pension funds have more latitude in the use of their funds than do life insurance companies or savings and loan associations. Accordingly, they use a substantial portion of their funds to purchase corporate stock, i.e., to make investments rather than loans. By the end of 1969, almost 60% of the private pension funds' asset holdings were in the form of corporate stock. The trend is towards more stock holdings. For example, the quoted 60%-figure for 1969 compares with stock holdings in the amount of 42% a decade earlier.

4. Mutual Savings Banks

Mutual savings banks are located primarily in the Northeastern United States. They are cooperatives in the sense that their depositors are not technically their owners (as would be evidenced by shares). In this respect the mutual savings banks differ from savings and loan associations. In other respects the two have several things in common. Both obtain their funds primarily from the small investor and both use their funds predominantly by making loans in the home mortgage market. In 1969, approximately 75% of the mutual savings banks' asset holdings were in the form of mortgages. About half of these were FHA and VA residential loans. Corporate stock holdings accounted for only 3% of their asset holdings.

All mutual savings banks are state chartered and subject to severe restrictions on the use of their funds. This may have contributed materially to their low annual growth rate of 6.3% over the past 24 years.

5. Finance Companies

There are two kinds of finance companies: sales and consumer. Sales finance companies are primarily in the business of providing loans for dealer financing of automobiles and other durable goods. They purchase consumer instalment contracts from dealers. Consumer finance companies, on the other hand, specialize in personal cash loans. However, in practice there is some overlapping in the use of funds of both types of finance companies. Some sales finance companies, such as the General Motors Acceptance Corporation, are captive companies controlled by the original manufacturer. These companies finance the sales of their own dealers.

The respectable growth rate of finance companies by 13.7% per year over the last 24 years is due in part to the increase in consumer credit purchases following World War II. Close to 95% of all asset holdings of finance companies are in the form of loans. The remaining 5% are demand deposits and currency required for the transaction of business. As far as their uses of funds are concerned, therefore, finance companies are exclusively in the credit market. On the liability side, finance companies obtain their funds primarily through debt, especially long-term debt. However, commercial paper and other short-term notes as well as bank loans are an important source of funds for finance companies.

State regulation of sales finance companies varies considerably. In some states there is no regulation. Consumer finance companies are usually subject to state small loan laws. Taken together, finance companies hold approximately 30% of the consumer instalment market. In this market they rank second to commercial banks which hold a market share of 41%.

6. State and Local Government Retirement Funds

Among the remaining three financial institutions that are listed separately in Table 1, state and local government retirement funds with assets at $51 billion hold a narrow lead over other insurance companies and open-end investment companies. Government retirement funds, like life insurance companies, aim at stability of principal and assured income. Accordingly, all but about 10% of their pension fund reserves are held in the form of debt instruments. The most important borrowers from these funds are corporations: Nearly 60% of the asset holdings of state and local government retirement funds are corporate bonds. Other debtors are the U.S. Government, individual consumers, and state and local governments. The annual growth rate of these funds since the end of World War II has been 12.9%.

7. Other Insurance Companies

This group covers a great number of diversified insurance companies, usually lumped together under the collective term property-casualty insurance companies. Some of these are highly specialized in narrow fields, others offer a variety of services such as fire, hail, and storm coverage (property coverage) as well as liability, glass, and burglary coverage (casualty insurance).

Property-casualty insurance companies differ from life insurance companies principally in the use of their funds. Since their financial obligations are not as easily predictable as those of life insurance companies, they carry upwards of 40% of their assets in highly liquid form, i.e., in demand deposits or government securities. By contrast, only about 5% of the assets of life insurance companies are carried in this form. Roughly about one third of the asset holdings of property-casualty insurance firms were held in the form of corporate stock in 1969.

8. Open-End Investment Companies

These companies exist for the purpose of collecting investment funds from the small-time investor. These funds go toward the purchase of a wide range of securities, thus spreading the risk of investment. The name "open-end" refers to the fact that these companies, also called mutual funds, issue new shares to the public on demand. Closed-end investment companies, on the other hand, have a fixed number of shares; they hold less than $5 billion in assets and are, therefore, of minor importance.

By the end of 1969, open-end investment companies had asset holdings in the amount of $48.3 billion, down $4.4 billion from the preceding year. This reduction in asset holdings is a reflection of the 1969 stock-market decline. Since almost 85% of their asset holdings are corporate shares, open-end investment companies are very vulnerable to the vagaries of the stock market. Still, the overall annual growth rate of 16.7% over the past 24 years is the highest of all nonbank financial institutions.

9. Other Financial Institutions

Among the other financial institutions two deserve mention. The first, credit unions, held assets in the amount of $13.7 billion in 1969. Almost all of these were in the form of consumer credit. If titles to real property, e.g., corporate shares, were excluded from the asset holdings in Table 1, credit unions would rank eighth among financial institutions, ahead of open-end investment companies.

The second institution is security brokers and dealers. Their total asset holdings of $13 billion (1969) consist primarily of credit made available for the purchase of securities.

In comparing the volume of credit as shown in the flow of funds matrix in Table 15-1 and the asset positions of financial intermediaries in Table 1 of Appendix C, one point deserves discussion. In the first or credit table, only debt instruments have been considered. That is, Table 15-1 more nearly reflects the U.S. credit market than does Table 1. In Table 1, Appendix C, the asset holdings of the various financial institutions include corporate shares and money holdings (currency and demand deposits). Thus, if the year-end asset holdings of 1969 in Table 1 were added (excluding, of course, commercial bank assets), the resulting total would exceed the total asset holdings shown in column 10 of Table 15-1.

Appendix D
Short-Term
Credit Instruments

A few of the more important types of credit instruments will be listed on the following pages. In order to keep this list a manageable size, we will limit our discussion to short-term credits with instruments having a maximum maturity of one year. This market, although strictly speaking a credit market, is usually called the money market by the Federal Reserve System. We will, of course, use the term credit market, which is analytically more relevant.

1. Treasury Bills

Treasury bills first appeared on the market in 1929. They are sold competitively on a discount basis. The Federal Reserve System does much of the actual selling on behalf of the Treasury. Maturities vary from 90 days to over 20 years. Denominations run from $10,000 to $1,000,000.

There are new offerings each week. Bids are invited on Thursdays, the auction takes place on Mondays. Some noncompetitive bids are accepted, primarily from small investors. The noncompetitive price equals the average competitive bid price. The market is huge and has been known to absorb $3 to 4 billion without serious effects on the rate of interest. The Federal Reserve System's open-market operations are primarily through Treasury bills.

2. Tax Anticipation Bills

These bills made their appearance in 1951. They are sold competitively at auctions. The bills are designed to smooth the uneven flow of tax receipts. Primary purchasers of these bills are corporations who treat them as liquid investments. The Treasury accepts the bills at par in lieu of corporate taxes. From the Treasury's point of view, the sale of tax anticipation bills represents tax collections prior to the due date, but interest is paid to the corporations for this "advance tax payment."

3. Federal Funds

Interbank trading of reserve balances held with the Federal Reserve System had its beginning in the 1920s. In banking circles, deposit balances so traded are usually called federal funds.

Excess reserves yield no income. The federal funds market provides an income-yielding outlet for these funds. Let member-bank A have excess reserves and let member-bank B have a reserve deficiency. Bank B may approach bank A for a short-term loan of its excess reserves, for a fee, to cover its own deficiency. Since the reserve averaging period is one week for Reserve City Banks and two weeks for Country Banks, bank B may acquire more than its currently needed reserve funds to make up for past deficiencies. These transactions take place over the Federal Reserve System's wire network. Thus, there exists a nationwide market for these federal funds, with all banks having simultaneous access to it. Trading typically takes place in millions of dollars and loans are often ultra short-term: for example, overnight.

Both the number of banks participating in the federal funds market and the total daily volume of trading have increased steadily over the years, as illustrated in Table 1.

The major significance of the federal funds market lies in the fact that it enables the commercial banking system as a whole to make full use of its reserve balances. This is illustrated in Figure 1 which shows that excess reserves have steadily declined from an average of nearly 5% of required reserves in 1950 to less than 1% in 1970.

With excess reserves reduced to a minimal 1% or less, open-market operations become more effective, at least in the tight-money direction. If the Federal Reserve System, through open market operations, reduces the reserve balances of commercial banks, very little of this reduction can be absorbed by a reduction of excess reserves, because these have already been trimmed to minimum levels.

Actually, the relevant safety cushion in this context is free reserves, which

Table 1
Trading in Federal Funds

Period	Number of Banks	Daily-Average Gross Purchases (in Millions of Dollars)*
1925–32	30– 40	100– 250
1951–53	75–100	350– 450
1955–57	125–200	800–1200
1960–63	175–275	1500–2500
1963–66	180–350	2000–3800
1966–70	225–400	3500–9000

*Amounts are partially estimated and approximate and include only active traders. Lower limits refer to earlier parts of designated periods.

Source: Federal Funds Market, Federal Reserve Bank of Boston.

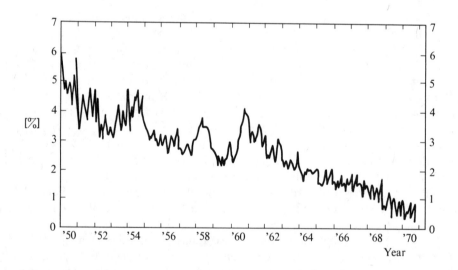

Figure 1   *Excess Reserves as a Percent of Required Reserves*

Source: Federal Reserve Bulletins.

are defined as excess reserves minus discount borrowing. Free reserves may be positive or negative, as shown by statistical data listed on the next page in millions of dollars.

		Reserves			
Date	*Held*	*Required*	*Excess*	*Discount Borrowing*	*Free Reserves*
Dec. 1967	25,260	24,915	345	238	+107
Sept. 30, '70	29,012	28,762	250	663	−413

4. Negotiable Certificates of Deposit

These instruments made their appearance in 1961. They were created by large commercial banks in an attempt to attract corporate funds. C.D.s are marketable receipts for funds deposited in a bank. Maturity terms and the rate of interest are specified. High denominations ranging from $25,000 to $1,000,000 reflect the banks' desire to attract only those funds that are destined for the credit market. That is, the switch from corporate demand deposits to C.D.s is discouraged.

A strong secondary market for C.D.s assures the acquiring corporation of a relatively high degree of liquidity. This and the fact that the term of maturity is negotiable and thus may be set to suit the individual corporate buyer make C.D.s attractive to corporate financial managers. As with all savings accounts held by commercial banks, the rate of interest payable on C.D.s is subject to a ceiling as set by the Federal Reserve System's Regulation Q. Therefore, when short-term interest rates exceed the maximum allowable interest rate on C.D.s, the latter are no longer competitive.

5. Prime Commercial Paper

While this instrument is relatively old, direct placement with investors was initiated by the General Motors Acceptance Corporation in 1920. Prime commercial papers are short-term promissory notes sold either through dealers or directly to institutional investors. These notes are usually unsecured; hence only corporations with impeccable credit ratings sell them. The advantage to the seller of these notes, or, what is the same thing, to the borrower of funds, is that the interest rate charged on prime commercial paper is normally less than the prime interest rate charged by banks. The notes are used primarily to finance consumer loans.

6. Bankers' Acceptance

This type of credit instrument is used in financing United States exports and imports. It is one of the oldest instruments traded on the market. In the United States, it precedes the Federal Reserve System, which was created in 1914. Maturity terms range from 30 to 180 days.

The actual transactions involving bankers' acceptances are a bit complicated. This is probably the reason why these are the least understood credit instruments. For our purposes it will suffice to note that these credit instruments finance international trade by having a well-known bank co-sign (or accept) a promissory note. To the foreign dealer, the bank's signature on the promissory note is added assurance of the credit-worthiness of the original issuer of the note.

7. Federal Agency Securities

In addition to the Treasury, several federal agencies and government corporations are legally empowered to issue their own securities. The Federal National Mortgage Corporation is one such agency. An example of a federal government corporation that has sold securities is the Tennessee Valley Authority. In 1966, the volume of total securities issued by federal agencies or corporations was $19 billion.

Appendix E
Sample Articles
from the Wall
Street Journal

Reserve Could Damage Its Public Image
By Early Discount-Rate Cut, Analysts Say

by Richard F. Janssen, Staff Reporter of The Wall Street Journal—Washington   The Federal Reserve Board would risk some unfavorable political and psychological reactions if it decides to cut its 6% discount rate very soon, analysts here say.

They note that widespread expectations of a cut in this rate the Reserve System charges on loans to member commercial banks assume a motive that also is political: to aid the Nixon Administration by signaling to the public before next month's Congressional elections that the trend is strongly away from the painfully tight credit of recent years.

"It could come down any time," one monetary source concedes. But he cautions this would first require that a majority of board members be convinced that further weakness in the economy is a greater danger than further inflation and that the public needs a strong reassuring "signal" that the slump won't be allowed to get out of hand.

Reprinted by permission of *The Wall Street Journal;* from the Oct. 2, 1970 issue.

But the sheer fact that speculation about a politically motivated rate cut is so rife, sources say, could well sway the Reserve Board to hold off any move until after Nov. 3 in order to avoid blemishing its image of aloofness from partisan considerations. Significantly, there isn't any sign that Administration officials are pressing the board, either publicly or privately, to cut the bellwether rate even though they do rank it as a move that would help blunt Democratic charges that Republicans are saddling the nation with onerous interest charges.

"The board must be aware that any cut would be treated as a political action," one Washington observer says, even if it were dictated strictly by financial and economic considerations. For fear of the long-run damage this would do the board's standing with Congress and with the financial community, he suggests, the board would be very reluctant to lower the rate unless the nonpolitical case is clearly compelling.

Only One Republican Member

That the seven-man board would want to serve the GOP cause is a dubious assumption, anyway, a board-watcher cautions, because the only Republican member is Chairman Arthur F. Burns. The six others are either Democrats or independents with past ties to Democratic Administrations. So any "political" motivations, others add, more likely would be in a narrower Washington sense of improving the board's relations with the White House.

The purely financial conditions could change enough in coming weeks, however, Government economists here hasten to add, to induce the board to brush aside the public-image objections that apparently have dissuaded it from a rate cut so far. The key factor, some suggest, would be a clear-cut and apparently long-lived slide in short-term money market interest rates that would leave the Reserve System's discount rate looming as an unrealistic and outdated reminder of the more stringent conditions of the recent past.

If the discount rate were to long remain significantly higher than the "Federal funds" rate at which banks deal in excess reserves among themselves, monetary specialists explain, it would amount to a "penalty" rate and, thus, unintentionally convey to banks the idea that they're no longer welcome to tide themselves over temporary cash binds by discount-window borrowings from the Federal Reserve.

But barring a sharp downtrend in other short-term interest rates, some experts say, the technical reason of keeping the discount rate reasonably well aligned with market rates is unlikely to prove compelling. It is more narrowly below the "prime" rate that banks charge their best customers now that this rate has come down to 7.5% from the 8% that it had been for a long time, they note. And they express great doubt that the board would want to trim the discount rate in order to pressure banks into a further prime-rate cut soon.

While last week's prime-rate cut is the main factor spurring talk of a "confirming" discount-rate reduction, of course, Washington officials are well aware that many commercial bankers went along with the move very reluctantly, expressing fear to them that "inflationary psychology" could well be revived as a result. This would be all the more true, if the Reserve System were to lower its own rate, too, some bankers add. They cite such inflationary perils ahead as climbing auto prices, still-strong wage settlements and a possible early 1971 economic rebound following the current auto strike.

Other Possibilities are Cited

If the board wants to ease money somewhat more without the dramatic "announcement effect" of a discount-rate cut, it has plenty of other means to do so. It could continue pumping out more money through its basic "open market" purchase of Treasury securities, or it could post further reductions in reserve requirements. This is a potent, but usually less-publicized, tactic that frees for lending funds banks otherwise would have to keep idle. The board also could let banks compete more vigorously for deposits by raising the ceilings on interest rates they pay.

As a practical matter, experts say, the extra discount-window borrowing that would be induced by a discount-rate cut wouldn't amount to much. The discount-window credit outstanding has been running in the $600 million range and lower lately, one notes. This is only a small fraction of the $10 billion, or so, of daily private "Federal funds" transactions that transfer excess reserves from some banks to others anxious for the extra lendable cash.

The discount rate has been held at its current 6% since early April of 1969, despite sharp swings up and down in money-market rates.

For several years the board has had in hand an internal report suggesting that much more frequent changes, smaller than the usual half-point movements, be made. But the board hasn't found conditions placid enough to implement the reform. Insiders are once again starting to examine the possibilities for using this means of stripping the discount rate of its sometimes awkwardly excessive headline-getting role. But indications are that this won't begin with the next month or so.

U.S. Banks Had "Free Reserves" In Latest 7 Days

*New York Reserve Asserts $27 Million
Surplus Was First Excess in 2 Years;
Four-Week Borrowings Down*

by a Wall Street Journal Staff Reporter—New York   For the first time in more than two years, the nation's commercial banks found themselves with "free reserves," according to statistics released yesterday by the Federal Reserve Bank of New York.

The New York Reserve bank estimated the nation's banks averaged free reserves of $27 million in the week ended Wednesday. That contrasted sharply with net borrowed reserves of $413 million in the preceding week.

Member banks are required to set aside reserves equal to a percentage of their customers' deposits. Some banks may have to borrow from the Federal Reserve to meet their requirements while others may have reserves in excess of their needs. When total borrowings of some banks exceed surpluses of others, the difference is termed "net borrowed reserves." Conversely, when surpluses exceed borrowings, it is termed "free reserves."

It was the first time the banks registered a free reserve position since the week ended July 10, 1968, when free reserves averaged $21 million.

Analysts frequently use reserve position figures as a very rough guide to monetary policy. But bankers cautioned that reserve position figures can fluctuate widely from week to week, and a one-week figure can be highly unreliable. They also noted that the Federal Reserve System itself looks closely at numerous other monetary statistics and money market indicators in carrying out credit policy.

In the four weeks ended Wednesday, net borrowed reserves averaged $268 million, down from $485 million in the preceding four weeks.

Borrowings Drop Sharply

In the latest statement week, member bank borrowings from the Federal Reserve dropped to an average of $396 million from $663 million the previous week.

Several major factors contributed to the easing of the banks' reserve position. The first factor was a $408 million drop in the average amounts of reserves that banks were required to keep idle behind deposits.

Analysts attributed about $350 million of this decline to new reserve-requirement rules on bank-related commercial paper, or IOUs, and certain deposits. The new rules went into force two weeks ago and entered the statistics for the first time this past week. Those rules imposed — for the first time — reserve requirements on bank-related commercial paper. But at the same time they reduced the percentage of reserves required on deposits left with a bank for a specific period of time. The two rule changes, taken together, cut by about $350 million, the amount of funds banks must keep idle.

Check "Float" Increases

A second factor contributing to the easing in reserve position was a $20 million average increase in the "float" of checks in the process of collection. Banks obtain reserve credit for such checks; thus, an increase in float adds to reserves of the banking system. The increased float came somewhat as a surprise, because normally declines are registered in the early part of a month.

The Federal Reserve itself moved to counteract the expansionary factors by reducing its holdings of Government securities by an average of $208 million. Sales of securities takes funds from the banking system because buyers pay for their purchases by drawing on the commercial bank accounts.

Other statistics released by the Federal Reserve yesterday showed an increase in the nation's money supply, but a slight decline in the so-called adjusted credit proxy.

The money supply — private demand, or checking account, deposits plus cash in the public hands — averaged a seasonally adjusted $205.4 billion in the week ended Sept. 30. That was up from $204.3 million the previous week.

The adjusted credit proxy dipped to $323.1 billion in the Sept. 30 week from $323.4 billion the week earlier. The figure represents total member bank deposits plus certain nondeposit items, such as bank related commercial paper.

Loan Demand Sluggish

In another area, the latest statistics indicated that loan demand continued sluggish in the week ended Wednesday. The Reserve bank reported that commercial and industrial loans on the books of the 12 leading New York City banks dropped $314 million in the statement week. That compared with a $281 million increase the previous week and an $84 million decline in the like 1969 week.

Analysts said the latest week's decline might even be overstating true loan demand. They noted that in recent weeks loans on the books of bank affiliates have been declining sharply, because of customer repayments and because banks themselves have been repurchasing loans from their affiliates. Banks earlier in the year had sold the loans to their affiliates to raise additional lendable funds.

In the week ended Sept. 30, for example, while business loans on the books of the 12 banks rose $281 million, loans on the books of their affiliates dropped $403 million. That left a net decline of $122 million.

European Currency Plan Gains in Common Market

by a Wall Street Journal Staff Reporter—Luxembourg   Financial experts completed work on proposals for the first three-year phase of a nine-year plan for full economic and monetary union among the six European Common Market countries.

The committee of experts from West Germany, France, Italy, Belgium, the Netherlands and Luxembourg, made their proposals final at a 17-hour working session.

Their 32-page report will be sent to the Common Market Council of Ministers next week.

Phase one of the plan is expected to be put into effect Jan. 1.

It calls for a narrowing of exchange rates among the six countries as they move towards a common European currency by 1980 to rival the U.S. dollar.

Federal Reserve Report
Assets and Liabilities of 12 Weekly
Reporting Member Banks in New York City
(in millions of dollars)

Assets:	Oct. 7 1970	Sept. 30 1970	Oct. 8 1969
Total loans and investments	56,278	55,779	52,875
Federal funds sold and securities purchased under agreements to Commercial & Industrial loans	26,401	26,715	25,938
U.S. Govt. securities—total	4,855	4,832	4,046
Obligations of States and political subdivisions:			
Tax Wts, short-term notes, bills	1,686	1,630	899
All other	4,681	4,705	4,537

Other bonds, corporate stocks, and securities:
  Certificates representing participations

in Fed'l agency loans	63	64	98
All other (incl. corporate stks)	834	852	506
Cash items in proc of collection	13,225	16,036	14,791
Reserves with F.R. Bank	4,395	4,901	4,374
Currency and coin	419	405	368
Balances with domestic banks	1,045	1,158	295
Other assets	4,841	5,038	4,717
Total assets-liabilities	80,536	83,649	77,691

Liabilities:

Demand deposits – total (a)	39,186	43,092	38,069
Time & svgs deposits – total (b)	17,864	17,661	12,947
Federal funds purchased and securities			
sold under agreements to repurchase	4,247	3,364	4,723

Borrowings:

From F.R. Bank	0	259	177
From others	193	187	415
Other liabilities	11,711	11,754	14,258
From own foreign branches	7,033	7,159	9,810
Reserves for loans	1,191	1,191	1,051
Reserves for securities	0	0	3
Total capital accounts	6,144	6,141	6,048

Memoranda:

Demand deposits adjusted (f)	16,164	15,612	16,035
Negotiable time CD's issued in denominations			
of $100,000 or more included in time and			
savings deposits – total	6,164	5,938	2,155

    (a) Includes certified and officers checks not shown separately. (b) Includes time deposits of U.S. Government and foreign commercial banks not shown separately. (f) All demand deposits except U.S. Government and domestic commercial banks, less cash items in process of collection.

Member Bank Reserve Changes

    Changes in weekly averages of member bank reserves and related items during the week and year ended October 7, 1970 were as follows (in millions of dollars).

		Chg fm wk end	
	Oct. 7	Sept. 30	Oct. 8
Reserve bank credit:	1970	1970	1969
U.S. Gov't. securities:			
Bought outright – sys acc't	59,366	− 165	+5,336
Held under repurch. agreemt.	178	− 18	− 123
Acceptances – bought outright	34	− 2	− 4
Held under repurch. agreemt.	15	− 9	− 20
Loans, discounts and advances:			
Member bank borrowings	396.	− 267	− 571
Float	2,586	+ 20	+ 270
Other Federal Reserve Assets	1,692	+ 380	−1,532
Total Reserve Bank credit	64,292	− 83	+3,305

Reserve bank credit:	Oct. 7 1970	Chg fm wk end Sept. 30 1970	Oct. 8 1969
Gold stock	11,117		+ 750
Treasury currency outstanding	7,062	+ 7	+ 281
Total	82,871	− 77	+4,736
Money in circulation	54,823	+ 194	+3,369
Treasury cash holdings	457	+ 9	− 209
Treasury dpts with F.R. Bnks	874	− 216	− 38
Foreign deposits with F.R. Bnks	135	+ 10	+ 1
Other deposits with F.R. Banks	729	+ 34	− 232
Total	59,351	+ 107	+3,536
Member bank reserves			
With F.R. Banks	23,521	− 182	+1,201
Cash allowed as res. (est.)	5,256	− 53	+ 423
Total reserves held (est.)	28,777	− 235	+1,624
Required reserves (est.)	28,354	− 408	+1,340
Excess reserves (est.)	423	+ 173	+ 284
Free reserves (est.)	27	+ 440	

Twelve Federal Reserve Banks' Position
(in millions of dollars)

Assets:	Oct. 7 1970	Sept. 30 1970	Oct. 8 1969
Total gold certificate reserves	10,819	10,819	10,036
U.S. Gov't. securities:			
Bought outright:			
Bills	23,876	24,110	19,313
Notes	32,758	32,758	31,357
Bonds	2,732	2,732	3,468
Total bought outright	59,366	59,600	54,138
Held under repurch. agreemt.		375	162
Total U.S. Gov't. securities	59,366	59,975	54,300
Total assets	82,654	83,300	77,592
Liabilities:			
Federal Reserve Notes	48,467	48,087	45,517
Total deposits	24,807	25,992	23,018
Gold Reserves	11,117	11,117	....

Monetary Aggregates
(four-week daily avg., seasonally adj., in billions)

	Sept. 30 1970	Sept. 2 1970	Oct. 1 1969
Total member bank deposits	307.6	304.0	285.0
Money supply	205.7	304.0	285.0
Bank time deposits	217.2	212.3	194.1

CD Rates Drop, Spurring Talk Of Cut in Prime

Three Large Banks Act; CIT and GMAC
Reduce Commercial Paper Rates;
Soft Loan Demand Reflected

by a Wall Street Journal Staff Reporter—New York   Rates that banks pay on negotiable certificates of deposit registered another sharp drop yesterday, reflecting sluggish loan demand and general rate declines on other money market instruments.

Among those lowering their CD rates yesterday were New York's Chemical Bank, Chase Manhattan Bank and Bankers Trust Co.

Chemical posted a new scale of $5^3/_4\%$ on CDs due in 30 to 59 days; 6% on 60 to 89 days; $6^1/_4\%$ on 90 to 179 days, and $6^3/_8\%$ on longer maturities. It previously quoted a range of 6% to $6^1/_2\%$. Chase went to a scale of $5^3/_4\%$ on 30 to 59 days; $6^1/_8\%$ on 60 to 119 days, and $6^3/_8\%$ on longer maturities.

An even lower rate scale was posted by Bankers Trust, which quoted 5.70% on 30 to 59 days; $5^3/_4\%$ on 60 to 89 days; 6.15% on 90 to 179 days; $6^1/_4\%$ on 180 days to one year, and $6^3/_8\%$ on longer issues.

Negotiable CDs represent deposits, generally $100,000 or more, left with banks for a specific period of time.

In other money market developments, C.I.T. Financial Corp., the nation's largest independent finance company, cut to $6^3/_8\%$ from $6^1/_2\%$ its rate on commercial paper due in 90 to 270 days. Commercial paper is the money market designation for short-term unsecured promissory notes issued by corporations and sold to investors, mainly other companies.

General Motors Acceptance Corp., the finance arm of General Motors Corp., currently closed by a strike, reduced its commercial paper rates by $1/_8$ percentage point. It posted a new schedule quoting $5^7/_8\%$ on 30 to 89-day paper; $6^1/_8\%$ on 90 to 179 days, and $6^3/_8\%$ on 180 to 270 days.

Money market and credit conditions are moving into an area where a further reduction in the banks' prime rate "wouldn't be surprising," a New York bank officer said yesterday.

George A. Murphy, chairman of Irving Trust Co., and other officers of the bank said at an economic briefing that banks generally are reporting softening loan demand. At this time of year, demand for credit usually rises.

With the prime rate at $7^1/_2\%$ since last September, Mr. Murphy said, the "supply (of bank credit) is equal to demand, if not a little in excess of it." George W. McKinney Jr., chief economist for the bank, a subsidiary of Charter

New York Corp., said he expected short-term interest rates to continue declining next year while the economy stages a moderately paced recovery.

Mr. McKinney said the time is logical for a cut in the Federal Reserve
System discount rate—the rate charged on loans to member banks, currently
6%. He noted that yields on three-month Treasury bills, a key rate, have fallen
below the discount rate, and that rates on commercial paper also have tumbled.
Historically, he said, this would indicate a cut in the discount rate is imminent.

However, Leif H. Olsen, senior vice president and economist of First
National City Bank, said at a separate press briefing that he doubts if the
Federal Reserve will change the discount rate now. He said that the central
bank hasn't made much effort in recent years to keep the discount rate in line
with other market rates. The current 6% rate has been in effect since April
1969.

The First National City economist further stated that it appeared the Federal Reserve was trying to "peg" at about 6% the going rate of Federal funds—
uncommitted reserves that banks lend to each other, usually overnight. If
that's the case, he said, there would be little reason to drop the discount rate
below 6%.

Reserve's Open Market Committee Backed "Some Easing" of Credit at August Parley

by a Wall Street Journal Staff Reporter—Washington   The Federal
Reserve Open Market Committee voted nine to three "for some easing of
conditions in credit markets" at its Aug. 18 meeting.

The committee, however, reaffirmed its earlier-stated target of a growth of
the money supply at about a 5% annual rate with the provision that any deviation should be "in an upward rather than a downward direction."

The committee's majority, including Federal Reserve Board Chairman
Arthur F. Burns, said monetary policy should be "sufficiently stimulative to
foster moderate growth in real economic activity, but not so stimulative as to
risk a resurgence of inflationary expectations." They placed "considerable
stress . . . on the need to encourage an adequate flow of credit to the housing
industry and to state and local governments if a satisfactory rate of growth in
overall activity were to be achieved."

Thus, the majority concluded that open market operations "should be
directed at some easing of conditions in credit markets and growth in the money
stock at a rate somewhat greater than that of the second quarter."

Reprinted by permission of *The Wall Street Journal;* from the Nov. 17, 1970 issue.

In the third quarter, it turned out, as previously reported, that the money supply rose at about a 5.1% annual rate, up from the 4.2% pace in the second quarter.

But at the August meeting the committee said its analysts suggested that if prevailing money market conditions were maintained the money supply growth would only have been at a 4% annual rate in the third quarter and into the fourth period.

But Reserve Board Member Andrew F. Brimmer, Darryl R. Francis, president of the St. Louis district bank and Alfred Hayes, president of the New York Fed, dissented.

They claimed that "such easing was not presently required for the purpose of encouraging a satisfactory rate of expansion in economic activity, and it would involve an unduly large risk of rekindling inflationary expectations."

But the three dissenters all stated different reasons for their objections. Mr. Brimmer said "he was deeply troubled by the rapid recent and projected growth rate in bank credit," and that he favored a more "modest rate" of growth. But Mr. Hayes said the "sizable increase" in bank credit recently had been appropriate in view of the shrinkage in commercial paper following Penn Central's liquidity problem, and added he "would be troubled by continued rapid growth in bank credit now that the commercial paper market seemed to be stabilizing."

Mr. Francis said the committee should focus on the growth rate of money instead of bank credit.

Directives of the Federal Reserve Open Market Committee are released about 90 days after each meeting.

Business Group Asks Wage-Price Guidelines To Cut Risk of Long Economic 'Stagnation'

by a Wall Street Journal Staff Reporter—Washington　　　　A blue-chip business group called on the Nixon Administration to start a voluntary wage-price guidepost policy to reduce the risk of long economic "stagnation."

The report, which seems sure to heighten the policy debate within the Administration, was issued by the Committee for Economic Development, a group of 200 top corporate executives and educators. If the Administration continues seeking to squelch inflation almost solely through budget and monetary policies, the CED declared, the cost in terms of lost jobs, profits and output "is likely to be substantially greater than the American people would or should tolerate."

Separately, a group of 58 House Democrats urged President Nixon to call a conference of labor and management leaders to work out "long-term guideposts for noninflationary wage-price behavior." The Democrats, all members of the liberal-oriented Democratic Study Group, also asked Mr. Nixon to "stand ready" to use a law enacted last year giving the President authority to temporarily freeze wages, prices, interest rates and rents. "Such a freeze is necessary if labor is going to be asked to use restraint," the lawmakers said.

In their letter requesting the President to take "vigorous action to save the economy," the Congressmen also advocated steps to increase housing and general construction and to convert defense industries to peacetime uses.

The group recommended that the Administration consider creating a three-man Board on Prices and Incomes to develop "norms of noninflationary behavior" and to publicize "important deviations" by business and unions. "Our own observations suggest that major firms wouldn't be insensitive to official requests that they take the public interest in price stability into specific account when they make price and wage decisions," the panel asserted.

While some executives dissented sharply on the ground that guideposts failed during the Johnson Administration, most argued strongly that the "cost-push" kind of inflation it finds prevailing now would be more susceptible than the kind due to "excess demand" in the late 1960s. The majority believes such efforts "might make a useful contribution to the reconciliation of price stability and high employment and that they should be tried," said Emilio G. Collado, executive vice president of Standard Oil Co. (New Jersey) and co-chairman of the 50-member Research and Policy Committee.

Although general fiscal and monetary policies should remain the most important anti-inflation measures, the CED report said, "inflation is too serious a problem to permit us the luxury of ignoring potential weapons for curbing it that are at our disposal." The report, while welcoming President Nixon's initiatives of last June in setting up a productivity commission and a Federal Regulations and Purchasing Review Board and asking his Council of Economic Advisers to issue "inflation alerts," politely chided the Administration for not making "much more determined" use of these means.

The report could prove influential on the Administration, observers reasoned, as it comes at a time when the Federal Reserve Board chairman, Arthur F. Burns, and some Administration aides are stepping up their efforts to persuade President Nixon to reverse his early rejection of guideposts. Also, they state, the report goes well beyond the recent requests of members of the Business Council for White House pressure on wages alone, a position that Administration men could dismiss as unrealistically one-sided. There's considerable overlap in membership between the CED and the Business Council, which doesn't take formal positions.

The CED, in addition to its stress on the wage-price policy issue, called for selective credit controls; "basic structural and institutional changes which would increase competition in markets for labor and products"; "intensified Federal action" to provide jobs, training and welfare; reduction of Federal subsidies; easing of credit policy, and acceptance of a budget deficit caused by lagging incomes and profits.

Leading Indicators Rose 1% in November; Gain First Since July

by a Wall Street Journal Staff Reporter — Washington   The Government's composite index of leading economic indicators rose last month for the first time since July, the Commerce Department reported.

The leading indicators, which tend to foreshadow broad movements in the economy, climbed 1% in November to 115.2% of the 1967 average following an 0.3% drop in October. The last previous monthly increase, in July, was 1.4%.

But Government analysts cautioned that the November figure might be revised, noting that October's initially was reported as an 0.8% increase. Some of the leading indicators aren't available when the preliminary report is compiled, and thus the outcome can be changed sharply later.

Of the eight leading indicators that were available, five rose last month and three declined. Increases were registered in the average workweek, new durable-goods orders, new building permits, plant and equipment contracts and the average initial weekly claims for state unemployment insurance. The jobless benefits claims actually fell in November, but are treated inversely in the index.

Declines were recorded last month in industrial-materials prices, the average price of 500 common stocks and the ratio of price to unit labor costs of manufacturers.

Index

Accelerator principle, 180–181
Aggregate consumption function, 79–81
Aggregate demand, components of, 77–97
Aggregate demand curve, 112–113
    and price-level changes, 113
Aggregate production function, 60–65
Aggregate supply, 67–75
Aggregate supply curve, 60–75
    and cartels, 71–73
    derivation, 67–71
Aggregate supply and demand, 56–58
Anti-inflationary fiscal policies, 141–143
Anti-inflationary monetary policy actions, 149–150
Antitrust laws, and cartels, 162, 162n
Arbitrage operations, 228–231
Automatic stabilizers, 181–182

Balance of payments, 211–213
Balance of trade, 45–46
Bank reserves, 193
Bankers' acceptances, 262
Banking, chain and group, 215
Banking system, American, 214–217 (see also Banks)
Banks: assets, 215–217
    branch banks, 214–215
    cash assets, 216
    commercial banks, 201, 214–215
    creation of money, 193–194
    Federal Reserve Banks, 198, 201–202
    investment securities, 216
    loans, 193–194, 195, 216
    minimum reserve balances, 194, 196
    minimum reserve requirements, 194, 196–197, 206–209
    mutual savings banks, 255
Bond market, 114 (see also Credit market)
Bonds: interest rates of, 226–228
    long-term and short-term, interest rates, 224–225
Borrowing, to finance government spending, 137–139

Brimmer, Andrew F., 273
Burns, Arthur F., 264, 272

Capital gain or loss, 80–83
Cartels: and the aggregate supply curve, 71–73
    and antitrust laws, 162, 162n
Cash assets, of banks, 216
Certificates of deposit, 228–231, 261
Chain banking, 215
Collado, Emilio G., 274
Commercial banks, 201, 214–215 (see also Banks)
    "free reserves," 266–268
Commercial deposits, interest rate drop in, 271–272
Committee for Economic Development, 273–275
Commodity market, 79
    effect of government spending financed by taxes, 136
    equilibrium in, 91–97
Commodity-market equilibrium curve: and interest rate change, 93–94
    and price-level changes, 95–97
Common Market countries, proposed currency plan, 268
Consumer finance companies, 255
Consumer price index, 9–14
Consumer purchases; see Consumption spending
Consumption spending, 26–28, 43–45, 78, 79–86
    and accumulated wealth, 83
    consumption functions, 79–81, 248
    determinants, 79–84, 248–249
    effect of aggregate income on, 248–249
    effect of reduction in, 123–126
    expectations of people, 80, 83–84
    and interest rate, 83, 85–86, 93–94, 249
    and net incomes, 80, 85
    and price-level changes, 95–97
Corporate tax cuts, 139–141
Cost of living, measure of, 9–14

Cost-push inflation, 157, 159–163
  wage settlements as example of, 164–168
Credit, 219–232 (*see also* Credit instruments;
    Credit instruments, short-term)
  credit matrix, 221–222
  easing of, 272–273
  financial intermediaries, 222–223, 250–257
Credit instruments: (*see also* Credit instru-
    ments, short-term)
  arbitrage operations, 228–231
  interdependence of interest rates, 228, 231
  rates of interest, 224–231
  with and without repurchase clause,
    223–224
  risks and interest rates, 226–228
  types of, 231–232
Credit instruments, short-term: bankers'
    acceptances, 262
  certificates of deposit, 228–231, 261
  federal agency securities, 262
  federal funds, 259–260
  prime commercial papers, 261
  tax anticipation bills, 259
  Treasury bills, 258
Credit market: credit instruments, 223–225,
    258–262
  credit-supply function, 114
  and price-level changes, 116–118
  savings function, 114
  size of, 219
Credit matrix, 221–222
Credit-supply function, 114
  and interest rates, 115–116
Credit unions, 257

Debt financing, government, 139
Deficit spending, 42–43, 137–141, 143
  ceiling on public debt, 146, 175
  to finance wars, 173
  induced, 181–182
  national debt, 172–175
Demand deposits, 206–207, 216–217
Demand-pull inflation, 157–159, 160–161
Depreciation allowance, 21–22
  calculation of, 21n
Depressed economy; *see* Economy, de-
    pressed
Depressions, 2, 39–40, 41–43, 81 (*see also*
    Economy, depressed)
Discount-rate reduction by Federal Reserve
    Board, article on, 263–265
Discount window, 196, 205–206
Dissaving, 182
Dollar, devaluation of, 211n
Durable goods, 44–45

"Easy-money policy," 195
Economic growth, 20n
Economic indicators, 153, 161, 275
Economic policies, long-term, 234–238
Economic theory, Keynesian, 185–187
Economy: automatic stabilizers, 181–182
  cost-push inflation, 157, 159–163, 164–168
  in equilibrium, 67, 121–123
  equilibrium aggregate demand, 108–110
  macroeconomic model, construction of,
    54–58, 60–65, 77–97, 100–118
  price-level fall and, 68–69
  price-level increase and, 69–70
  size and complexity of, 1–2
  and unemployment, 161–162
  wage-price spiral, 163–164
Economy, depressed, 120–131
  excess-money-supply situation, 125–126
  income-adjustment model, 124–130
  and interest rate, 125–127
  price-level effects, 128–130
  reduction in consumer spending, 123–126
  stimulation, 147–149
Equilibrium aggregate demand, 108–110
European currency plan, proposed, 268
Excess-money-supply situation, 125–126
Expansionary money policies, 147–149

Farm income, 30
Federal agency securities, 262
Federal funds, 259–260
Federal National Mortgage Corporation, 262
Federal Open Market Committee, 200, 204,
    272–273
Federal Reserve Bank float, 213
Federal Reserve Banks, 198, 201–202
Federal Reserve Board discount-rate reduc-
    tion, article on, 263–265
Federal Reserve policies: changes in reserve
    requirements, 196–197, 206–209
  loans to commercial banks, 196, 205–206
  open market operations, 196, 200, 202–205
Federal Reserve System, 166–167, 197
  administration of monetary policies, 147–
    148, 152
  Board of Governors, 198–199, 208
  credit matrix, 221–222
  discount window, 196, 205–206
  factors changing bank reserves, 209–213
  Federal Reserve Bank float, 213
  gold sales and purchases by, 211–213
  interbank trading of reserve balances,
    259–260
  minimum reserve requirements, 194, 196–
    197, 206–209

Federal Reserve System (continued)
  monetary policies, 196–197, 202–213
  money multiplier, 213–214
  money supply, 102, 102n, 107, 108, 110,
    113, 124–125, 147, 191, 192, 193
  Open Market Committee, 200, 204, 272–
    273
  report on member banks in New York City,
    268–270
  structure and organization, 198–202
Final product, value-added concept, 32
Final purchases, 26, 28
Finance companies, 255–256
Financial intermediaries, 250–257
  credit unions, 257
  finance companies, 255–256
  life insurance companies, 250–251
  mutual savings banks, 255
  open-end investment companies, 257
  private pension funds, 254–255
  property-casualty insurance companies, 256
  savings and loan associations, 251, 254
  security brokers and dealers, 257
  state and local government retirement
    funds, 256
Financial sector; *see* Banks; Financial inter-
    mediaries
Fiscal policies, 132–143 (*see also* Govern-
    ment expenditures)
  anti-inflationary, 141–143
  government projects, 132–133
  implementation problems, 237
  increase in government spending financed
    by borrowing, 133, 137–139
  increase in government spending financed
    by taxation, 133, 134–137, 143
  military spending, 133
  recession-induced, 141
  stimulation of private spending by tax cuts,
    139–141
Float, Federal Reserve Bank, 213
Flow variable, 4–5 (*see also* Income)
Francis, Darryl R., 273
"Free reserves," 266–268
Future income, computation of present
    value, 7

General Motors Acceptance Corporation,
    255, 261, 271
*General Theory of Employment, Interest, and
    Money, The* (Keynes), 185–187
GNP (gross national product), 14, 14n
  consumer purchases, 26–28, 78, 79–86
  final purchases, 26, 28

GNP (continued)
  government expenditures, 29, 78, 90–91
  gross private domestic investment, 28–29
  investment spending, 28–29, 78, 86–89
  vs. national income, 34
  net exports, 29, 78, 78n
GNP accounts, 26–29
GNP-deflator, 14–16
Gold, dollar value of, 211, 211n 3
Gold holdings, changes in, 211–213
Government debt financing, 139
Government expenditures, 29, 41–43, 47,
    78, 90–91 (*see also* Fiscal policies)
  financed by borrowing, 137–139
  financed by taxation, 134–137
  funding of, 133–134
Great Depression, 39–40, 41–43, 81
Gross national product; *see* GNP
Gross private domestic investment, 28–29
Group banking, 215
Growth models, Harrod-Domar model, 235–
    236, 236n

Harrod-Domar national growth model, 235–
    236, 236n
Hayes, Alfred, 273
Hicks, J. R., interpretation of Keynes' theory,
    186

Income: derived from human labor, 6, 6n
  derived from productive equipment, 5–6
  distribution, 34–36
    Lorenz chart and curve, 34–35
  income stream, 5–6
  vs. money, 104
  national, as flow variable, 5
  real income, 8–9
Income tax cuts, stimulation of private
    spending by, 141
Induced deficit spending, 181–182
Inflation: cost-push, 157, 159–163, 164–168
  demand-pull, 157–159, 160–161
  vs. full employment, 161–162
  Phillips curve, 182–185
Insurance companies, property-casualty, 256
Interest rates, 50–52, 83, 85–86
  of bonds, 226–228
  on credit instruments, 224–225
  and credit-supply function, 115–116
  in depressed economy, 125–127
  and money demand, 105–106
  and price-level changes, 113, 116–118
  and risk, 226–228
Inventory changes, 45

Investment companies, open-end, 257
Investment multiplier, Keynesian, 178–179, 179n
Investment securities, 216
Investment spending, 28–29, 78, 86–89
  accelerator principle, 180–181
  aggregate investment function, 89
  Keynesian multipliers, 178–180
  opportunity cost, 87–88, 237–238
Investment tax credits, 139

Keynes, John Maynard, 43, 57, 185–187
Keynesian investment multiplier, 178–179, 179n
Keynesian multipliers, 153–154, 178–180
Keynesian theory, Hicks' interpretation of, 186

Labor force and price-level changes, 67–70
Labor market, 66–67
Lags, 146–147, 150–153
Life insurance companies, 250–251
LM curve: effect of price-level changes on, 110–111
  and supply of money, 107–111
Loans, 193–194, 195, 216
  decreased demand for, 267–268
Lorenz chart and curve, 34–35

Macroeconomic concepts, 177–187
Macroeconomic issues, current, 157–175
Macroeconomic model, construction of, 54–58, 60–65, 77–97, 100–118
Macroeconomic problems, long-term, 234–238
"Market basket," 9
McKinney, George W., Jr., 271–272
Monetary policies: anti-inflationary actions, 149–150
  expansionary money policies, 147–149
  lags in, 146, 150–153
  quantification of policies, 153–154
  stimulating a depressed economy, 147–149
Money, 190–217
  bank reserves, 193
  creation by banks, 193–196
  vs. income, 104
  mechanics of, 192–197
  types of, 193
Money demand, 103–107
  and interest rates, 105–106
  transactions demand for money, 104–105
  variables determining, 104–106

Money market, 101–111
  demand for money, 103–107
  effect of government spending financed by borrowing, 137
  effect of government spending financed by taxes, 136
  supply of money and the LM curve, 107–111
Money-market equilibrium curve (LM curve), 107–111
Money multiplier, 153, 196, 213–214
Money supply, 102–103
  annual growth rates, 236–237
  changes in currency holdings, 209–210
  changes in gold holdings, 211–213
  changes in Treasury deposits, 210–211
  foreign and international deposits, 211
  and LM curve, 107–111
Monopoly(ies), 159–160, 161–162
  and the aggregate supply curve, 72–73
Monopsonies, and the aggregate supply curve, 71–72
Multipliers: Keynesian multipliers, 153–154, 178–180, 179n
  money multiplier, 153, 196, 213–214
Murphy, George A., 271
Mutual savings banks, 255

National debt, 172–175
  ceiling on, 146, 175
National income: definitions, 17–22, 31–32
  finished goods, 32–33
  hypothetical economy as example, 18–22
  income distribution, 34–36
  as measure of aggregate wealth, 5
  measurement problems, 31–34
  net addition to capital stock, 32
National income accounts, 26–36
  compensation of employees, 29–30
  corporate profits, 30
  interest payments, 31
  proprietors' income, 30
  rental income, 30
National wealth: government vs. private operation of activities, 237–238
  growth models, 235–236
  implementation of fiscal policies, 237
  opportunity cost, 237–238
  short-term vs. long-term maximization, 234–235
Net investment, 20n
New York Reserve Bank "free reserves," 266–268
Nondurable goods, 43–44

Olsen, Leif H., 272
Open-end investment companies, 257
Open Market Committee, of Federal
    Reserve, 200, 204, 272–273
Opportunity cost, 87–88, 237–238

Pension funds, private, 254–255
Per capita real wealth, 3
Personal consumption expenditures, 28
Phillips curve, 182–185
Present-value tables, 239–247
Price controls, 168–172
    resource-allocation problem in, 170–171
Price-earnings ratio, 81
Price index, 9–14
    mathematical expression of, 10n
Price level and inflation, 157–161
Price-level changes, 66
    and aggregate demand curve, 113
    and consumer spending, 95–97
    and credit market, 116–118
    and interest rate, 113, 116–118
    and labor force, 67–70
    and money-market equilibrium curve, 110–
    111
Price-level effects in depressed economy,
    128–130
Price-level rises and GNP-deflator, 14–16
Prime commercial papers, 261
Principal, consumption of, 17–18
Private spending, stimulation by tax cuts,
    139–141
Property-casualty insurance companies, 256

Real income, 8–9
Real wages, 65–66
Real wealth, 3
Real-wealth effect, 96
Recession-inflation; *see* reflation
Recessions, 45, 150–152, 153
Reflation, 41, 164–165
Reserve balances, 194, 196
Reserve requirements, minimum, 194,
    196–197, 206–209
Risk, 226–228

Sales finance companies, 255
Savings function, 114
    and interest rates, 115–116
Savings and loan associations, 251, 254
Security brokers and dealers, 257
Stabilizers, automatic, 181–182
Stock market, 80–81
Stock variable, 4–5

Supply and demand, 55–56
Supply and demand, aggregate; *see* Aggre-
    gate demand; Aggregate supply

Tax anticipation bills, 259
Taxation, to finance government spending,
    134–137, 143
Tennessee Valley Authority, 262
Time deposits, 216–217
    reserve requirements, 207
Total output, 60–61
Transactions demand for money, 104–105
Treasury bills, 258
Treasury deposits, changes in, 210–211

Unemployment, 2, 47–50, 66
    anti-inflation policies in, 162
    levels of, 74
Unemployment compensation, 181
Unions, and the aggregate supply curve, 72
US Department of Commerce, 33, 39, 45 (*see
    also* GNP; National income accounts)
US Department of Labor: price index, 9–14
    wage changes, in collective bargaining,
    165
US economy, past history of, 39–52
    economy during World War II, 40–41
    government expenditures, 41–43, 47
    Great Depression, 39–40, 41–43, 81
    gross private investment, 41, 43, 45, 47
    interest rates, 50–52
    small-scale recessions, 41
    unemployment, 47–50

Value-added concept, 32–33

Wage control, 168, 170
Wage and price controls, 168–172, 273–275
Wage-price spiral, 163–164
Wage settlements as cost-push inflationary
    force, 164–168
Wages and price-level changes, 66
Wall Street Journal, The, articles from, 263–
    275
Wealth, 4–23
    Department of Commerce concept of,
    4n, 5, 6
    as flow variable, 5, 16
    as stock variable, 5
Wealth, individual, 7–9
Wealth maximization, short-term vs. long-
    term, 234–235
Wealth, national; *see* National wealth
Welfare of the people, 2–3